The NEW Option Offense for
WINNING
BASKETBALL

A.L. "Lee" Walker, MS
Jack Donohue
Basketball Canada

Leisure Press
Champaign, Illinois

Developmental Editor: June I. Decker, PhD
Copy Editor: Wendy Nelson
Assistant Editors: JoAnne Cline, Phaedra Hise
Production Director: Ernie Noa
Projects Manager: Lezli Harris
Typesetter: Yvonne Winsor
Text Design: Keith Blomberg
Text Layout: Tara Welsch
Cover Design: Conundrum Design
Cover Photo: Rick Stewart/Focus West
Illustrations By: Bill Eckmann
Printed By: Braun-Brumfield

ISBN: 0-88011-307-3

Copyright © 1988 by A. L. Walker and Jack Donohue

Library of Congress Cataloging-in-Publication Data

Walker, A. L., 1916–
    The new option offense for winning basketball.

    Includes index.
      1. Basketball—Offense. 2. Basketball—Coaching.
I. Donohue, Jack, 1931–   . II. Title.
GV889.W343   1988   796.32′32   87-33879
ISBN 0-88011-307-3

Printed in the United States of America

10 9 8 7 6 5 4 3 2 1

Leisure Press
A Division of Human Kinetics Publishers, Inc.
Box 5076, Champaign, IL 61820
1-800-342-5457
1-800-334-3665 (in Illinois)

To all the "Boys of Winter," those great coaches and players of basketball in the United States, Canada, and everywhere.

Acknowledgments

To Herman L. Masin, publisher of *Scholastic Coach*, Elmer A. Blasco, publisher of *Athletic Journal*, and Parker Publishing Company for their timely copyright and reprint permissions.

To colleagues in Canada and the United States who have always shared their thoughts and knowledge about basketball and shown an interest in ours.

To my wife, Lucia; our son Jon and his wife, Mary; our daughter Susan and her husband, Dave Luckman; our son Christopher; and of great importance to basketball coaches in the future, grandchildren Brynn Walker, Justin Luckman, Jordan Luckman, and Sarah Luckman.

A.L. "Lee" Walker

To Mary Jane, Carol, John Joe, Kathy, Mary Beth, Bryan and Maura and to Coaches Joe Lapchick and Red Saracheck.

Jack Donohue

Contents

Preface

The title of this book, *The New Option Offense for Winning Basketball* suggests that an innovative offensive system, with its accompanying defensive plan, is successful because the essential feature of having *options* is the central theme. The foundation for the Option Offense was laid during the 1950s. Over thirty years later, encompassing an intervening wealth of coaching experiences at different levels of competition, the philosophy, basic composition, and operating procedures remain much the same. Revisions and modifications have been made, however, reflecting personal observations and experiences, changes in the rules of the game, and the worthwhile suggestions and advice that have been received from coaches at all levels. Since 1973, parts of this option-oriented total program have been subjects for articles in *Athletic Journal* and *Coach*, and in 1977 a work that treated the option offense of the 1970s, *The Option Offense for Winning Basketball*, was published by Parker Publishing Company.

In the New Option Offense of the 1980s, the main features of the total program continue the past emphasis on purposeful movement of players and ball in planned, patterned routes, during which options unfold and are rejected until an option arises that offers the optimum high-percentage field goal attempt. Simplicity and attention to basic fundamentals remain the cornerstones of the offense. With its 32Z Goose Egg Combination

Defense and the 32Z Trap, the New Option Offense program is adapted to all rules of play pertinent to the 45- and 30-second clocks and to the constantly changing situations and trends of basketball.

Because this book includes materials pertaining to defense, it provides a total program. Chapters 7 and 8 promote the 32Z Goose Egg Combination Defense and the 32Z Trap. The latter is an exciting, imaginative half-court zone trapping scheme that is particularly effective given the clock rules (30- and 45-second) and the recent NCAA introduction of the three-point line.

Initial chapters deal with the installation of the three series of the New Option Offense. Their nomenclature, "Red," "White," and "Blue," has not changed over the years. The Offense is of equal importance to men and women and is applicable to all levels of competition. The only variations to be expected would be in the quality of performance at differing levels. A drills chapter that relates specifically to the installation and perfection of the offense is a major feature, and chapter 11 is an extensive survey of over 75 drills that improve offensive skills in general.

One of the highlights of this book is chapter 5, which furnishes "sure fire" plays for game situations. Included are two-point and three-point plays for out-of-bounds situations, various other situational plays, and a number of three-pointers. All were utilized during recent past seasons of play, and the three-point plays are interesting because they were competition-proven in various leagues and championships even before the universal adoption of the three-point line. The assumption in chapter 5 is that situational two-point and three-point plays, some of which are memorized to preclude costly time-out orientation, should be a part of a team's repertoire and playbook. In particular, the receipt of the ball from an official at an out-of-bounds location is a *gift*, not to be taken lightly; to make a desultory, nonobjective inbounds pass is the waste of a *bonus*!

An Early Offense in chapter 6 rounds out the survey of the New Option Offense. Early Offense is a well-planned, well-practiced part of the offense, and players appreciate the option to "push the ball" when the oportunity arises. It will be noted that natural screens, screen-rolls, back-door cuts, give-and-go moves, and high-low passing, all earmarks of the regular patterns of "Red," "White," and "Blue," are in the format of Early Offense, and that the players rotate smoothly and naturally to their half-court sets if the Early Offense is unproductive.

"War at the Window," chapter 9, contains material on rebounding and includes practice drills to make every player feel that he or she is a part of the rebounding team. Many successful coaches declare that rebounding is the major factor determining the outcome of a game and that successful rebounding depends on total five-player desire, contribution, and effort. This chapter, emphasizing basic fundamentals and aggressive, competitive exercises and drills, is a reflection of that school of thought.

Six model sheets are included in chapter 12's discussion of how to prepare and maintain statistical records. Throughout the season, coaches need cumulative information about the proficiency and performance of players in both practice and games. The ideas in this chapter, and the worksheet forms, should be significant.

A glossary concludes this book. Its purpose is to define terms, language, and expressions that are singularly pertinent to the New Option Offense.

This work was some years in the making, and it is finished with the lament "It wasn't easy." Blood, sweat, and tears notwithstanding, the goals that were set in the beginning have been fulfilled if *The New Option Offense for Winning Basketball* proves useful and worthwhile to the coaching profession.

Presenting the New Option Offense

The purpose of this chapter is to furnish a general orientation to and analysis of the New Option Offense, including only its basic sets, formations, and initial movements and the early development of the patterned routes. Scoring options and specific explanations, with illustrations, will be detailed in following chapters.

General Information

Establishing the New Option Offense is a demanding task. Coaches "lay it on the line" on the opening day of practice and operate from a well-prepared practice plan organized with certain daily objectives in mind.

Players arrive on time, ready to go to work and aware that this is a rules-oriented, disciplined program with high expectations and demands. During the practice sessions the "laws of learning"—*explanation, demonstration, and application*—dominate the teaching methods. Players become familiar with the omnipresent chalkboard, on which the following symbolizations are drawn to expedite the explanation of drills, patterns, and plays:

- – – → Pass
———→ Path of player
———⊣ Pick, or screen
〜〜〜→ Path of dribbler
1 Offensive player
③ Initial location of basketball with player.
◎ Basketball symbol, used at times
× Defensive player
×⁴ Designated defensive player
= Hand-back, or hand-off pass
⊣ ⊢ Rebounding triangle

Composition and Procedures

The New Option Offense consists of three series, called Red, White, and Blue, all activated by cues or keys that are usually the responsibility of the team's floor leader. An entry pass in the half-court attacking area usually acts as the cue or key, although in some instances the floor leader calls out the series that is to be initiated.

Depending on the opportunities for field-goal attempts during their development, the Red and White series each can progress into a wheeling, mixing supplement called *Rotary*. Blue, considered the most effective of the three series against zones, does not employ the Rotary addition.

All three series start the players in the same initial positions, as illustrated in Figure 1.1, after giving attention whenever possible to an Early Offense (see chapter 6). Players reach these set positions in the operational front court as efficiently and rapidly as possible, unless timing dictates otherwise or help is needed against a full-court press. Red, White, and Blue move "full speed ahead," with no loitering or sauntering permitted. Entry passes are sometimes made while players are moving into positions.

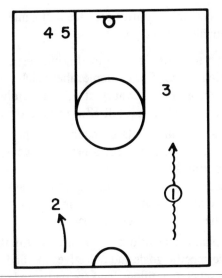

Figure 1.1. Identical sets of Red, White and Blue.

Assignments Plan and Characteristics of Players

Positions in the offense are referred to by number. The traditional designations guard, forward, and center are not applicable. When the squad, through cuts and attrition, is reduced for the season ahead, a Position Form is prepared (Figure 1.2) with numbered positional assignments included; this form is posted on the gym bulletin board and made available to the players.

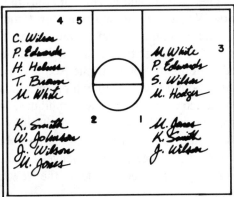

Figure 1.2. Position Form.

The numbering system simplifies practice and game situations and has the following valuable advantages:

1. Substitution procedure is more intelligible, especially at the height of an exciting game. For example, the coach gives simple directions: "Steve, go in for Maury at 3," or "Judy, go in for Mary Jones. You play at 2, and tell Kim to take over at 1."

2. Confusion during time-outs is reduced. Sometimes in the heat of battle the coach will grope for a name; however, using the positional numbering system, he or she simply states, "1, take the ball out of bounds; 4 and 5 stack up under the basket like this; 2 and 3, set up like this." Numbers and symbols are quickly and clearly drawn on the coach's diagram board.

3. Aware of planned positional assignments for the season ahead, players have specific goals and objectives in mind, know where they stand in the scheme of things, and are motivated to concentrate their efforts on the skills that are applicable to the assignments.

4. The numbering of positions, and the format of the worksheet (Figure 1.2), point out the positive aspect of *interchangeability*: "If you can play 3, you can play 4 and 5; if you play 1, you can play 2, and vice versa. So practice and play that way!" Interchangeability affords the coach a wealth of options in her or his substitution plan and compensates for inevitable injury and ineligibility problems; in the future interest of players, it demands effort in different skill areas, not just in specialized ones.

Players are characterized as follows. Player 3 is a key player. He or she is one of the bigger players and capable of adjusting to multidimensional requirements. We expect 3 to substitute for 4 and 5 if necessary, to play wing and high post in the Red and White series, to play the wing in Blue, and to be mobile enough to operate on the outside in the wheeling techniques and patterns of Rotary in the Red and White series. We want 3 to go to the rebound triangle, to exhibit excellent outside jump-shooting skills, and to execute triple-threat techniques. In short, there is no specific label for player 3. He or she operates at times as a power forward, then again as a finesse forward, an aggressive rebounder, a point player, a high post player, a shooter, and a "weaver" in the outside Rotary weave. Player 3 is a truly important member of the New Option Offense!

Players 4 and 5 are totally interchangeable; in fact, they may trade places at any time, by mutual communication. They are the biggest, strongest players, trained in the aggressiveness of low post operations for Red and White, and for both low and high post techniques in the Blue series. We expect both to be proficient in setting picks (screens), making acceptable passes off defensive rebounds, and going to the offensive boards with either finesse or power. They must be competent turn-around jump shooters and familiar with the possibilities of the hook shot. Players 4 and 5 are combative, "mean," and recalcitrant about offensive rights of ownership around the low post blocks, and they are taught to be resourceful if defensive denial is applied in these areas, in the spirit of the motto "There is a reaction for every action." Although familiar with the position requirements at the player 3 spot and skill-trained to operate there, players 4 and 5 are primarily inside players charged with inside responsibilities. Only secondarily should either of them be considered as resources for the position at 3.

Players 1 and 2 are the guards and, as a two-person force, act as the prime movers in pushing the ball downcourt and activating the half-court offense. Player 1, at position 1, could be considered the traditional point guard, and player 2, at position 2, would be the off-guard. Player 1 is the floor leader, an adept dribbler and passer, the "coach" on the floor. He or she designates the attacking series and, as a proficient shooter, is one of the players encouraged to attempt a three-pointer. Certainly, player 1 is urged to take outside two-point shots as the Red, White, Rotary and Blue options unfold. Players 1 and 2 are trained in the concept of interchangeability. Player 2 is expected to substitute for 1, and 1 changes over to 2, as necessary. Both players like to pass and cut, flash *back-door*, split the post, rotate from point to wing to point, dribble-drive, and take the outside shots.

Activation of Red

Figure 1.1 shows the set of Red. Its initial movement, activated by 1's dribble down the side or by verbal call, is drawn in Figure 1.3. Player 3 clears the side and hustles to the high post, and 4 begins to cross the key to the opposite block (see chapter 2 for complete illustrations, examples, and explanation of options).

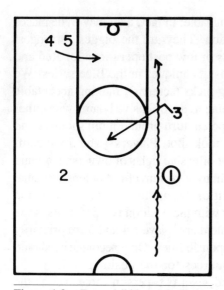 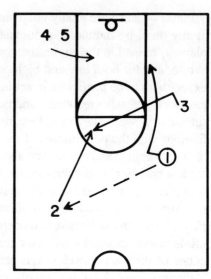

Figure 1.3. Entry dribble, early Red routes.

Figure 1.4. White series entry pass, early moves.

Activation of White

White's set and initial moves are illustrated in Figures 1.1 and 1.4. Players 1 and 2 bring the ball downcourt. Player 3 receives the entry pass from 2 at the high post. As this pass is made, 1 cuts back-door, down the cleared side. The back-door pass from 3 to 1 is the first planned option of the White Series. (See chapter 3 for a detailed account of the White action.)

Development to Rotary

Figure 1.5 shows the rotation of players into Rotary, applicable to both Red and White series. Up to this time, players have traveled their pat-terned routes, and no field goal attempt has transpired; automatically, the team has moved into the 1-2-2 Rotary set of Figure 1.5, with a point player holding the ball, two wing players, and a double low post. Figures 1.6 and 1.7 depict the first "wheeling" stage of Rotary. When 3 passes to the wing (Figure 1.6), he or she has the option of moving opposite the pass to screen for the wing on that side (Figure 1.6) or cutting down the key, hoping for a give-go return pass (Figure 1.7). Notice that 4 and 5,

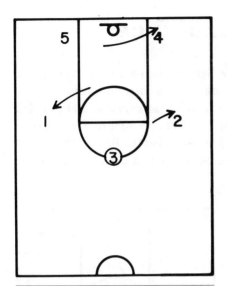

Figure 1.5. Development to Rotary.

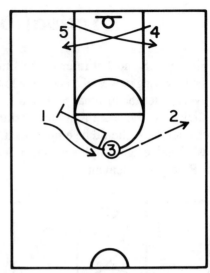

Figure 1.6. Point player's option, Rotary.

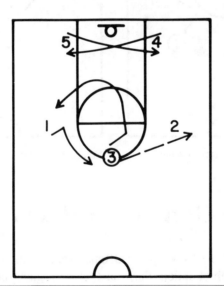

Figure 1.7. Another option.

with natural screens, exchange block positions hoping for an open pass from a wing. (See chapters 2 and 3 for detailed descriptions of Rotary and its options.)

Activation of Blue

Figures 1.8 and 1.9 refer to the Blue Series. The pass from 1 to 3, and the following moves of 5 and 4 out to high post and corner positions, respectively, alter the original set into a 1-3-1 and into an *overload* on that side; obviously, the stage is set for ensuing "anti-zone" offensive action (see chapter 4). It should be emphasized, however, that the Blue Series is just as effective against player-player defenses and that it does not commit to a Rotary supplement.

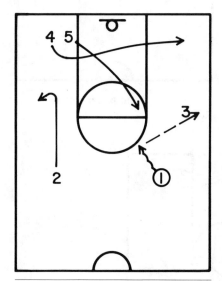

Figure 1.8. Entry pass, first moves, Blue.

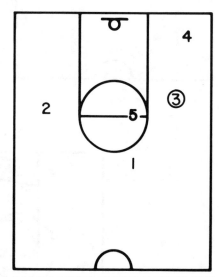

Figure 1.9. Ball at wing, Blue.

Utilization Plans

All three series of the New Option Offense are classified as multiple; that is, with their wealth of options they function well against both player-player and zone defenses. The Blue Series, however, is considered the "workhorse" against all types of zones, especially if Red and/or White are in difficulty. The three series are adaptable to any number of pregame plans, some of which are listed below:

- Utilize all three during the game in alternating fashion, no matter what type of defense is encountered; delegate to the floor leader the responsibility of cueing (keying) Red, White, and Blue.
- Against a team that changes defenses during the flow of game, combine Red *or* White with Blue; use Red *or* White in player-player situations, and use Blue against zone defensive sets.
- "Keep it simple," and use only Blue as the multiple offense against both player-player and zone.
- Change the combinations at halftime or during a time-out.
- Attach a few memorized special plays (to be "called" by the coach and/or floor leader) to the game plan.
- Detach Rotary from Red and White and use it as an independent 1-2-2 entity. Especially give consideration to its employment as a separate unit against certain zone defenses and in ball-control, protect-the-lead, and use-the-clock situations.

Summary

The New Option Offense is comprised of three separate units of attack, all three usually generated by the floor leader's cue or key. The offense lends itself very well to adaptations, depending on the varying needs of different teams and coaches. It operates with the *option* concept, in which "if something doesn't work, something else will." The set positions are numbered and apply identically to all three series, and the numbering procedure carries over to player designations as well. "Player 3" refers to both player and position, replacing the traditional terms "guard" and "forward." The use of numbers is in no way dehumanizing; rather, it serves to *clarify*, to save time, and to ensure that there is sanity and comprehension during substitutions and time-outs in a game.

Interchangeability of players, position to position, is a salient feature of the New Option Offense. It is a positive factor in morale and motivation, and it adds to the team's effectiveness and success.

Installing the Red Series

The Red Series features a player directing the team into its offensive pattern with a dribble instead of a pass. This player is player 1, the floor leader, premier ball handler, and proficient dribbler. Player 1 favors the use of the Red Series because, as illustrated in Figure 2.1, he or she is in control with a penetration-dribble down the right side of the floor. The primary hope here is to take one defensive player along one-on-one, into the basket area, because that side of the court has been cleared (Figure 2.1). If unsuccessful in driving all the way, 1 suspends the dribble, selects an open teammate (passes A, B, or C in Figure 2.2), and the Red Series is in full swing, with simple, individual routes and continuous ball and player movement within a team pattern.

Basketball players like simplicity, which is understandable. They should not be restricted on offense by "having to think too much." With this in mind, the Red Series is comprised of simple, purposeful routes; minimum rules; a good, workable balance between the inside and outside game; and an allowance for individual creativity within that balance.

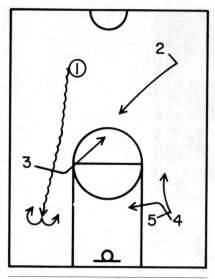

Figure 2.1. Red starts.

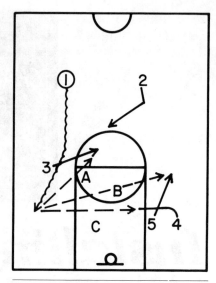

Figure 2.2. Pass options for 1.

The Rotary component of the Red Series is identical to that of the White Series, although the sequence, flow of action, and option choices should vary.

The Red Series is effective against both player-player and zone defenses. (The summary at the end of this chapter has an additional note about this aspect of the offense.)

The Start

The Red Series begins (Figure 2.1) with player 1 keeping possession of the ball and dribbling down the side, crossing with teammate 3 at about the free throw line extended. Supposing that he or she is halted short of a lay-up, player suspends the dribble, stops, turns, and *reads* the floor quickly. That is the situation at the end of Figure 2.1.

The Read: Three Passes

Figure 2.2 shows three excellent passes (A, B, and C) that player 1 may make, all three made possible by disciplined player movement in the Red

Series pattern. Players 5 and 4 moved out of their stack positions, with 5 stepping out toward a wing-posting position, weak-side; player 4 crossed with 5 down low, starting a move into the key area; and player 3 arrived at a high post position, facing the basket, hoping for a swing-type pass from 1.

Each of the three passes, A, B, and C, will be dealt with in turn as separate choices by 1, including many scoring options that are produced after each pass is made.

Consequences of Pass A

Figure 2.3 shows player 3, facing the basket, receiving pass A at the top of the key while route movements of teammates continue. Player 5 retreats to the near low post block; 4 continues across the key, heading for the block and hoping for a high-low pass from 3 on the way as he or she crosses with 1. Player 1 is traveling a route toward the opposite wing area, also hoping for a pass along the way. Meanwhile, player 2 is "cutting across the grain," going over the top of 3 at the high post. Figures 2.4 through 2.7 detail the alternatives and options of player 3, and Figure 2.4 indicates 3's decision to make the short pass to 2, set a pick (screen), and roll to the basket. Using 3's screen against player-player defense, or the creation of an overload against a zone defense, 2 has a jump shot, a dribble-drive, or a pass to 3 on the roll.

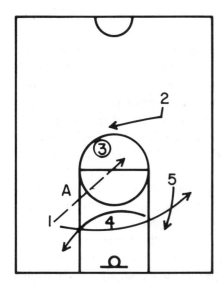

Figure 2.3. Pass A to 3.

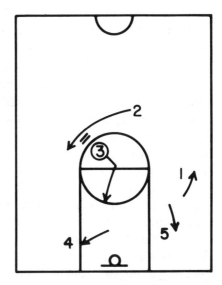

Figure 2.4. Hand-off to 2 option.

Figures 2.5 and 2.6 show 3's decision to reject 2 and instead pass down to 4 or 5. These high-low passes are very effective; 4 takes advantage of the earlier screening actions by 5 and 1, and 5 takes advantage of an unexpected opportunity to jab into the key, target hand extended, asking for the ball.

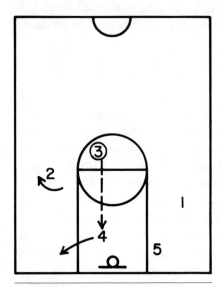 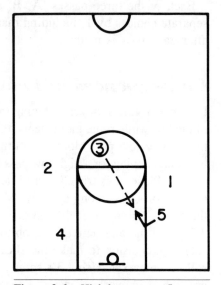

Figure 2.5. High-low pass option.   **Figure 2.6.** High-low pass to 5.

A Feature of Pass A Sequence

Figure 2.7 depicts the back-door option, a feature of both Red and White series. This is one of the most exciting maneuvers in basketball. Coach Ralph Miller's Oregon State teams stand out as classic practitioners, although back-door has been a traditional, universal weapon for years.

Back-door is particularly effective against a defensive team that is running behind on the scoreboard, needs the basketball, and is therefore crowding and overplaying, anxious to "shoot the gap" for interception of passes. Proper execution of the back-door option requires extremely skilled passing, cutting, and deception. The deception comes explicitly from the cutter, who contrives for a half-step advantage with a jab and head-shoulder fake, and/or gets inside position at the start of the drive.

In the Red Series and its Rotary, as well as in the White Series in chapter 3, back-door is not merely regarded as a play; instead, it is an integral part of the pattern. Usually, but not always, back-door signals the beginning of Rotary. If it doesn't work at that stage, it may be tried again dur-

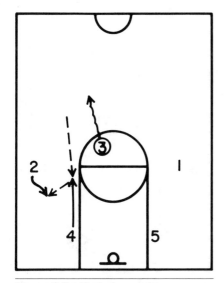

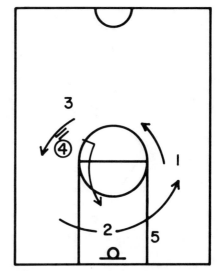

Figure 2.7. Back-door option.   **Figure 2.8.** Over the top.

ing the flow of action on either side of the court. To rerun back-door, all the playmaker has to do is give the signal or key, usually a backward dribble, which resets the team quickly at any time.

In Figure 2.7, player 3 had passed up the other options and, mindful of the 5-second limitation on the time that one can hold the basketball while being guarded, dribbled a few steps backward on the right side. This signaled low post player 4 to pop out; 3 passed to 4, who turned to feed 2 on the back-door cut. Simple as that. The flow has gone into Rotary by natural development from the initial Red, and Rotary is taking over!

In Figure 2.8, player 4 refuses 2's cut and decides to hand off to 3 coming over the top. The wheeling, rotating circulation of players should be noted here, as 4 flips the short pass to 3 for a jump shot, dribble-drive, or return pass to 4, who is rolling to the basket.

Completing the turn and facing the basket, 4 decides to pass down to 5 instead of giving the ball to 3 (Figure 2.9). In Figure 2.10, player 4 has refused all options, including those of dribble-driving or jump-shooting, and passes the ball out to 1 with the implication of starting over. Figure 2.11 shows a new formation of Rotary, and Figures 2.12 through 2.15 carry out Rotary options identical to those in Figures 2.7 through 2.10 on the other side of the court.

With the 1-2-2 reset of Rotary, and with 3 having the ball at the point in Figure 2.16, we close our list of the "consequences" of pass A with examples of continuing action in Figures 2.17 through 2.19A.

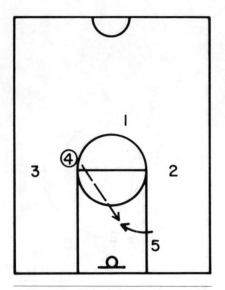

Figure 2.9. High-low option.

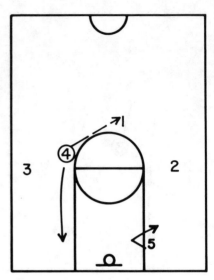

Figure 2.10. Start over.

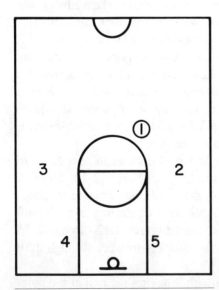

Figure 2.11. Set for Rotary.

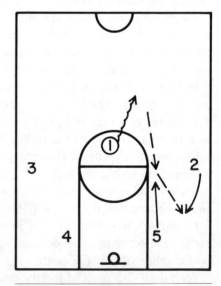

Figure 2.12. Back door.

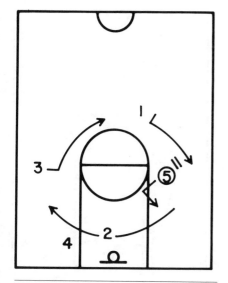

Figure 2.13. Routes, player 5 with ball.

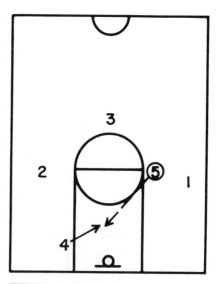

Figure 2.14. High-low option.

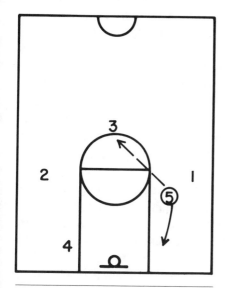

Figure 2.15. Start over.

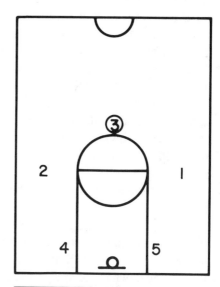

Figure 2.16. New Rotary set.

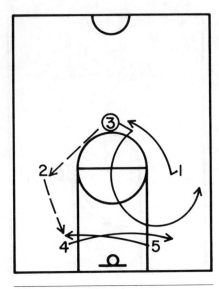

Figure 2.17. Give-go.

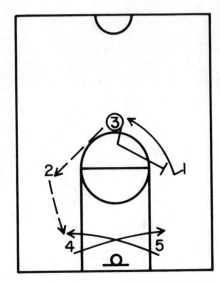

Figure 2.17A. Pass and screen option.

In Figures 2.17 and 2.17A, when the point player passes to a wing, two alternatives are furnished as routes in the team pattern: (a) Go down the key, as shown in Figure 2.17, ask for the give-go return pass, and emerge on the other side, replacing the wing player; or (b) cut across the key as in Figure 2.17A and set a screen for the weak-side teammate. The point player may alternate these two options in any manner during a game. With both options, there is a new positioning (replacement) at the wing and point spots. These Rotary options apply also to the White Series Rotary.

When the wing receives the pass in Figures 2.17 and 2.17A, she or he squares up quickly, looks down at the block, and goes into a triple-threat stance. The primary hope is that she or he will be able to pass to the low post, although the other two triple-threat options of passing or shooting remain.

If the low post player is not open for a pass from the wing, he or she calls "break" and cuts across the key, exchanging with the opposite post player. The exchanging, natural-screening action by the two low post players is mandatory, as the ball rotates from side to side (Figures 2.17 through 2.19A). Cross-court skip-passing is highly encouraged, and delivering the ball down to the low post teammate from the wing is a top objective.

We now go back to refer to Figure 2.2 and pass B.

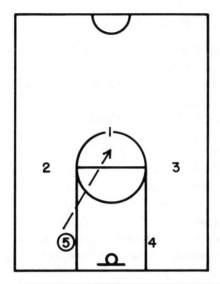

Figure 2.18. Pass out to 1.

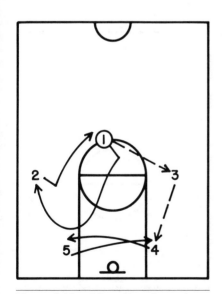

Figure 2.19. Other side, wing to low post.

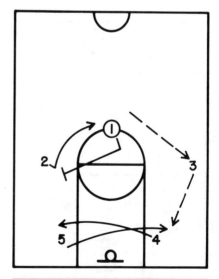

Figure 2.19A. Some passes, screen opposite.

Outcomes of Pass B

Figure 2.20 reviews pass B, as playmaker 1 suspends the dribble and decides to skip-pass across to 5. Notice that 1 follows the pass, generally, in Figures 2.20, 2.21 and 2.22, and may receive a hand-off pass and/or a screen from 5 (Figure 2.22) for a jump shot. Although the drawings may suggest otherwise, 5 won't be standing still, waiting for 1, but instead will be feinting, faking, trying to get a jump shot, dribbling, or passing to an open teammate (as in Figure 2.22). Player 1 should be warned, therefore, to get over to 5 in a hurry if hoping to receive the hand-back.

It is important to note here that 1's route is the *same general path traveled in pass A action* (see Figure 2.3); this is an example of the fact that the play options in these series are based on "simplicity with purpose."

Against a zone defense, the relationship of 5 and 1 in Figure 2.22 creates an outnumbering situation in an area; against player-player, 5 screens for 1 who is coming over the top.

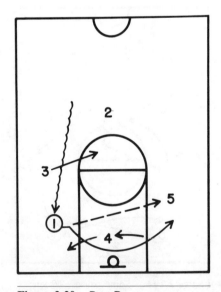

Figure 2.20. Pass B.

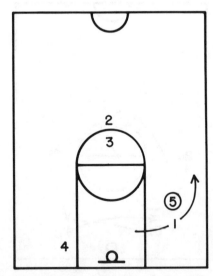

Figure 2.21. Player 1's route.

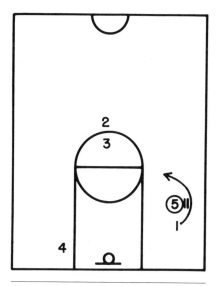

Figure 2.22. Hand-off option to 1.

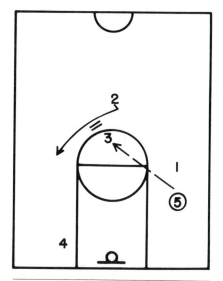

Figure 2.23. Player 5 passes out to 3.

Figure 2.23 shows 5 refusing 1 and swinging the ball out to 3. As with pass A in Figure 2.4, player 2 rides over the top of 3, receiving the handback pass. For the sake of an example of continuity, however, Figure 2.24 shows 3 holding the ball and 2 going on to a wing position. When 5 slides down, the flow of action has become Rotary. Player 3 passes to wing 1 as an example of a beginning, and option routes for 3, as well as the exchange routes for 4 and 5, are shown in Figures 2.25 and 2.25A.

Receiving the ball at the wing, 1 has Rotary choices, three of which are drawn in Figure 2.26. The first option is to pass down to the low post teammate; the second is to skip-pass across to 3; and the third is to swing pass out to 2. Player 1 also has the option of trying to dribble-drive and jump-shoot.

Any one of the three passes in Figure 2.26 could lead to a review of developing Rotary options. Some examples were drawn for pass A, numerous ones will be included in the following pass C discussion, and chapter 3 (White Series) will add many more. Remember, "Rotary options are Rotary options," no matter whether discussed in terms of the Red Series (this chapter) or in terms of the White Series (Chapter 3).

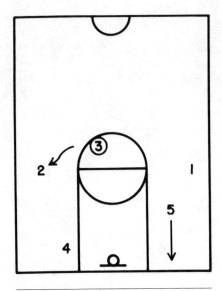

Figure 2.24. Into Rotary.

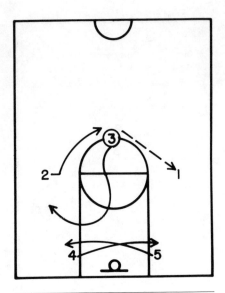

Figure 2.25. Point to wing.

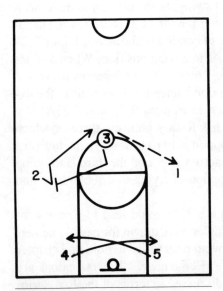

Figure 2.25A. Some pass, screen opposite.

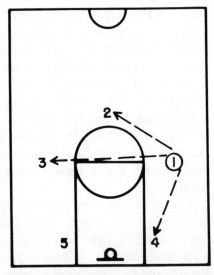

Figure 2.26. Pass options for 1.

Results of Pass C: 1 to 4

Player 1's pass to 4 in Figure 2.27 is a classic example of effective screen-and-cut basketball. As 1 suspends the dribble, 5 automatically sets a screen for 4 and then rolls out; 4 drives hard, crosses the key, and asks for the ball. The consequences of pass C should culminate right there, because 4 will open for the close-in shot, whether against player-player or against zone.

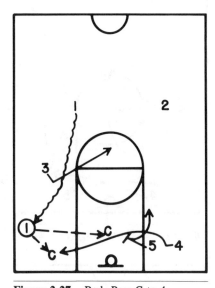

Figure 2.27. Red. Pass C to 4.　　**Figure 2.28.** Pass options for 4.

Development: Three Pass Choices for 4

With the assumption that 4 received the pass but did not shoot, three interesting pass possibilities are pointed out in Figure 2.28. Each of the three is referred to below, and a few Rotary examples are included.

4's First Choice. At the block in Figure 2.29, 4 passes out to 2 at the wing. Player 2 has had the advantage of 3's screen and, in addition, is a part of the overload on that side of the floor against a zone defense. This is a highly desirable pass, because it gives ball control to a player facing the basket and surveying all the good movement of teammates. Player 2 has triple-threat options, but with a pass back out to the point (Figure 2.30), Rotary action follows, as shown in Figures 2.30 and 2.30A.

Player 3 swings the ball over to 1 at the wing. Following the rules of Rotary, 3 cuts down the key and out to the opposite wing (Figure 2.30), or cuts opposite across the key to screen for 2 (Figure 2.30A). Player 2 replaces 3 at the point. Player 1 passes the ball down to 4 (Figures 2.30 and 2.30A),

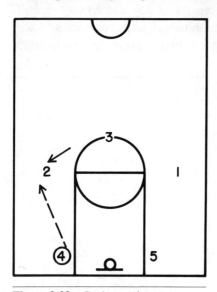

Figure 2.29. Back to point.

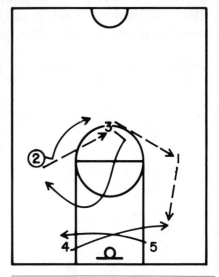

Figure 2.30. Player 3 hopes for give-go.

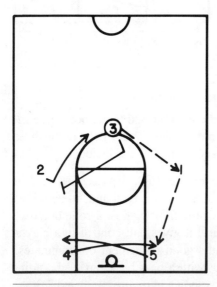

Figure 2.30A. Player 3 passes, screens opposite.

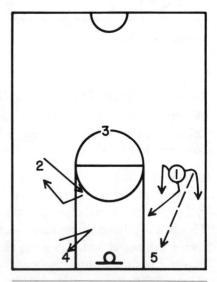

Figure 2.31. Two-player game.

who has exchanged blocks with 5. What does 4 do with the ball? One simple solution, an enjoyable one, is to challenge the defensive player one-on-one!

4's Second Choice, and One Rotary Example.   Referring again to Figure 2.28, 4 makes a cross-court skip pass to 1, who has had a natural screen with teammate 5. Against a zone, 1 is entering a relatively undefended weak-side area, and the skip pass will be very effective. If he or she doesn't shoot after receiving the pass, player 1 may dribble-drive but also has many passing choices, all within the purview of the Rotary movement. One passing choice is presented here, when, after receiving the pass, 1 squares up and reads the low post area. In Figure 2.31, 5 retreats to the block and asks for the ball; 1 passes down to 5 in Figure 2.31, and in a two-player game, 1 tries to get open for a return pass and jump shot. The maneuver was successful, as 5 gives 1 a return pass for a high-percentage jump shot (Figure 2.32).

Note: Figure 2.33 is included here to illustrate, in one example, the desired triangular method of offensive rebounding. With the ball in the air (1's jump shot), players 3, 4, and 5 converge automatically to form the triangle, as shown; 1 and 2 retreat, for floor balance. The rule: 3, 4 and 5 rebound offensively; 1 and 2, get back!

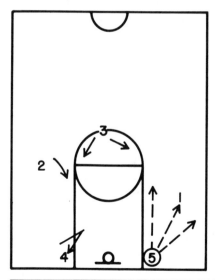

Figure 2.32.   Jump shot by 1.

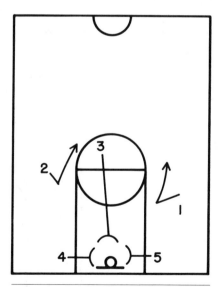

Figure 2.33.   Triangular offensive rebounding.

4's Third Choice, With Rotary Example.   Returning to Figure 2.28, 4 passes cross-key to 5. This pass is also shown in Figure 2.34, with the implication that 5 has choices but is encouraged to work hard in this close-in, weak-side area for a shot, without giving up the ball. On the other hand, 2 and 3 will be asking for the ball; so, for the purpose of demonstrating one more Rotary option, we have 5 passing across to 2 in Figure 2.35. Receiving the pass, 2 decides on a pick-and-roll effort, using 4 as a screen. Player 2's dribble toward the corner in Figure 2.36 is the signal; 4 comes out and sets a screen for 2, then rolls for the basket, looking for a pass on the way.

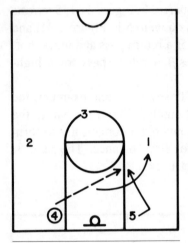

Figure 2.34.   Pass to 5.

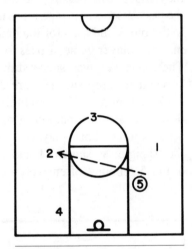

Figure 2.35.   Pass option for 5.

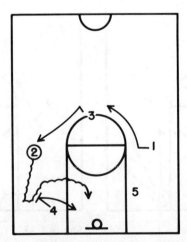

Figure 2.36.   Pick-and-roll option.

Coaching Guidelines

There are several elements coaches must stress for successful execution of the Red Series.

1. The first stage of the Red Series, if executed properly (Figures 2.1 through 2.10), will produce enough effective shooting opportunities that the transition to Rotary is not always necessary. The team should have confidence in this.
2. The reverse pass from 1 to 3 (pass A in Figures 2.2 and 2.3) will be subject to interception. Player 1 must pass to the outside, target hand of 3, away from the defensive player. The "Push, Pull, Pass" technique (chapter 11) must be practiced in order to combat defensive overplay, anticipation, and "cheating."
3. In Rotary, players 1, 2 and 3 must work on fundamentals that pertain to action at the wings. Upon arriving there in Rotary rotation, hoping to receive the ball from the point, the wing must (a) ask for the ball with an extended outside hand, receive it by *meeting* it, make an aggressive *jump stop* with both feet planted on the floor, and (b) assume the *square-up* (attack) position quickly and aggressively after receiving the pass from the point, protect the ball, maintain body balance, read the floor, and consider the triple-threat options of shooting, passing, or dribble-driving.
4. The *break* maneuver by 4 and 5, in which they exchange low-post areas, is vitally important to the offense because it overcomes defensive *fronting*. An excellent drill for proficiency is included in chapter 10, drill 10.8.
5. An excellent drill for becoming expert at Rotary continuity (rotating, wheeling without shooting) is included in chapter 11, drill 11.25.
6. The Coaching Guidelines and Reminders sections in the White and Blue chapters are also applicable to the Red Series.

Summary

The Red Series is workable against both player-player and zone defenses, with the main focus and emphasis on the former. It is activated against the right side of the half-court defense when player 1 dribbles and penetrates that area. If unable to drive all the way for a short jump shot or lay-up, player 1 stops, turns, and expects to have at least three pass possibilities, in the open-player concept: pass A, B or C. These passes are the subjects of this chapter, including the possibilities and consequences of each of the three.

As options unfold and are discarded during the flow of ball and player movement, the transition to Rotary from pass A, B, or C becomes the subject, including an example of just one outstanding choice that a player can make after receiving one of these passes.

The Red Series is geared to meet most needs and situations. It may operate, by signal, in alternating combination with both of the other two series (White, Blue) in a game; it may team up with just one of the others (say, with Blue if there are unusual problems against a zone defense); or it may be used on its own as a complete, independent entity.

Using the White Series

This chapter describes the potent White Series, which attacks the center of player-player and zone defenses and is effective against both. The White Series is the focus of the New Option Offense article in *Athletic Journal* (October 1985) and can be detached from the total New Option Offense and used as a complete, valid offensive entity in its own right. The series is signaled and activated by the quarterback, player 1; player 2 makes the entry pass to 3 while flashing to the top of the key, and players 4 and 5 hurry to their set positions. Figure 3.1 depicts this early action.

Simple to teach and install, this series can be broken down into a study of three obvious continuations or steps. Phase 1 features the individual back-door and over-the-top routes in the search for good shooting opportunities. Phase 2 continues the hunt with an inside high-low game; phase 3 naturally and smoothly develops into the 1-2-2, double-low-post, wheeling, rotating Rotary operation, which is common to both Red and White Series.

Phase 1 and Options

With 2's pass to 3 in Figure 3.1, player 1 changes speed to go back-door, receiving pass C. The essence of back-door is finesse, and deception is part and parcel of finesse. The deceiver is 1, who manages to gain a half-step advantage on the defensive player with a head-shoulder fake, V-jab, and "shifting of gears." Other parts of finesse are especially apparent and impressive in the teamwork relationship of 3 and 2, and in the play of 3 at the high post after receiving 2's pass. In a player-player defensive situation, 3's defensive opponent is forced to make decisions. Should he or she overplay all the way from wing to top of the key and try to deny the pass from 2 to 3? If 3 receives the pass, should the defensive player back off, play tight, or play the ball side of the post? Once 3 pivots with the ball and faces to pass to the driving 1 and/or continues the pivoting and turning movement to face the basket, does the defensive adversary tighten up and play tough, or back off? While the opponent is having such defensive thoughts, 3 is thinking in terms of offensive finesse; this is where all the hard work involved in learning high post fundamentals comes into play.

If a two-player-front zone defense (such as the 2-3 or 2-1-2) challenges this first option (back-door), it must make hurried defensive adjustments and decisions when 3 explodes across from the wing to split the two-player defensive front. Is there aggressive defensive denial as this move occurs? If the ball gets in to 3, do both the front defenders pinch in, in a kind of trapping technique, at the expense of leaving the wings open? Do the back defensive partners slide up to defend the wings? Doesn't this weaken the low post defensive areas? Instead of having the front defenders slide over to defend the high post, could the middle person in the 2-3 or 2-1-2 slide up to challenge? But wouldn't this reaction weaken the inside area? What is the formation and configuration of the zone team when 3 is meeting the pass in the middle while 1 is cutting down the side, asking for the ball? In addition to all this, the second option is coming up, without a break in the action!

If rejected by 3, player 1 continues a route as shown in Figure 3.2, coming out to a wing position on the other side. An option materializes as 2 cuts over the top of 3 to accept the hand-back pass and subsequent screening action from 3. Here 2 gets the opportunity to free-lance and create, with the options of a jump shot, a dribble-drive, or a return pass to 3 (as 3 rolls down the key). These possibilities are drawn in Figure 3.2. Against

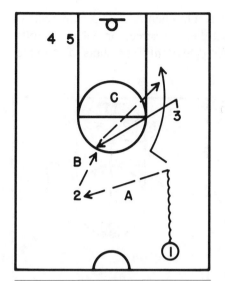

Figure 3.1. Initial action, White.

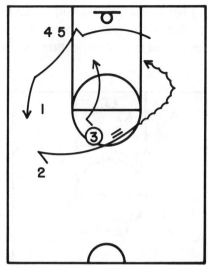

Figure 3.2. Phase 1 continues.

a player-player defense, offensive teammates 2 and 3 hope that X2 and X3 will switch and/or fail to communicate properly. A defensive switch in this situation, of course, results in a size and position mismatch, making the pick-roll (by 3) that much easier. A more plausible defensive adjustment, and one the offense must expect, is for X3 to call out "slide through" and then step back, allowing X2 to do just that: slide through, evading the screen and sticking with 2.

A zone defense finds itself in an *overload* dilemma at the top of the key. It should also be noted that the entire right side of the floor has been cleared out for 2 if the ball is put on the floor in a dribble-drive.

Phase 2: The Inside Game

Phase 2 evolves with options drawn in Figures 3.3, 3.3A, 3.4, and 3.4A. When 3 refuses 2 and continues turning to face the basket, Figure 3.3 shows player 5 setting a rear screen on X4 as 4 slides into the key. If X5 and X4 fail to communicate defensively, 4 will be open in Figure 3.3A because X5's attention will be fixed on 5, leaving 4 open for the high-low pass from the top of the key. The point is, if the defensive players do not switch, 4 will be open.

Figures 3.4 and 3.4A illustrate the result when X4 and X5 *do* switch. In Figure 3.4, player 5 steps up to set the rear screen on X4. As 4 rolls across and behind this action, X5 calls, ''Switch!'' and shuts off 4 in the

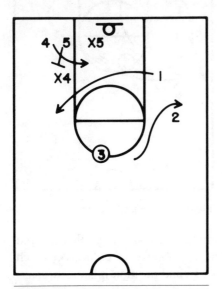

Figure 3.3. No switch.

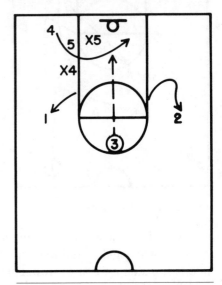

Figure 3.3A. High-low inside game.

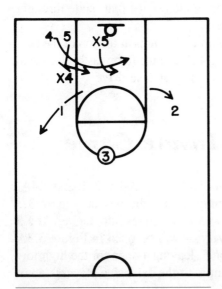

Figure 3.4. Switch.

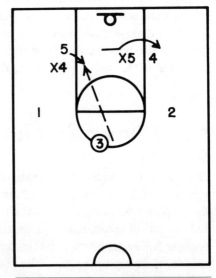

Figure 3.4A. High-low inside game.

key; however, X4 is fixed in place by 5's assertive rear screening action and cannot react when 5 asks for the ball with the left, target hand and arm extended into the key. In Figure 3.4A, player 3 makes the high-low pass to 5; if the defensive players do switch, 5 is open!

The development of inside options against zone defenses must be encouraged, just as against player-player situations. Interestingly enough, screens and picks do work against zone defenses. Additionally, 4 and 5 are instructed to always look for open seams and spots while running their designated routes. They may improvise in the key, taking advantage of defensive mistakes and lapses, as long as they operate in their own general areas.

Notes: Players should be reminded of the following: (a) Along with working on other high-post techniques, player 3 must work on high-low passing, including the soft, deceptive bounce pass, and the jumping, overhead, two-handed ''dump'' pass down to both 4 and 5; (b) player 5 must establish ownership of the block area along the foul line (5's ''turf''); (c) player 5 must learn to use hip and body to fix the defensive opponent in place behind or to the side; and (d) player 5 must remember to ask for the ball with outstretched target arm and hand.

Notice that V-cuts (jabs) are drawn in the individual routes (usually at the beginning) in Figures 3.1 through 3.4 and in all others that follow. You must conduct practice drills for this required foot movement and demand the execution of this basic fundamental, along with the head-shoulder fake. When installing the New Option Offense, including the White Series, the coach must stress that no player on the team moves in a straight line to meet a pass, cuts for the basket in a straight line, or travels in a circling *banana route*. It is mandatory for a player to execute the head-shoulder fake and the V-jab at the start of, or during, every move without the ball.

The action described for Figures 3.1 through 3.4A is a trademark of finesse teams, which are unusually disciplined in running programmed, individual routes and team patterns, and steeped in the team concept. They like to surprise the defense with back-door action, sometimes in multiple, consecutive attempts on alternating sides of the floor, and to use outside screens (including natural and flash screens) for gaining jump shots and dribble-drives. Outside and inside pick-rolls are emphasized, and from the vantage point at the top of the key the high post player looks inside and passes down to teammates who have become open under the basket. One is reminded of the great, ruling teams at UCLA, the philosophy and methods of John Wooden, and the style of Oregon State teams under Coach Ralph Miller.

Phase 3: Rotary Options

Figure 3.5 shows the development of the early routes of the White Series to a new 1-2-2 set, the freewheeling Rotary. Player 3 has the ball out at the point and chooses to begin the mix in Figure 3.6 with the cue to a back-door try: a backward dribble on 5's side, which signals 5 to flash out for a pass while 1 goes back-door.

The back-door options shown in Figures 3.6 and 3.9 as activators for Rotary are only *examples* of how it may start, and are not mandatory. That is, a pass from point to wing (as in Figure 3.13) could activate the mix just as well; it all depends on reading the floor. Throughout Rotary, back-door may occur at any time, keyed by the point player's backward dribble.

In Figure 3.7, player 5 refuses the back-door pass to 1, who continues on through the other wing. Player 3 follows the pass to 5 with a cut over the top, receiving the hand-back pass in Figure 3.7 for a jump shot, a dribble-drive down the cleared area, or a return pass to 5 on a pick-roll.

Figure 3.8 indicates that 5 refuses 3, squares up, faces the basket, reads the floor, and passes down to 4, who has jabbed into the key asking for the ball with outstretched target arm and hand. In Figure 3.7, player 2 has replaced 3 out at the point, in the standard operating rules of Rotary.

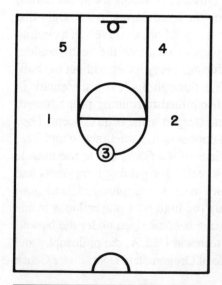

Figure 3.5. Phase 3 sets up.

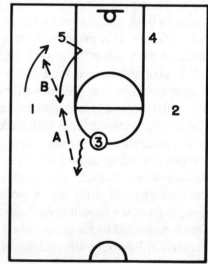

Figure 3.6. Back-door.

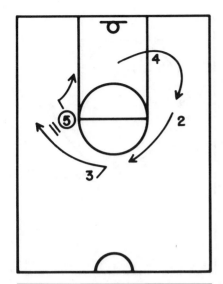

Figure 3.7. Over the top again.

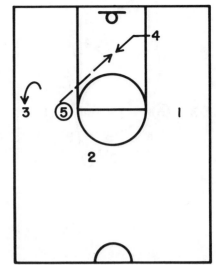

Figure 3.8. High-low to 4.

Figure 3.9 is an example of "starting over." With no workable options within the five seconds he or she could hold the ball while being guarded, player 5 passes back out to the new point player 2, who tries a new back-door sequence on the right side. Player 5 moves down to the low post position.

Figures 3.9, 3.10, and 3.11 repeat the actions of Figures 3.6, 3.7, and 3.8 on the opposite side of the floor as Rotary continues. In Figure 3.12, player 4 decides to start over. Figure 3.13 shows player 3 passing to the wing, moving down through the key, and replacing 2 at the opposite wing, as 2 becomes the new point player. The same pass to the wing, 3's move across the key to screen for 2, and 2's rotation as the new point, are shown in Figure 3.13A.

Figures 3.13 and 3.13A are reminders of a Rotary rule: If you pass to a wing, either go through the key and ask for the ball, or go opposite your pass and screen for the wing on that side. The wing you replace becomes the new point.

Figure 3.14 points out the wing-to-low-post pass and option, and also brings up another rule: If you receive the pass at the wing, square up quickly, read the low post area, and be aware that 4 and 5 are exchanging, trying to get open for your pass, inside. For purposes of example, Figure 3.15 shows 4 passing the ball back out to the point, although 4 may have had other options after receiving the pass from the wing, including those of his or her own low post action.

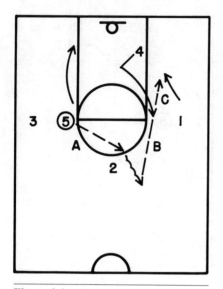

Figure 3.9. New back-door.

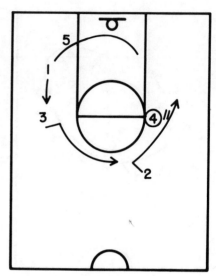

Figure 3.10. Hand-off to 2.

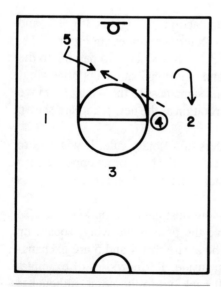

Figure 3.11. High-low option.

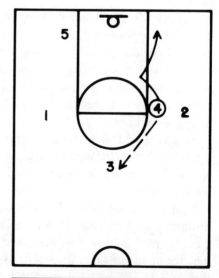

Figure 3.12. Back out to 3.

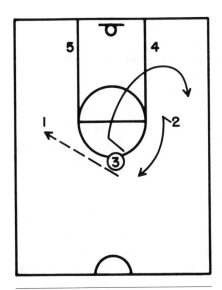

Figure 3.13. Pass and go.

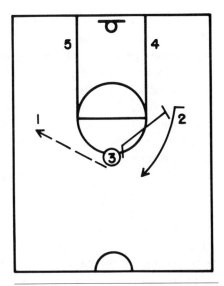

Figure 3.13A. Pass and screen opposite.

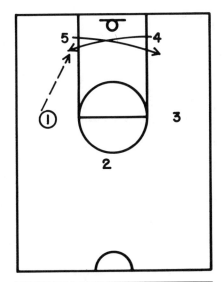

Figure 3.14. Inside game.

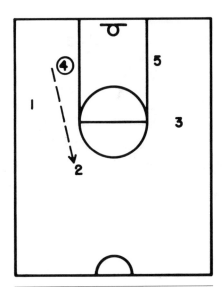

Figure 3.15. Pass back out.

With the ball now at the point in Figure 3.16, the Rotary continues with the example of 2's pass to the wing. This figure also further illustrates the routes of the outside players at this particular time and the inside, natural-screening exchange of players 4 and 5. Coaching points and reminders for this action: (a) When player 4 arrives at a new block position after the exchange, she or he must be *asking* for the ball, with target hand out, and absolutely refusing any denial of the block area; 4 must want the ball, and there must be nothing tentative or perfunctory in his or her attitude; (b) if 4 is open, 3 passes there as a primary objective, unless there is better reason to do something else with the basketball within the pattern; we want the ball down to the low post area as much as possible; (c) the passer, 2, and the replacement, 1, make V-jabs with head-shoulder fakes, and ask for the ball (give-go fashion) from the wing as they drive down the key (Figure 3.16); however, they must always remember the option of going to screen opposite the pass to a wing player (refer to Figure 3.16A); and (d) player 1 jockeys for good shooting range upon replacing 2 and asks for the ball with a target hand. There is always the danger of pass interception when this pass is made from wing back out to the point.

It has been stated that we want the ball passed down to the low post as much as possible because the inside game is the area of success for any offensive system; Figure 3.17 shows the pass from 3 to low post 4

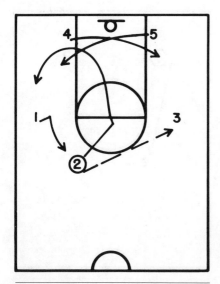

Figure 3.16. Pass to wing and movement.

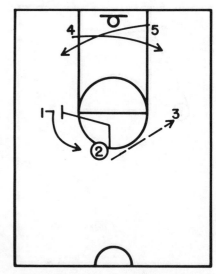

Figure 3.16A. Same pass, screen option.

as *primary*, as it should be. However, there are viable alternatives (which 3 is trained to recognize): (a) pass B, which is a Rotary-pattern swing pass out to 1 for, it is hoped, an open jump shot; (b) passes C and D, which are *skip* passes, very effective against zone defenses; and (c) player 3's right to go one-on-one against a defensive player, with a dribble-drive or jump shot.

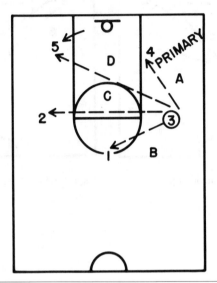

Figure 3.17. Pass options.

Windshield Wiper

Figures 3.18, 3.19, and 3.20 depict the "windshield wiper," the freewheeling, mixing, rotation feature of Rotary. All three figures show the point player cutting down the key (give-go). No additional figures will be drawn to remind about the point player's pass-and-screen-opposite option.

The Rotary windshield wiper of Figure 3.18 points out passes A, B, C, D, and E; the rotation moves of outside players; and the exchange of 4 and 5 as the team works patiently for an open, close-in shot. This is *not* a called play; the windshield wiper is really only the natural movement of player and ball in Rotary, with options and choices encouraged.

Rotary yields high-percentage jump shots at the top of the key and wings against both player-player and zone defenses, as set forth in Figure 3.19. The rule of asking for the ball in give-go is the example in Figure 3.20.

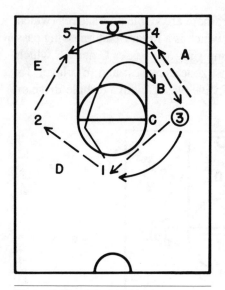

Figure 3.18. Windshield wiper.

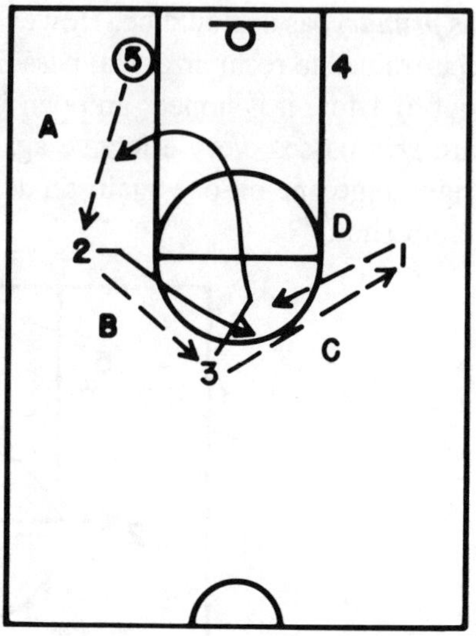

Figure 3.19. Jumper at the top.

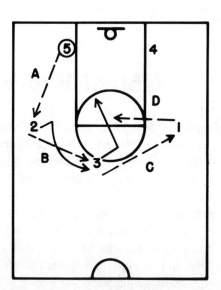

Figure 3.20. Give-go.

Response to Fronting the Low Post

Since *fronting* the low post is such an increasingly popular defensive ploy, an offensive reaction to it must be included in White Rotary and should be a part of Rotary in the Red Series as well. In Figures 3.21 and 3.21A, the point player, 3, passed to the wing, followed an option route, and replaced 2 at the opposite wing. Player 2 rotated to the top of the key. Now, in Figure 3.22, player 1 looks down, ascertains that 4 is being fronted by a defensive player, fakes a couple of passes, and suddenly passes back out to 2 (pass A in Figure 3.22). At this precise instant, 4 turns to the right, pivots on the right foot, and snares (fixes) X4, the defensive fronter, on hip and rear. Leaning forward, 4 asks for the ball with target hand extended into the key and receives the pass from 2 at a "sweet spot" for a lay-up. If defender X5 releases from 5 and moves in to help, 4 dumps the ball over to 5. Defender X4 has been taught a lesson about what has sometimes been called "cheating," a defensive action has been stymied, and Rotary has demonstrated yet another weapon in its arsenal!

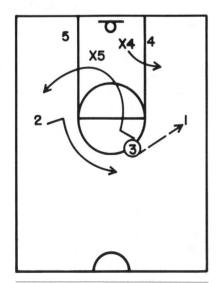

Figure 3.21. Pass to wing. Player 4 is fronted.

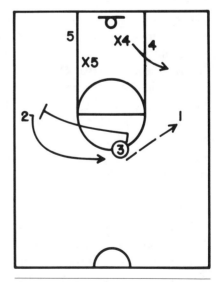

Figure 3.21A. Same pass, screen opposite.

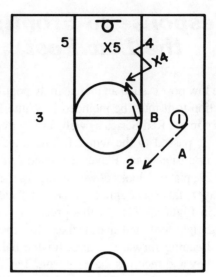

Figure 3.22. Defender X4 is trapped.

A Special White Series Play

One special play is programmed into the White Series. It is activated simply by communication between players 1 and 2 as they bring the ball downcourt. The other players, 3, 4, and 5, do not require the cue or communication; they go to their usual sets in the White Series. The play follows the *open player* concept with its skip-pass tactic. The ball swings quickly and directly across the floor to the weak side, skipping the teammate at the top of the key and catching the zone defense leaning toward the strong side. This play is doubly effective because both 1 and 2 are trained as excellent deceivers, and in traditional roles as backcourt operators they are not hesitant about shooting from the wing areas. Against player-player defense, the play traps cheaters, who anticipate usual pattern passes. Pass B in Figure 3.23 shows the skip pass from 2 to 1. This is a kind of "alley-oop" pass and is especially effective against 2-3 and 2-1-2 zones, not only because of the leaning but because of the open seam tendency and vulnerability of both defenses when they react to 3's clear-out move to the high post. In Figure 3.24, if shut off after receiving the pass, player 1 skip-passes cross-court to 2, an example of improvisation.

For a further example of improvisation, assume that 2 also has no shot; in Figure 3.25, 2 swings the ball out to 3, and, obviously, the movement has evolved into 1-2-2 Rotary.

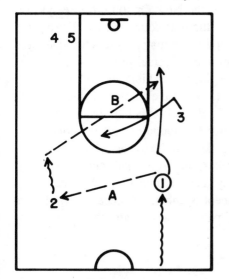

Figure 3.23. Skip-pass play.　　**Figure 3.24.** Skip option.

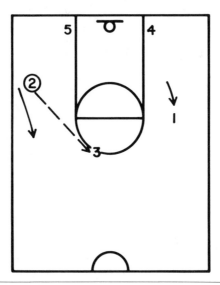

Figure 3.25. Rotary develops.

Summary

The White Series, a central feature of the New Option Offense system, initially concentrates on the center of the half-court offense. During the search for high-percentage shooting options, it may progress through three phases (outside, inside, and Rotary) and a special play.

White is a comprehensive offensive plan that exhibits the following positive characteristics to a high degree: (a) All the elements of floor balance are present, throughout the action; (b) there is excellent triangular positioning for both offensive and defensive rebounding; (c) the continuous movement of ball and players is varied and produces back-door cuts, give-go, high-low action, penetration, screens, pick-rolls, high-percentage jump shots at the wings and top of the key, and an unusual number of lay-up opportunities; and (d) the team concept is enhanced, because all players get to "feel the ball" as routes and patterns unfold and there are offensive options for all.

Defeating the Zone and Player-to-Player: Blue Series

This chapter introduces the Blue Series, the last of three series that comprise the New Option Offense. Blue is a comprehensive, multipurpose offensive component that is effective against both player-player and zone defenses, with emphasis on the latter. To an even greater extent than Red or White, the Blue Series can "stand on its own two feet" as a separate, all-purpose entity, if the coach prefers such a plan. In many games it is used on its own. When employed in conjunction with the other two series, it is simply called or signaled, as necessary, against overly troublesome zone defenses. If the White Series is the "focus" of the New Option Offense (chapter 3), then Blue deserves the title "work-horse," because its anti-zone characteristics complement its anti-player-player qualities and it is called upon most extensively.

Players are enthusiastic about the Blue Series. There is a definite feeling of purposeful movement and teamwork; there will be no problems with the simple but interesting routes. All five players know they will get to touch the ball in the team concept, and they know the coach's philosophy, which allows them to improvise and take advantage of openings that present themselves during the structured movement. Of additional importance, much of the passing and movement is concentrated along, or close to, the three-point line; the true "gunners" will need little encouragement from the coach to exploit the shooting opportunities as Blue unfolds.

Objectives

The initial set shown in Figure 4.1 is similar to the formations of the Red and White series, but the developing team pattern of Blue differs markedly. In spite of the differences, however, the circulation of ball and players progresses with identical goals and objectives: (a) Keep constant pressure on the outside, especially along the three-point line, through the exchanging, rotating, wheeling actions of players 1, 2 and 3, and (b) bring heavy pressure on the inside with the constant position-exchanging activities of 4 and 5, especially as the ball swings from one side of the court to the other.

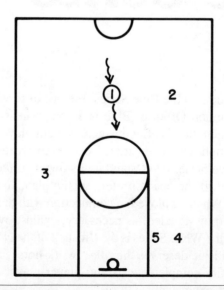

Figure 4.1. Blue set.

The Blue Series is more concerned than White or Red with one aspect of the assault on zone defenses: overloading (outnumbering) a given part of the floor, delivering the ball to that area, and then shifting the overload, and the ball, from side to side.

Activation

If put to use in combination with the other two series, Blue gets to work when playmaker 1 calls "Blue" or gives a hand-signal. Figure 4.1 shows the initial formation (the same as for Red and White), with 1 and 2 bringing the ball downcourt, 3 reaching the wing position on the right side, and the side-by-side set of 4 and 5.

Choice of Entry Passes

In Figure 4.1 the ball has been brought downcourt, and 1 recognizes the opponent's zone defenses. For the sake of this chapter, we'll say that the offensive reaction is to call "Blue," although there is no need for a signal if the Blue Series is being used exclusively. Players move to their initial positions (Figure 4.1) and an entry pass from 1 may go to either wing. In Figure 4.2, wing player 3 receives the pass; in Figure 4.3, the pass goes to the opposite wing, player 2.

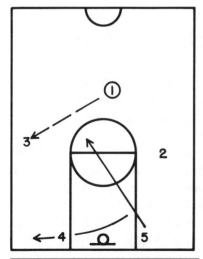

Figure 4.2. Entry pass to right wing.

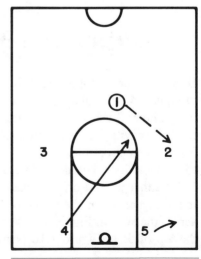

Figure 4.3. Entry pass to left wing.

Pass Options for Wing Players

In Figure 4.4, wing 3 has two passing options: a short one, usually a short bounce pass to 5 at the high post elbow, or down to 4 in the corner. If the entry pass was to 2 at the opposite wing, there are similar passing options: to 4 at the high post, or to 5 in the corner (Figure 4.5).

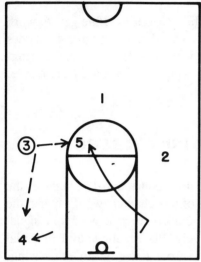

Figure 4.4. Pass options for 3.

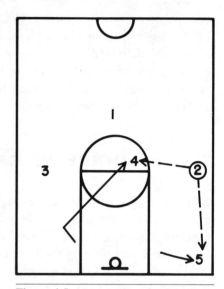

Figure 4.5. Pass options for 2.

Structured Motion Options

Basic structured motions of the outside players 1, 2 and 3 are the subjects of Figures 4.6 through 4.10, showing both sides of the floor. In Figure 4.6, wing player 3 and point player 1 are given movement options, whether the ball is with 5 at the high post or with 4 down in the corner. Player 3's movement options (Figure 4.6) are either to go over the top of 5 or to go back-door, behind 5. In either case, 3 is looking for the ball from 5, by either a hand-off or a back-door pass. If 3 had passed down to 4 in the corner, he or she would be hoping for a give-go pass while cutting across the key. In Figure 4.8 (same side of the court), 3 chose to go over the top of 5; in Figure 4.10 (same side), 3 chose back-door.

If 3 does not receive the ball after passing to either 5 or 4, his or her destination is the other wing, replacing 2, who rotates to the point.

Now we turn to the options of player 1, also in Figures 4.6, 4.8, and 4.10, and it should be pointed out that 1's movements are synchronized with those of 3, following the rule "The passer goes first." With the ball either at the high post or in the corner, 1 has the following route options: cut over the top of 5, hoping for a hand-back pass and a jump shot at the three-point line, or cut behind 5, using 5 as a screen-pick. If the ball is located in the corner, 1 hopes for a pass from 4 as he or she moves, whether over the top of 5 or behind 5. If player 1 does not receive the ball, the route continues to the wing spot vacated by 3.

The main purpose of Figures 4.8 and 4.10 is to clarify Figure 4.6; they separate the "scissors" action option of 1 and 3 (Figure 4.8) from the details of 3's back-door option (Figure 4.10).

Figures 4.7, 4.9, and 4.11 depict identical action if the entry pass goes to 2 at the other wing. Figure 4.7 shows the route options of 1 and 2, with the ball at the high post or the corner; Figure 4.9, the scissors option of 2 and 1; and Figure 4.11, player 2's back-door route option.

All diagrams show that the weak-side wing rotates to the point.

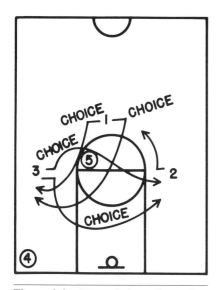

Figure 4.6. Route choices, players 3 and 1.

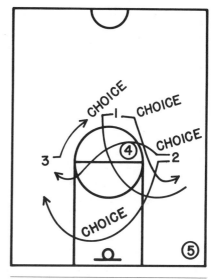

Figure 4.7. Route choices, players 2 and 1.

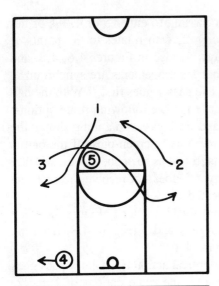

Figure 4.8. Players 3 and 1 go over the top.

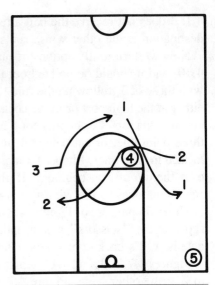

Figure 4.9. Players 1 and 2 go over the top.

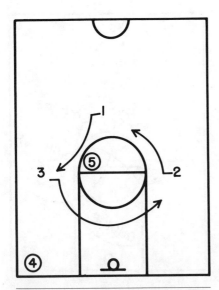

Figure 4.10. Movement, players 1, 2 and 3.

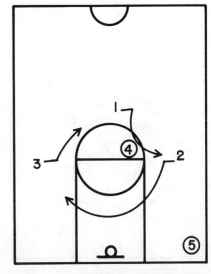

Figure 4.11. Same movement, other side.

The Scissors

Many coaches disagree with the validity and effectiveness claims made for the traditional "scissors" maneuver (criss-crossing and "splitting the high post"). This was bread-and-butter for the legendary Boston Celtics under Coach Arnold "Red" Auerbach years ago, but modern criticism states that "it's too old-fashioned, defensive switching negates it, and against zone defenses no screening action takes place anyway, so why do it?" The truth is that, if executed properly, splitting the high post remains effective against all defenses. Against player-player defense, players are "rubbed off" on the post player; against zones, our Blue offensive players emerge from the high post area, with deception, along the new three-point line, entering and leaving overloaded areas, forming temporary triangles, and looking for a pass. Even if a pass is not always forthcoming, the scissors points the players in the right direction in their routes, and the team pattern continues.

The high post players in the Blue Offense are also important in the options that develop out of the routes and pattern. The actions and options of players 4 and 5 are set forth in Figures 4.12 and 4.13. In Figure 4.12, player 5 can hand off to 1 or 3 as they come by in the scissors procedure, and 5 always rolls down the key as shown, asking for a pick-roll pass.

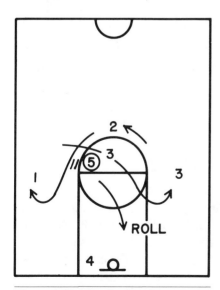

Figure 4.12. Hand-off options.

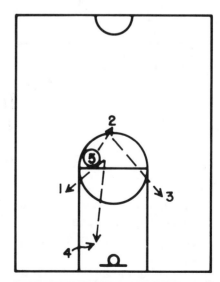

Figure 4.13. More options.

As another option in Figure 4.13, 5 elects to turn, square up, and pass down to 4 (high-low pass action), breaking into the lane. This action would be a part of the triple-threat stance; the other parts would be 5's delay pass to either 1 or 3 (Figure 4.13), her or his own jump shot from the stance, or the dribble-drive to the basket. Player 5's last option, the pass back out to the new point player, is shown in Figure 4.14, and the implication is that the Blue offense starts over (Figure 4.14) when 5 returns to the low post.

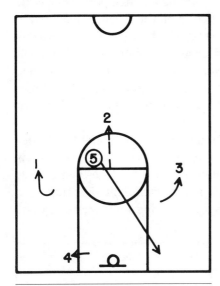

Figure 4.14. Pass back out.

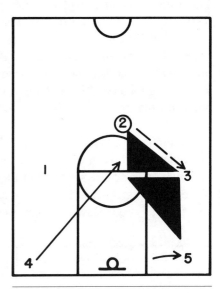

Figure 4.15. New start, opposite side.

A New Start

"Starting over," with 2's pass to 3 in Figure 4.15, we will go through complete sequences and examples of Blue is order to further clarify its operation and comment about significant features. When player 2 passes to 3, low post player 5 goes to the strong-side corner, and 4 blasts out diagonally to the high post, strong side. The two resultant overload triangles, 2-4-3 and 3-4-5, are shaded in Figure 4.15, and 3 has the two passing options (to 4 or 5) shown in Figure 4.5.

The shaded areas in Figure 4.15 also serve as examples of the general rule that defensive areas are best overloaded by purposeful ball and player movement; players in Blue are taught to move in and out of overload areas according to planned routes, never standing still and, if in possession of the ball, always looking for the open player in an unguarded, open seam or in an outnumbered sector.

The Wing Passes to the Corner

In Figure 4.16, player 3 decides to pass down to corner 5 and cut over the top of 4. At least two triangles can be shaded in as examples of players moving in and out of overloaded sectors, forming new, shifting triangles as they pass and move. Player 2 looks for a pass from 5 and a jump shot; 3 looks for a pass while coming over the top of 4; and 4 hopes, with all the movement and defensive adjustment, to be open for a pass from 5.

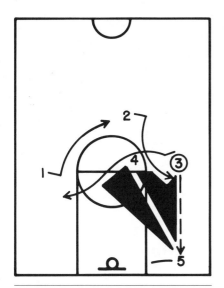

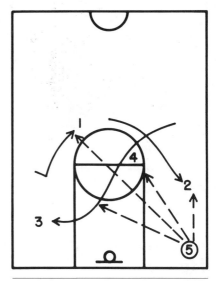

Figure 4.16. Pass to 5. Over the top.

Figure 4.17. Passing options of player 5.

The situation might also call for a great three-pointer by 4! These are excellent options, drawn in Figure 4.17. If loosely guarded, 5 might be tempted to take the ball to the basket via the baseline or to attempt a field goal from the corner. The latter option, however, ranks low in preference and percentage; if the shot misses, the rebound usually favors the opponent's getaway on a fast break.

The same pass from wing to corner is made in Figure 4.18, but this time 3 cuts behind 4, looking for a return, give-go type pass from 5. The same options accrue that were cited in Figures 4.6 and 4.7, as 2 gets a screen from 4, player 3 completes his or her route, and 1 rotates to the point. One shaded triangle of overload is drawn. Skip-pass options, such as from 5 out to 3 at the wing and from 5 out to 1 and 4, are drawn in Figure 4.17. Player 2 is also looking for a pass. *Hit the open player!*

The ultimate destinations of 2 and 3 are the same as in Figure 4.16; as indicated by the movement arrows, they move to the opposite wings, if no pass is forthcoming from 5.

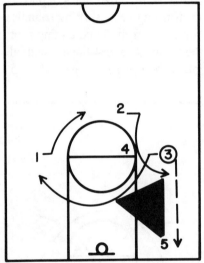

Figure 4.18. Pass to 5. Split the high post.

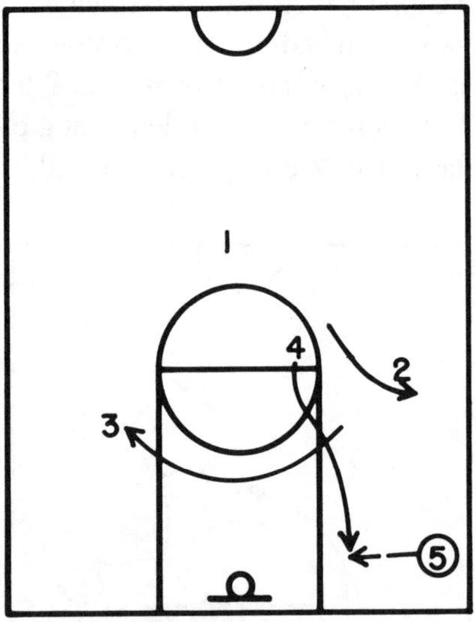

Figure 4.19. High post slides down.

One Important Additional Move, High Post

In a previous paragraph describing the actions of the high post player, one move was saved until now for discussion. The move, an important one when the ball is in the corner, calls for the high post to *slide down* to the block after the scissors by the outside players has taken place. This move down from high post to low post is cited in Figure 4.19. A corner-to-low-post pass from 5 to 4 is also shown and furnishes 4 with the options of a two-player game with 5, a personal one-on-one game at the low post, or a pass out to an open teammate.

In Figure 4.20 we have developed the sequence to include new wings and point. The ball is shown at low post player 4; for purposes of continuity, 4 passes the ball out to 1 at the point and moves across the key to his or her customary low post block.

When 1 passes to wing 2 in Figure 4.21, the signal is clear for 4 to flash out again to the high post elbow, where the pass is received from 2. Figure 4.22 demonstrates 2's option of cutting over the *top* of the high post in the scissors option. Figure 4.23 is a reminder of the alternative route; to go behind 4 and across the key to the opposite wing. Two additional shaded overload triangles are also drawn in 4.23, demonstrating their shift with ball and player movement.

Figure 4.24 reviews a few of the options available to high post 4, who is in control of the ball. Player 4 may (a) hand off to either 1 or 2; (b) turn, square up, and make a delay pass to either 1 or 2; (c) pass down to 5, who is cutting for the basket; (d) take a jump shot or dribble-drive to the basket; or (e) pass back out to the new point player. In Figure 4.25, player 4 refused all these options and passed the ball out to 3, who will start a new sequence on the other side.

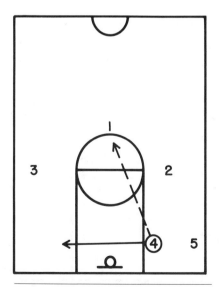

Figure 4.20. Ball to low post. Rotation example.

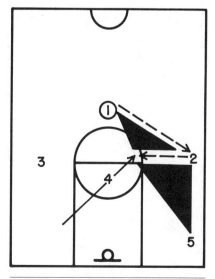

Figure 4.21. Point to wing to high post.

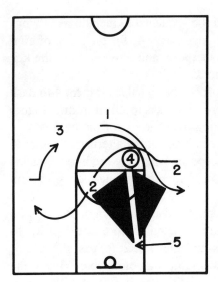

Figure 4.22. Movement after pass.

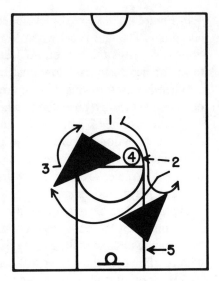

Figure 4.23. Player 2's back-door after pass.

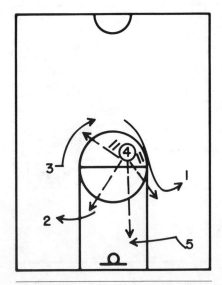

Figure 4.24. Options of high post.

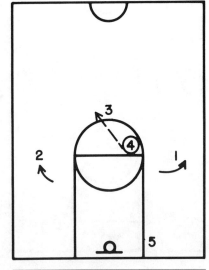

Figure 4.25. Start over.

Shifting Overloads, Rotations and Options

A distinctive earmark of Blue is the shift and formation of overloads and triangles by the simple reversal (swing) of the ball from one side to the other. The post players 4 and 5 flash diagonally from high post to corner, to and from, while the outside players run routes and rotate their positions at point and wings. Player routes, options, and choices are identical, right side and left side.

Figure 4.26 marks the beginning of an example of the reversing, rotating, side-to-side features and, along with the succeeding diagrams through 4.33, serves to demonstrate the right-side operation, with routes, options and objectives identical to those of the left side.

Player 3 passes to 2; player 4, who was at the high post in Figure 4.25, swings down to the strong-side corner, criss-crossing with 5, who is coming out as the new high post. The right side is now overloaded. (Figure 4.26).

In Figure 4.27, player 2 decides to skip-pass over the top of 5 to player 1 at the opposite wing. This, of course, is the quickest way to reverse the ball, and it many times catches a zone *leaning*, to the extent that weak-side offensive players are temporarily unguarded.

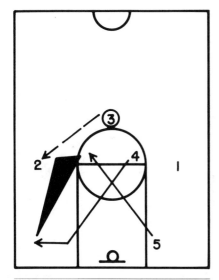

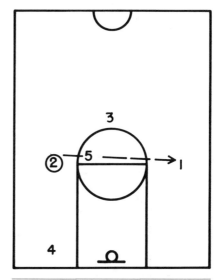

Figure 4.26. Player 3 passes to opposite wing.

Figure 4.27. Player 2 decides to skip-pass.

When player 1 receives the skip pass, 4 blasts out to the high post and 5 retracts to the strong-side corner (Figure 4.28).

The action continues in Figure 4.29 as player 1 refuses both 4 at the high post and 5 in the corner, and instead passes back out to 3. Without breaking the continuity, 3 passes to 2 at that wing, 5 pops out to the high post, and 4 slides down to the strong-side corner where he receives pass C from 2.

We are familiar with the wing's choice of driving over the top of the high post and splitting it with the point player, as shown in Figure 4.30. Major pass options of the corner player, with the ball, are sketched in Figure 4.31; these are similar to actions on the opposite side that were drawn and described in preceding paragraphs.

Figure 4.32 points out the slide of the high post player down to the low post, giving 4 another option after he has refused everybody in their routes. If 4 passes in to 5 at the low post, they may play a two-player game, or 5 may play a typical low post game, with individual moves and/or passes out to the open teammate.

To discuss Figure 4.33, we go back to Figure 4.29 and player 2. Instead of passing down to corner 4, player 2 passes to the high post and chooses to cut back-door behind 5. Routes of 3 and 1 are also drawn in Figure 4.33. The options of 5, with the ball in Figure 4.34, are impressive. They have already been diagramed and described for the action on

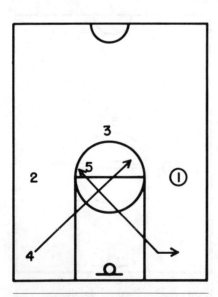

Figure 4.28. Moves of 4 and 5.

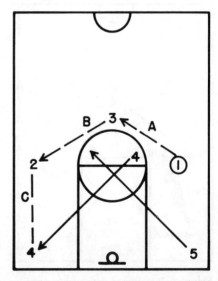

Figure 4.29. Perimeter passing.

the other side of the court and will not be reviewed here. The remaining option of passing back out to 1 is shown in Figure 4.35, indicating that the offense continues from that point.

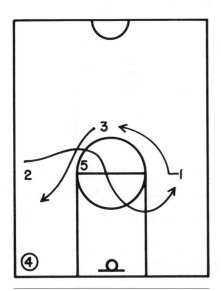

Figure 4.30. Ball in corner.

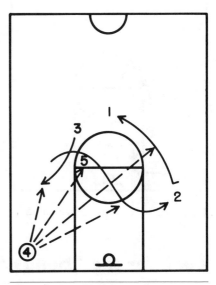

Figure 4.31. Player 4's options.

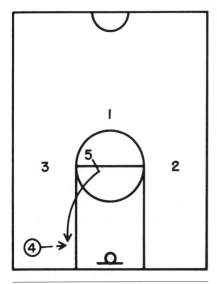

Figure 4.32. Player 5 slides down.

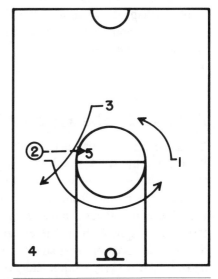

Figure 4.33. Perimeter passing. Refer to Figure 4.29.

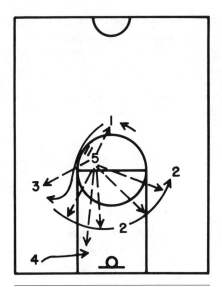

Figure 4.34. Options of high post 5.   **Figure 4.35.** Start over.

Look for the "Bonus Babies"!

A continuity-type offense like Blue, operating with motion in an option concept, will get bonus (unplanned, free-lance) opportunities that result from improvisation and unexpected openings during the course of movement. Perhaps the openings should not be too unexpected; they exist in one way or another in every defense and need only to be recognized and exploited. Outstanding past examples are drawn in Figures 4.36 through 4.39.

A Pass to the Open Player

In Figure 4.36, the ball is passed to the wing as the entry pass in the Blue Series, and the weak-side low post player, 4, is on the way, diagonally, to the high post. Many unanticipated times he or she will be open for just an instant along this inside route; a head-shoulder fake and a V-cut help, too! The wing player 2 must recognize the opening, be aware, and pass to the open spot without "telegraphing" the pass. Player 4 takes what the defense gives or what she or he can create: a turn-around jumper, a drive to the basket, a hook shot, or a pass to 5, who is moving around to get open in 4's general vicinity.

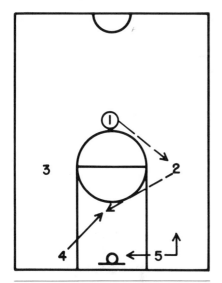

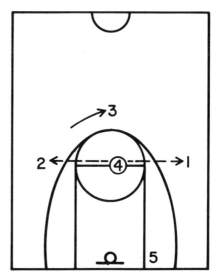

Figure 4.36. Surprise: Inside bonus.   **Figure 4.37.** A three-point bonus.

A Simple Three-Pointer

Figure 4.37 suggests a three-point play that presents itself off the regular pattern. After the pass from wing to high post and the scissors action by 2 and 1, player 4 makes a delay pass to either 1 or 2 along the three-point border. This is a simple way to acquire a three-point attempt, as needed. Just run the offense.

Penetrator

Figure 4.38 shows an improvised, free-lance penetration-dribble by the point player. We shout encouragement for the move because it is an uncomplicated, quick-opening way to deliver the ball to high-percentage shooting areas. The extent of the penetrator's dribble-drive, however, may depend somewhat on the opponent's type of zone defense. A one-player front zone (1-2-2, 1-3-1) will surely challenge the dribbler early, with fierce reaction. A two-player front zone (2-3, 2-1-2), on the other hand, cannot react as quickly; if the point player can dribble and wedge between them and/or draw them in, she has at least six vulnerable passing avenues, as drawn in Figure 4.38. Two of the passing lanes relate to the three-point border line; the other four are inside pass possibilities. Figure 4.39 gives an example against a 2-3 zone. If the defensive wing players converge on her, player 1 dumps a pass to either 2 or 3 for a jump shot, possibly a three-pointer. If player 1 drives through or penetrates, the middle defensive X has to come up to meet her, exposing vulnerable passing lanes leading to 4 and 5.

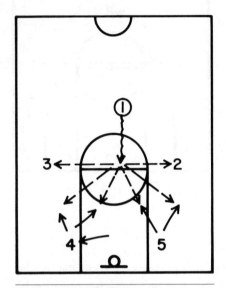

Figure 4.38. Penetrator.

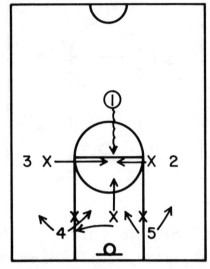

Figure 4.39. Against a 2-3 zone.

Coaching Reminders to Players

Coaches should stress the following points when players are running the Blue Series:

1. Recognize the opponent's zone defense quickly and look at the coach for a signal, although you may be on your own. If Red or White is to be used, no signal or call is necessary; if Blue is to be used, call it.
2. Do not walk the ball downcourt. Even when not in an Early Offense, all players should rush down to their set positions in the offense. The first (entry) pass, initiating the offense, can be made while players are nearing, or just arriving at, their set positions.

3. Do not let the defense intimidate and take a set position from you. There is no deviation from the designated positions at the wings: horizontally level and even with the free throw line extended, and half-way between the side line and the foul line. If the defense over-plays and tries to prevent, work out a back-door signal with the point.

4. The Blue Series is not so rules-oriented that players can't use imagination as they run their routes. Use V-cuts and head-shoulder fakes, square up to the basket at every opportunity when you have the ball, always look inside, always think dribble-drive, and keep moving.

5. Be patient against a zone. Pass to the *open player* as the routes are traveled.

6. Work extensively on jump-shooting skills, mainly from the wing areas and the top of the key.

7. Always begin routes with a V-cut (jab).

8. Do not amble or loiter in routes; when you don't have the ball, move aggressively and with purpose. If a free-lance opening occurs in the area of your route, take it.

9. Players 3, 4 and 5 are the main offensive rebounders. Players 1 and 2 may infiltrate for an offensive rebound, but these two players must always be thinking of floor balance and getting back when a teammate takes a jump shot.

10. Players 1 and 2 get back on defense and maintain floor balance.

11. Players 4 and 5 must concentrate on the following posting-up techniques:

   a. The jump stop and reception of a pass;

   b. The pivot-turn, with ball, to face the basket (triple-threat position); and

   c. The mastery of all passing methods from the post positions.

Additional coaching reminders are listed in chapters 2 and 3. Most, if not all, are applicable to the Blue offense.

Summary

The Blue offense gives notice early on that it is anti-zone, as necessary, when a triangle is formed on the strong side, comprised of the high post, wing, and corner players. Since all three players represent a threat, the zone defense stretches and expands, attentive to the outside perimeter. The defensive attention to the *outside* triggers the Blue *inside* game as players 1, 2, and 3 run routes that take them inside, through the key area, while players 4 and 5 exchange and rotate from corner to high post to low post, looking for the ball. There are reverse-shuffle principles that shift the overload triangles from side to side, maintaining pressure around the perimeter and offering three-point field goal attempts with little or no adjustment. The continuity-motion concept keeps the defense on the move, flexing, contracting, and flailing about, susceptible to screens, cuts, drives, and high-percentage jump shots. All five players are unusually involved in the Blue Series, which is applicable for use against player-player defenses as well as zones.

Being Prepared: Special Plays

The worth of planned, practiced plays in the repertoire and play book of a team's offensive system is unquestioned. The coach should have an appropriate set of prepared, situational two-point and three-point plays ready for use when necessary during the game.

This brings to mind the classic story of an NBA coach, selected as a coach by management, not because of expertise, experience or cerebral qualities, but by reason of his great career and popularity as a long-time player in the NBA. With seven seconds to go, one point behind, and his team in possession of the ball, the coach wisely called for a time-out, and his players ran for the bench, ready to digest the game-winning strategy. Drawing board and pen in hand, but unsuccessfully groping and reaching back in his memory for something, anything, with his players looking at him expectantly, he finally yelled, "Okay, guys, let's go out there and kick some butts!"

In different game situations, in one way or another, the New Option Offense system runs plays. These plays, whether for two points or three, are activated as follows:

1. The floor leader calls out the number of the play as the ball is brought down the floor.
2. The team huddles at the free throw line before a free throw is attempted.
3. The floor leader calls out a number when the team has possession of the ball out of bounds.
4. The coach calls out a number from the bench as the ball is being advanced downcourt.
5. The coach calls a time-out and organizes a play on the clipboard, insofar as possible, one that has been rehearsed, memorized and practiced beforehand. Sometimes, however, the play will be a new one from the coach's prepared notebook, fitting a particular situation.
6. The team is aware of certain cues (other than verbalized) that trigger special plays. For example, in both the Red and White series, a backward dribble by the point player cues a back-door action.

In most cases, New Option Offense special plays are initiated from sets that resemble, or copy, the start of the Red, White or Blue series. If the play doesn't work, or no workable free-lance opportunity evolves, the floor leader calls out "Set Red!" or "Set White!" or "Set Blue!" and the team scrambles to get into one of the patterns without confusion or interruption.

The special plays in this chapter are proven, successful ones that may call for some memorization by the players in some cases and for time-out orientation in others. "Keep it simple" is totally important; no player should be expected to memorize a number of special plays to fit all game situations. Without a time-out orientation, however, each player should be expected to execute at least one two-point, sure-fire play; one out-of-bounds, under-the-basket play; one side-court out-of-bounds play; one three-pointer; and one procedure that beats the press.

At any rate, the following abbreviated listing of plays should furnish ideas and material for special ways to put points on the scoreboard at a time when they are most needed.

A Surefire Two-Pointer

Figure 5.1 shows an easily memorized two-point play that sets up in the initial part of the White Series. Four passes are shown, A, B, C, and D, with the latter finding 2 open in the under-basket area. After pass B, which is a return to 1, player 2 sprints down and uses the double screen of 4 and 5 to emerge in the key for pass D. Notice that player 4 pops out to the top of the key after player 2 swings around, giving 3 an option. This play works well against both player-player and zone defenses.

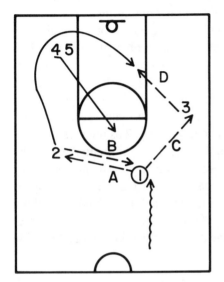

Figure 5.1. A surefire two-pointer. **Figure 5.2.** Clear out for the alley-oop.

Clear Out for the Alley-Oop

In this play (Figure 5.2), player 1 has options besides the alley-oop pass to 3; player 1 may pass to 4 in the corner or to 5 popping out on the other side, and these two options have three-point implications. The primary pass, however, is the alley-oop to 3. Player 1 passes to wing 3 and follows the pass to the outside. Players 4 and 5 crisscross as shown, clearing out the under-basket area. Player 3 hands the ball back to 1, cuts, and circles down the key, looking for the return alley-oop from 1. This is a popular "called" play for the team. *Note.* The alley-oop pass is illegal in International Rules.

Side Court Out-of-Bounds Against Player–Player

This two-point play is easily memorized, so it should be called by the floor leader during the game, with no break in the action. A team should always "go for" a field goal directly upon receiving the gift of possession out of bounds. A desultory, nonobjective pass is not acceptable. In Figure 5.3, player 1 takes the ball out, calls a number or cue, and slaps the ball to activate the movement. Player 3 goes to screen for 2, players 4 and 5 crisscross, 5 goes to the strong-side corner, and 4 posts up, strong side. With the key area completely cleared, 3 rolls from her screen and looks for the primary alley-oop pass from 1. The main secondary pass is to 4; other passes may be to 5 in the corner, or to 2 as the safety valve. Players are encouraged to free-lance and get open, no matter where the ball is located. For example, if 1 passes (secondary) to 4, player 4 may turn to pass to 3, or 4 may hand the ball back to 1 as she comes by. If 1 passes to 5 in the corner, 4 may turn and cut for the basket, looking for a pass from 5. All of these option passes and movements must be practiced. Figure 5.3A illustrates the same action, other side. *Note*: This side

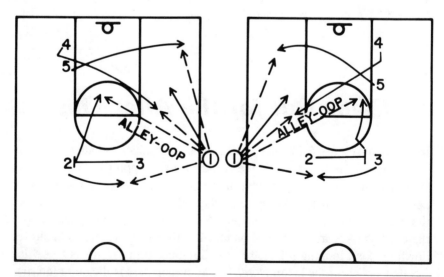

Figure 5.3. Four inbounds options, side.

Figure 5.3A. Other side, four options.

area (anywhere between the free throw line extended and the center line) is the site for the greatest number of inbounds passes during a game. This play is particularly effective against player-player defenses.

Side Corner Out-of-Bounds

These four diagrams show the movement of players when the ball is passed in from the side-corner area, out of bounds. Figures 5.4 and 5.4A show the action on the left side. Figures 5.5 and 5.5A picture the same action on the other side of the court. This play should be memorized, because the area between the baseline and free throw line extended furnishes a popular place for an errant ball to go out of bounds. In Figures 5.4 and 5.4A, player 1 slaps the ball and calls a number, activating movement. Player 5 crosses the key to screen for 4, then rolls back to the strong-side corner as 4 comes over the screen toward the ball. Players 2 and 3 criss-cross, with 2 moving into the key and 3 popping out. Figures 5.5 and 5.5A show the same action, right side.

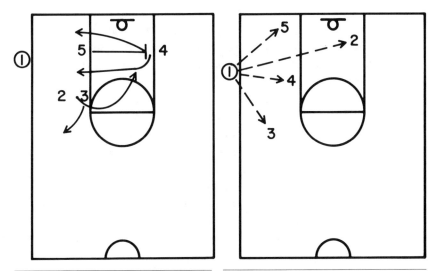

Figure 5.4. Out-of-bounds, side-corner position.   **Figure 5.4A.** Option passes.

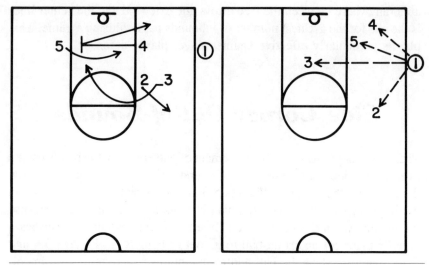

Figure 5.5. Out-of-bounds, other side.   **Figure 5.5A.** Pass options.

Line Up Under
the Basket Play

There is a recent trend for defensive teams to set up in a conventional zone in their under-basket area when the opposing team has possession of the ball for an inbounds pass. The rationale for the zone set is that player-player defense in this situation invites screening actions that result in easy, close-in field goals.

Figures 5.6, 5.6A and 5.6B furnish an answer to the zone defense. In Figure 5.6, players 2, 3 and 5 line up in a column along the side of the free throw line, facing 1, the inbounds passer. When 1 slaps the ball, 2 goes for the corner, 3 cuts into the key and out to the free throw line area, and 5 moves down into the vacated area. Player 4 is located on the weak side. In reaction to this movement, the zone has to expand. Figure 5.6A shows the option passes available to 1. Figure 5.6B points out the primary pass from 1 to 4, player 1's route, and the swing passes that bring the ball around to 1 for a jump shot. A cross-court skip pass from 4 to 1 would be even more effective.

A set of diagrams for each situation of inbounding is necessary, because the referee hands the ball to the inbounds passer on either side of the basket along the baseline. The team therefore must be familiar with the proper

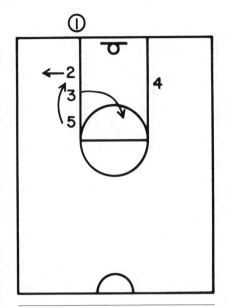

Figure 5.6. Under-basket line up.

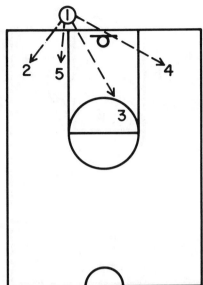

Figure 5.6A. Option passes.

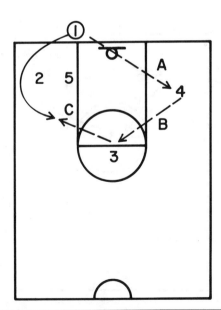

Figure 5.6B. Primary pass rotation.

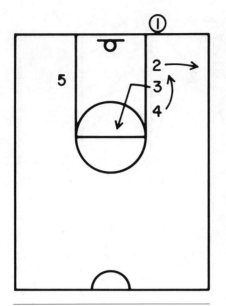

Figure 5.7. Line-up, other side.

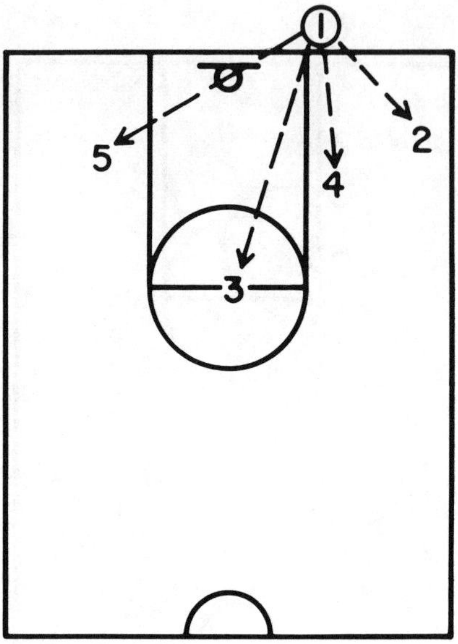

Figure 5.7A. Option passes.

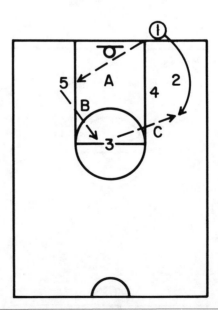

Figure 5.7B. Primary passes.

set and movement on either side, without confusion. Figures 5.7, 5.7A, and 5.7B show the formation and action when the official hands the ball to the inbounds passer on the other side of the basket. *Note*: Faking and feinting moves by both 1 and 5 (or 4) will usually result in a secondary inside pass for a lay-up. The zone has opened up, leaving the inside vulnerable.

Another Out-of-Bounds Play

This "fake to 5, pass to 3" play is added to the list of successful out-of-bounds maneuvers. In Figure 5.8, player 5 is the tallest player, and both 5 and 1 give every indication that the ball is going to be lobbed in to 5 for a lay-up. Player 1 does not glance at 3 or 4. As player 1 slaps the ball, 5 raises his or her hands and arms as if to receive the pass. Player 4 screens for 3 and continues out to the top of the key. The primary pass is a surprise to 3 under the basket. Player 2 is the secondary receiver, and if 1 passes to 2, the ball is rotated from 2 to 4 at the top of the key and then on to 1 for a jump shot. Player 1's route, after the pass, is shown. Figure 5.8A details identical action, other side.

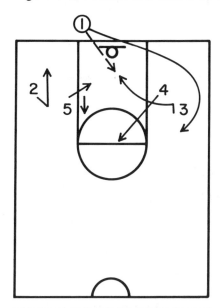

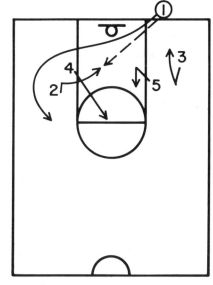

Figure 5.8. A second out-of-bounds play.

Figure 5.8A. Other side.

Three-Pointer for Player 3

Play develops out of a White Series set. As player 1 passes to 2, wing 3 flashes out to the high post, as in the White Series move. Player 4 sets a screen for 5 down low. After passing, 1 goes to the high post and screens for 3, who comes over the screen to receive primary pass A at the three-point line for a field goal attempt. Coming over 4's screen, 5 may receive the secondary option pass from 2 for a field goal attempt outside the three-point line (Figure 5.9).

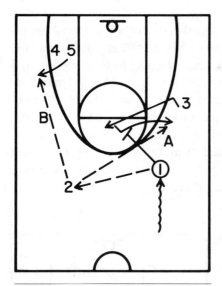
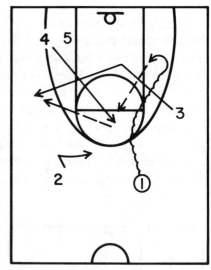

Figure 5.9. Three-pointer for player 3.   **Figure 5.10.** Another three-pointer for player 3.

Another Three-Pointer for Player 3

Player 3 clears the side for 1's dribble, as in the Red Series. Instead of rotating to the high post, however, 3 continues across to the opposite three-point line, making a natural screen with 4 as 4 blasts out to the high post. Player 1 suspends his or her dribble, pivots, turns, and passes out to 4 at the high post. Player 4 swings the ball over to 3 for the three-point attempt (Figure 5.10).

Screen the Back Line
for Three Points

Initial action and set resemble the White Series as 1 passes to 2 and moves toward 2's position. Player 2 passes down to 4 in the corner area and cuts down and across the key to act as a screen at the block. Player 4 rotates the ball back to 1, who swings it to 3 at the point, and 3 delivers the ball to 4 for a three-point attempt. Player 4 has used screens by 5 and 2 while cutting across the key. *Note*: Obviously this play is effective against a zone defense, as well as against player-player. There is an overload of players 1, 4, and 5 on the one side, and the sudden shift of passes to the weak side finds 4 open before the defense can adjust. Player 4's use of screening action is valid against both player-player and zone defenses. One passing option for 1 is to skip-pass over to 4 (Figures 5.11; 5.11A).

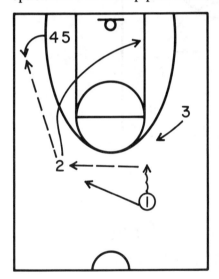

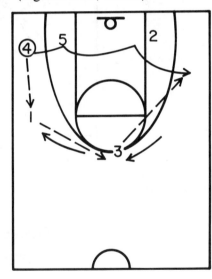

Figure 5.11. Screen the back line for three.

Figure 5.11A. Continued.

Scissors for Three Points

This proven three-point play features a scissors (splitting) action over the high post by the guards and a natural screen crisscross, affording the teammate with the ball the rare opportunity of looking at four options for a three-pointer. The initial appearance and set is that of the White Series. With 2's pass to the high post, players 1 and 2 scissor the post (passer goes first) and head for the three-point line. Players 4 and 5 crisscross as shown, and they aim for the same line. If player 3 is guarded closely, he or she will have to be aware of the five-second violation possibility, and 1, 2, 4, and 5 must move fast to get open, because they don't want 3 to hold the ball for over five seconds (Figure 5.12).

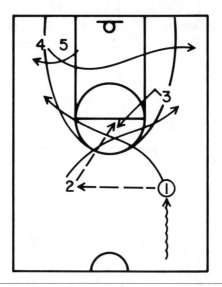

Figure 5.12.   Scissors for three.

Jam Down and Cross for Three Points

Again, the high post has the opportunity to find an open player along the three-point line from among four possibilities. The initial set and entry pass are identical to the White Series. Player 2 passes to 3 at the high post (Figure 5.13) player 4 uses 5's screen to cross the key, and then 4 and 5 come out (Figure 5.13A) to receive the jam-down screening actions of 1 and 2. Players 4 and 5 continue to the three-point line, hoping for a pass from 3. Players 1 and 2 move quickly after the screens, crisscrossing and heading for the corner three-point areas.

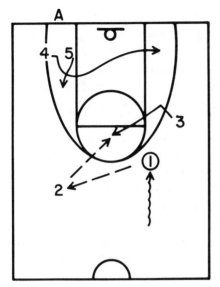

Figure 5.13. Start of play.

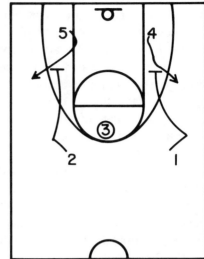

Figure 5.13A. Jam down, players 2 and 1.

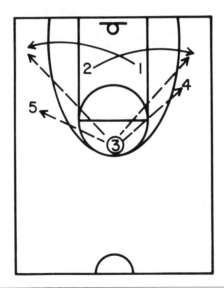

Figure 5.13B. Options for three points.

Notes and Coaching Points: This play features screening actions, so it may stand out as most adaptable and effective against player-player defenses; however, offensive picks and screens are encouraged against zone defenses, as well. Particularly against zones, a *flex* principle is inherent in this play, along with the screens. Figures 5.13A and 5.13B demonstrate passing options to the outside, causing defenses to expand and open up. At the same time, a defense must not disregard the danger of player 3 taking advantage of the expansion to dribble-drive for a two-pointer.

If player 3 is closely guarded while holding the ball at the top of the key, he or she must be trained to act within the five-second time limit in pass selection to a teammate and/or other aspects of the triple-threat principle. Players 4 and 5 must be very attentive regarding the following mechanics: (a) "popping out" off the down screens of 1 and 2; (b) coming to a jump stop, in body balance, with back to the basket, and receiving the pass from 3; and then (c) pivoting and squaring up to face the basket for the three-pointer.

Side Court Out-of-Bounds, Three Points

This play is designed for the out-of-bounds area between the free throw line extended and the center line. Usually called into play against zone defenses, it is also effective against close-checking player-player defenses because of its screening activity. Figure 5.14 shows the action on one side, and 5.14A depicts action on the other side. In the former, player 1 slaps the ball to activate the play and, primarily, passes in to 2. Players 4 and 5 crisscross down low, and 4 crosses the key to the strong side. Player 5 flashes out to the high post, top of the key. After the pass, 1 hurries down the side, through the kcy, and emerges on the weak side. Teammate 2 dribbles, looking for the open player. Option-passes include to 4 in the corner or to 1 on the other side. At the high post, 5 is the "safety valve."

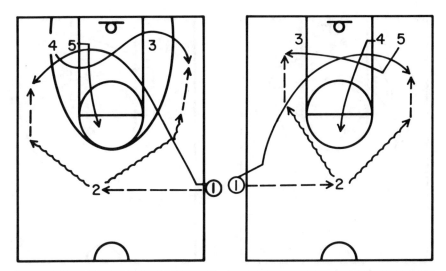

Figure 5.14. Out-of-bounds three pointer.

Figure 5.14A. Other side, three-pointer.

Five to Ten Seconds to Go

Five to ten seconds remain in the game, the team is one point behind, and the ball is out of bounds, ready for inbounding by 1. As 1 slaps the ball (or gives another signal), 4 and 5 set a stack along the free throw line, weak side, and 2 and 3 exchange, outside. Player 1 passes to 2, and 3 cuts down and around the stack. Teammate 2 dribbles down the side, looking for 3 to emerge over or under the stack. After passing to 2, player 1 had made a natural screen with the dribbling 2 and moved to the top of the key as a safety valve. Figure 5.15A pictures the same action for the other side (Figures 5.15; 5.15A).

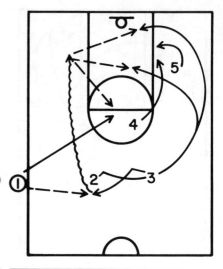

Figure 5.15. Five to ten seconds to go.   **Figure 5.15A.** Other side.

Last Chance

With one, two, or three seconds to go, one point behind, and in possession of the ball out of bounds near the illustrated locations (Figure 5.16),
player 1 slaps the ball to activate the movement. The primary pass is for
3's jump shot, just above the free throw line. Players 2, 4 and 5 converge
in screening action.

It should be noted that International Rules do not require that an official
handle the ball when it goes out of bounds in the backcourt; therefore,
there is no cessation of play, and the team awarded the ball by the official's signal grabs it quickly and usually tries to beat the other team to
the opposite end of the floor with an inbounds pass from the sidelines.
The only time the ball is taken out of bounds at the end line is after a
score. The inbounding team, of course, may call a time-out and design
a play such as the one in Figure 5.16, but the usual action is comprised
of a fast-moving, free-lance pass as the ball is secured.

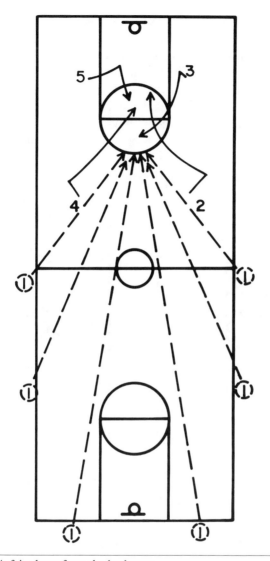

Figure 5.16. A faint hope from the backcourt.

Winning in the Last Second

This is a simple play for that winning field goal in the last second or two of play. Player 1 takes the ball out of bounds, and 2, 3, 4, and 5 line up facing 1. When 1 slaps the ball in Figure 5.17, player 5 steps out to set a screen for 2, and 3 and 4 crisscross in a natural screen. Players 3 and 2 drive on for the key area, looking back for the long pass from 1. Figure 5.17A shows identical action, other side.

There is always a possibility that the opposing team, ahead by a point, may lay back and not come out in this situation. If this happens when only a second or two remains, the team should go ahead with the planned set and run the play anyway, not attempting to get the ball inside to 2 or 3; instead, the ball should go in to 5 or 4 for an immediate, outside jump shot. (Of course, the other alternative is to call a time-out, if one is available, for the coach's strategic decision.)

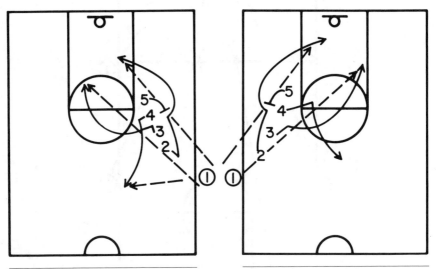

Figure 5.17. Side last-second play.   **Figure 5.17A.** Other side.

Defeating the Full-Court Press

A team needs a method, a Standard Operating Procedure (SOP), for defeating a full-court pressing defense. The SOP is carried out automatically, without the need for a time-out, so it must be memorized. The floor leader must exert leadership and authority in carrying it out. Properly planned and executed, one anti-press method should suffice, and it should be all-purpose, effective against both player-player and zone presses. In Figure 5.18 one of the post players, 4, takes the ball out after the opponent's score and immediately ascertains the press situation. He or she is taught to run the baseline and has five seconds of time (3 seconds in International Rules) to find an open teammate for an inbounds pass. Players 3 and 5 have started down court. Recognizing the press, 1 and 2 hurry to each side of the free throw lane and, to get open, may exchange as shown in Figure 5.18 or may meet and open up, as shown in Figure 5.18A.

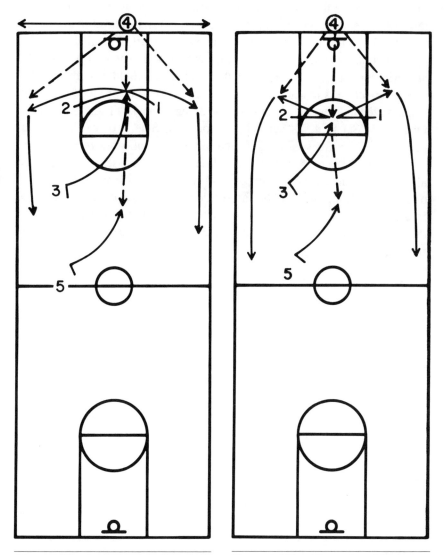

Figure 5.18. Anti-press 1 and 2 exchange.

Figure 5.18A. Players 1 and 2 meet, open up.

In either case, when 3 blasts back to the middle of the key, an opening exists in the vacuum and 3 posts up quickly, receiving the primary pass from 4. Secondary passes may be made to either 1 or 2, on the sides. Receiving the pass, 3 turns and passes down to 5, who is posting up in the middle farther down. If the secondary pass was made to either 1 or 2, they are instructed to look for 3 or 5 and, ideally, pass to one of them.

When 3 or 5 receives the ball in the middle (which is the desired location of the ball at this stage of the press breaker), the team is in the classic fast-break scenario, with both outside lanes filled and a player in the middle with the ball. As the ball starts to move downcourt, 3 or 5 should give up the ball and change fast-break lanes with 1 or 2. The best ball handler and dribbler, traditionally 1 or 2 in the fast break, should be in the middle.

The objective is to *score*. If the fast break does not produce, the team is instructed to keep the pressure on the defense; however, the floor leader must call "Set Red," "Set White," or "Set Blue," or call a play, as necessary. The press is not defeated unless the ball *goes in the basket*.

To review: Player 4 runs the baseline; 1 and 2 crisscross or open up after meeting in the key; 3 breaks into the middle; 4 may pass to 1, 2 or 3; 5 breaks into the middle farther down and receives a pass; and the fast-break lanes fill. Go for the fast break! Be quick, but don't hurry! Run the fast break the way you've been coached! If there is a choice between passing and dribbling, *pass*.

Pushing the Ball: An Early Offense

The New Option Offense program includes a modest Early Offense plan, and the coach encourages pushing the ball downcourt at every opportunity. The objectives of Early Offense are based on the concept that, confidence in the half-court patterns of the New Option Offense notwithstanding, pushing the ball is the quickest and simplest way to score. Certainly it is the most exciting!

Composition of Early Offense

Early Offense consists of the following meshing parts: (a) the aggressive, skillful defensive rebound of a missed field goal or free throw attempt; (b) the quick-release, accurate outlet pass; (c) the immediate establishment of lanes of hustling, "pushing" offensive players; (d) the cool leadership of the floor leader, no matter where he or she is; and (e) intelligent teamwork and moves at the end of the action, including instinctive decisions to call it off and go into an offensive half-court set of the New Option Offense such as Red, White, Blue, or a special play.

Coaching Note

In both practice drills and games, players should adhere to the axiom "Be quick, but don't hurry," and at least two familiar errors must be anticipated: (a) the tendency to attempt poor-percentage, hurried shots, and (b) the tendency to compound this error by attempting the poor shot with not one teammate in an offensive rebounding position.

The Early Offense is not necessarily a fast break. There are as many fast break plans as there are coaches, and the material in this chapter does not offer any extensive additional ideas in that area. Only one proven way of pushing the ball and three drills for installing general proficiency in full-court "sprint and hustle" are presented.

Features of Early Offense

The following illustrations of this one Early Offense operation disclose certain special features. Many similarities between Early Offense and parts of the Red, White and Blue series will be noted.

1. Players 4 and 5 are expected to be the primary defensive rebounders, and player 3 acts as a secondary rebounding force in the triangle.
2. Players 1 and 2 are the primary receivers of outlet passes, and one or the other becomes the middle player, pushing the ball downcourt.
3. Player 3 becomes the high post player, just as in the Red and White series, and gives the same attention to back-door, over-the-top handoffs, high-low passes, and triple-threat action from the top of the key.
4. Important natural screens are prominent throughout the movement, as the players develop downcourt routes which excmplify excellent team offensive floor balance; two players travel down each side of the court, and the fifth player pushes the ball down the middle.
5. Players 1 and 2 are recipients of the back-door pass, reminiscent of action in the Red and White series.
6. All players rotate smoothly and simply into a half-court set if no field goal attempt transpires during Early Offense.

Sequence and
Option Examples

The Early Offense is an effective means of pushing the ball down the floor and usually results in a high percentage shot. The steps of the Early Offense are outlined below.

Outlet Pass and Early Routes

In Figure 6.1, player 4 rebounds and turns to feed the outlet pass to 1 on that side. Players 2 and 3 make a natural screen, with 3 going to the

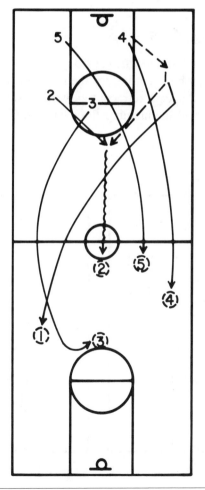

Figure 6.1. Outlet pass. Initial routes.

outside and 2 receiving the pass from 1 in the middle. Player 3 must accelerate and get downcourt ahead of 2's dribble. *Timing* is particularly important at this time. Players 4 and 5 must *dig in* and *go*. Just before turning to meet the entry pass at the high post, 3 makes a natural screen with 1, and 1 goes to the outside lane.

Option Pass to 1

Timing his dribble action so that all players are operating in the Early Offense, player 2 passes to 3, who is flashing in to the high post. Player 3 turns to feed 1 as he or she cuts back-door (Figure 6.1A).

Option Pass to 5

We assume here that 3 refuses the back-door pass option and instead turns to pass down to 5, who is cutting for the basket behind screening action from teammate 4. Player 1 retracts to a wing position, clearing out the under-basket area and maintaining floor balance (Figure 6.1B).

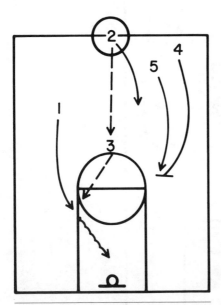
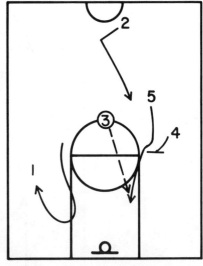

Figure 6.1A. Pass to high post. Back-door option.

Figure 6.1B. Pass to 5 off 4's screen.

Option Pass to 4

Player 5 was not open, so 3 held the ball and found 4 open for a high-low pass. Player 4 had "rolled" after executing a screen-barrier action. Note that 2 is following her pass to 3 (Figure 6.1C).

Hand-Off Option to 2

We assume that 4 was not open, so in this illustration 3 pivots back, sets a screen-barrier, and hands the ball to 2 coming over the top. Player 2 free-lances (jump shot, dribble-drive, or pass). If unable to pass to 2, player 3 is expected to resort quickly to the triple-threat stance (Figure 6.1D).

"Set!"

Assuming in our examples of options that 3 refused 2, we have 1 calling "Set" in this illustration. Player 3 rotates positions with 1, as necessary, by passing to 1 and following the pass. The team goes on to Red, White, or Blue, or a special play, depending upon cues and keys (Figure 6.1E).

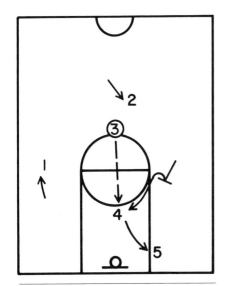

Figure 6.1C. Roll. High-low post.

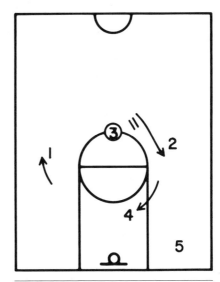

Figure 6.1D. Over the top. Hand off.

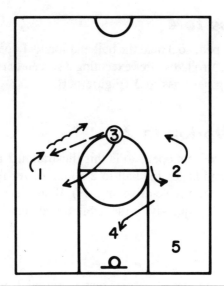

Figure 6.1E. Set.

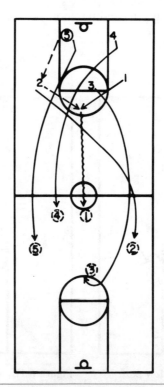

Figure 6.2. Outlet pass, other side.

Same Action, Opposite Side

Figures 6.2 through 6.2E are included in the interests of clarification and simplification, as they point out identical movements and options on the

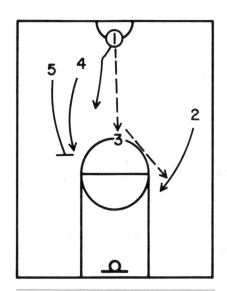

Figure 6.2A. Back-door.

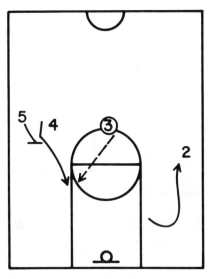

Figure 6.2B. Player 5 screens for 4.

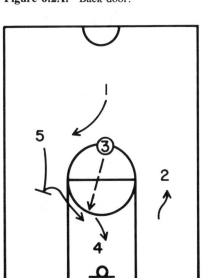

Figure 6.2C. Player 4 rolls. High-low pass.

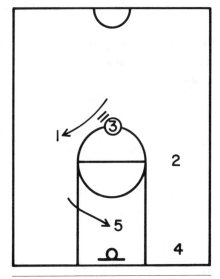

Figure 6.2D. Hand-off to 1.

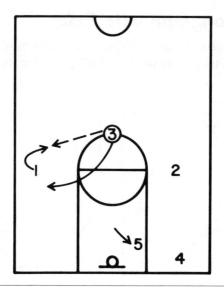

Figure 6.2E. Set.

opposite side of the court. No explanations accompany these time savers, which are drawn only to aid the busy coach.

Coast to Coast in High Gear

The following three drills are selected as teaching instruments for the Early Offense in its role as a component of the New Option Offense. They are not directly related to the one Early Offense plan described in this chapter; rather, their objective is to contribute indirectly to the preparation of the team for the installation of Early Offense. They promote the general concept of " 'git' up and go," so important in the team transition from defense to offense. The following are the main benefits derived from these drills:

- They instill and promote spontaneity in the transition from defense to offense.
- They enhance the skills required in 3-versus-2 play, both on offense and defense.
- They strengthen players' understanding of the concept and worth of pushing the ball downcourt and of applying offensive pressure against a defense, *outnumbered or not*.

Eleven-Player Sprint and Hustle

Other than the admonition to always fill the lanes, there are no designated routes or rules in this drill. Players 1, 2, and 3 start it, with the ball in the middle. They advance and play 3-versus-2 against XA and XB. Whether or not the shot attempt was successful, the rebounder teams with XA and XB in pushing the ball to the other end, against the defense of XC and XD. Players 4 and 5 become the new defensive players (formerly XA and XB), and two of the original offensive players rotate to the 4 and 5 positions. Similar action takes place at the other end, as the new offensive threesome descends on XC and XD (Figure 6.3). There are no breaks in this continuous drill, and no second attempts. The coach may want to announce jump shots only, or lay-ups only, for certain periods of time during the drill.

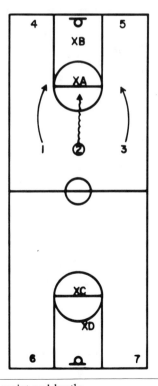

Figure 6.3. Eleven-player sprint and hustle.

Twelve-Player Dig In and Go!

There are designated routes and rules in this drill, and the six Xs (3 on each side of center court) remain on defense until changed to offense by the coach. The emphasis on timing, and the formation of natural screens, will be noted. Coach throws the ball out to 2 (simulated rebound), who passes to 1 in the middle. Player 1 dribbles down, aware of timing, as 2 and 3 fill the lanes. One X from each side of the court rushes out to defend, just as the ball crosses center court, and the action is 3-versus-2. At about the top of the key, a rule applies: As 1 passes to one of the wings, he goes on through "opposite," creating a natural screen. After a dribble or two (depending on timing), the under-basket pass is made to the other wing. Options are permitted and encouraged. Only one field goal attempt is allowed; the Xs return to the end of their respective lines at center court, and the three offensive players start for the other end. The next two Xs go out on defense. At the end of the round-trip, new offensive players (4, 5 and 6) rebound and take off as action continues without let-up (Figure 6.4).

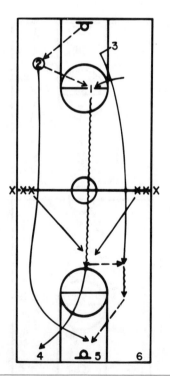

Figure 6.4. Twelve-player dig in and go.

Twelve-Player Crisscross

This drill is identical to the one described for Figure 6.4 except for the culminating offensive action. The routes of 2 and 3 cross in front of the dribbling 1, affording 1 the option of passing to either of the driving players for a lay-up field goal attempt (Figure 6.5).

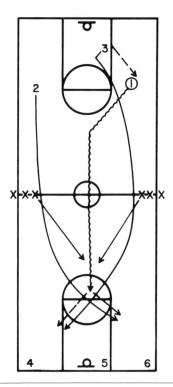

Figure 6.5. Twelve-player crisscross.

CHAPTER 7

Designing an Effective Defense: The 32Z Goose Egg

This chapter describes and illustrates a zone defense, the 32Z Goose Egg. This defensive plan joins the 32Z Trap of chapter 8, and the New Option Offense of chapters 2, 3, 4, 5, and 6, to comprise the foundation for a basketball program. Because of its title, this defense might tend to be dismissed as a gimmick, but that suspicion is not valid. It is rooted, conservatively enough, in the traditional 3-2 zone defense, retains the characteristics of that conventional defense, and adds some distinctive qualities of its own.

Favorable Aspects of Traditional 3-2

We'll begin by summarizing the positive traits of the traditional 3-2 zone defense. These features form the background for the success of the 32Z Goose Egg in its role as the defensive companion of the New Option Offense.

As drawn in Figures 7.1, 7.2 and 7.3, the initial set of the 3-2 naturally and easily slides into adjusted positions that react to the location of the basketball. For example, with the ball located at either side, and the middle threatened by cutters and/or an inside pass, X1 may slide down into a 2-1-2 alignment, as shown in Figure 7.1. If X1 must leave the initial set to step out a bit and pressure the ball (a move not necessarily advocated by 3-2 adherents), the zone may shift to a 1-2-2 configuration in Figure 7.2. If X2 or X3 has to go out for the same purpose on either side, X1 easily slides down to cover the open area, and the same 1-2-2 formation is the result. If the under-basket area or baseline needs strengthening, X1 may slide down as drawn in Figure 7.3, and the team is in a 2-3 defensive set.

These moves and slides by X1 are only examples of the ease of adjustment from the conventional 3-2 set. There are other sliding, defensive moves as the basketball moves; this is not a complete summary of the workings of this defense.

A defensive team, aware of the significance of the clock, lays back initially in the traditional 3-2 zone, enticing the offense to commit itself first. The primary objectives are (a) to compel the offense to operate outside the three-point line; (b) to deny inside passing lanes; (c) to incite hurried, low-percentage shots as the clock runs down; and (d) to *not* aggressively trap, double-team, or steal the ball. Later in this chapter, and in chapter 8's discussion of the 32Z Trap, however, we find that this 3-2 zone does lend itself to alteration of these objectives; it becomes a ball-hawking, strong-arming, combative, *combination-type* (player-player), trapping, double-teaming defensive instrument, and takes on new designations: "The 32Z Goose Egg" and "The 32Z Trap." The 3-2 forms easily into a fast-break opportunity, with the middle player and outside-lane players making a quick transition.

The 3-2 is especially strong at the high post and wings, which are considered critical defensive areas. With three-front outside defenders in linear deployment, this defense has the facility to shut off the high post and deny the wings, making entry passes most difficult if not impossible.

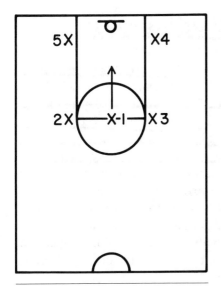

Figure 7.1. Slide to a 2–1–2.

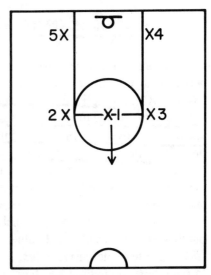

Figure 7.2. Slide to a 1–2–2.

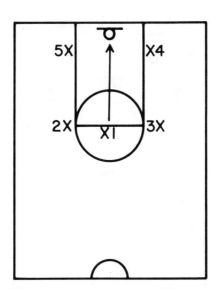

Figure 7.3. Slide to a 2–3.

3-2 Zone Weaknesses

Like all zones, the 3-2 has a weakness or two. There is a "horizontal seam" between the three front players (X1, X2, and X3) and the two back players (X4 and X5). Disciplined, purposeful offenses will send players into this vulnerability, hoping to receive passes. The seam, or seams, becomes wider and more uncovered if proper sliding adjustments are not made when any one of the three outside Xs goes out to meet an offensive threat.

The initial 3-2 set also discloses possible open areas on each side, in inside paint areas, and at the top of the key. Opponent jump-shooters will take a fancy to these places, especially along the arc of the three-point line. Figure 7.4 details the traditional 3-2 set and, with shaded areas, points out the general sites of initial vulnerability. Planned individual adjustment *slides*, and team defensive *shifts*, have to be especially efficient in order to overcome the natural shortcomings.

Offensive overloading, usually comprised of triangles formed by wing, high post and corner players, has been a major problem for the conventional 3-2 zone over the years. The corner areas are somewhat unprotected at times, although field goal attempts from the corners are not in the high-percentage category, and long rebounds from the misses tend to curl out to the free throw line, giving a fast-break opportunity to the defensive team. "Let 'em shoot from the deep corners" is a common defensive philosophy. Jump-shooting from the side areas and the top of the key, usually a result

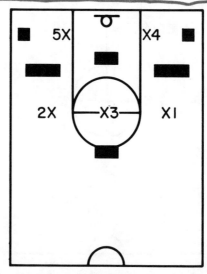

Figure 7.4. Initial 3–2 set and initial "seams."

of overloading, is a much more serious problem for the 3-2 zone, which has always depended on well-disciplined, sometimes complicated, sliding and shifting tactics from area to area for defensive success.

We turn now to the new 32Z Goose-Egg Zone Defense, based on the orthodox 3-2 zone. It is an innovative, uncomplicated, easy-to-install defensive plan.

The 32Z Goose Egg Zone: Coverage

Retaining the traditional initial set of the 3-2 in Figure 7.4, the players of the new 32Z Goose Egg Zone go into action, blanketing a designated area of the defensive half-court, operating in imaginary, oval enclosures (Figure 7.5) that overlap during the movements of offensive players and the basketball. Simulated "arrows" point out limits of responsibilities in all directions in each of the five "goose egg" ovals within the total collage. The arrows designated in each sphere are important and must be understood by the players. As a matter of fact, the introduction of this defense by the coach will be expedited if each player receives a copy of Figures 7.5 through 7.10 for orientation. Figures 7.6 through 7.10 single out each separate, individually assigned goose egg of responsibility and accountability.

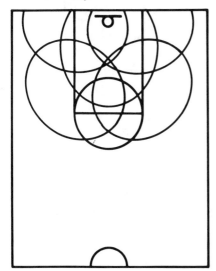

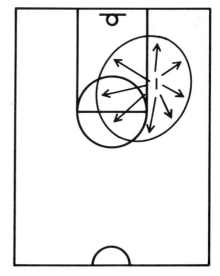

Figure 7.5. The goose eggs.

Figure 7.6. Player 1's zone, with arrows of responsibility.

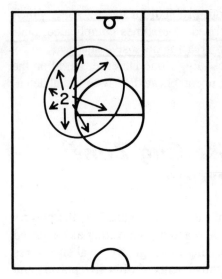

Figure 7.7. Player 2's goose egg.

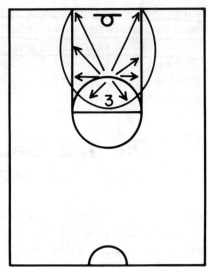

Figure 7.8. The inside goose egg of 3.

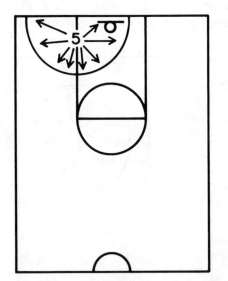

Figure 7.9. Player 5's area.

Figure 7.10. Player 4's responsibility.

Salient Feature

The essence of the 32Z Goose Egg is its *combination* concept, in which primary zone operation adds certain player-player actions, producing a defense that *appears zone* in totality, but utilizes player-player principles when the ball and/or a player is in any one of the enclosures. Any offensive player passing through a goose egg or standing stationary within it, with or without the basketball, is subject to tough, no-holds-barred defensive resistance. If the offensive intruder is passing through without the ball, the defender first orients the intruder, in a "personal" way, claiming ownership of the "turf"; then, the defender denies and prevents the reception of any pass, using *ball-you-player* techniques discussed later in this chapter. If the offensive player is a stationary potential threat, asking for a pass or posting up, she or he is fronted aggressively, with incoming pass avenues barred. Any offensive player dribbling into a goose egg meets individual player-player pressure, as the defender assumes a hard-nosed boxer stance, slide-stepping and shutting-off all the way. When this offensive player departs the goose egg to become another's responsibility, the erstwhile defender releases, remains in his or her goose egg, and pays strict attention to the imaginary arrows within it, as action continues.

Selected Situations: Ball at Wing

We turn now to working examples of the 32Z Goose Egg Zone. Different situations will be drawn and described, with planned defensive reactions. As the situations unfold, it will be noted that (a) the team zone shifts easily from the initial 3-2 set into other alignments, such as the 1-2-2, 2-1-2, and 1-3-1, when the ball moves from place to place; (b) one major example of overlapping and rotating is depicted when the ball is passed to the corner; (c) the system of installing imaginary directional arrows in oval zones, all leading to limits of responsibility, simplifies the defensive operation, obviously makes it easy to teach, gets a defender to the ball hastily, and closes off potential passing and infiltration lanes hastily; and (d) defensive players must be proficient in both player-player and zone techniques. In this combination defense, one player is hard at work, while teammates are playing zone; at other times, at least two players may be playing player-player while teammates are using zone defense methods in their respective goose eggs.

Demonstrations of the shifting characteristics of the 32Z Goose Egg Zone begin in Figure 7.11, when an entry pass is made from point to wing. X1 moves to the ball. If the ball is received just outside the three-point line (or at an estimated 20 feet from the basket, if the three-point rule does not apply), X1's defense is "soft." At the line or within it, X1 will apply heavier player-player pressure. Familiar with their arrows, the other four teammates slide in their goose eggs, as shown, moving in zone stance, denying passing lanes. The team has shifted into a distinct semblance of 1-3-1, with three players in a general line between ball and basket.

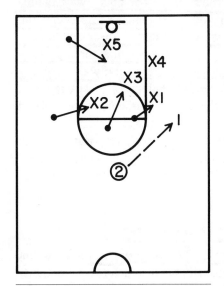

Figure 7.11. Point-to-wing pass.

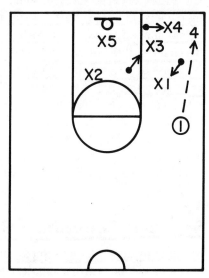

Figure 7.12. Ball in corner. X4, X3 reaction.

Defensive Reaction, Wing to Corner

The wing passes down to the corner in Figure 7.12. Player X4 glides out on an arrow to the limit of her responsibility, applying rather soft player-player pressure if the ball and player are in the deep corner, heavier pressure if they are closer than 20 feet from the basket. X3 slides down to replace X4, and fronts any offensive player who tries to post up at the low post. X5 slides over to the limit of her goose egg, protecting the under-basket area. The adjustments of X3 and X5 are examples of overlapping action. X2 drops down in the key, and X1 is thinking *intercept* if the corner player looks to pass back out to the wing area. Generally, the team has shifted to a 1-2-2 or 2-1-2 alignment, with X3 and X4 playing player-player, and the other three playing zone.

A Defensive Rule

The illustrations of Figures 7.11 and 7.12, showing the fronting tactics of X4 and X3 at low post and in the lane, point out the important defensive rule that no pass is permitted inside: none to a moving player, and none to a stationary player, especially if she is posting up at the low post. Put another way: absolute denial is the rule inside, ball and player alike!

The Skip-Pass Challenge

In Figure 7.13, with the defense shifted to the strong side, the corner player 4 was able, somehow, to deliver a skip pass to the opposite side. X2 travels over to the limit of his goose egg and plays player-player defense. Other players move according to their arrows, transferring to a team alignment of 1-3-1. This skip pass poses a definite threat, especially if the receiver is in good shooting range. It tests the ability of the defense to react quickly, and much defensive *desire* and aggressiveness must be exhibited in getting to the potential shooter.

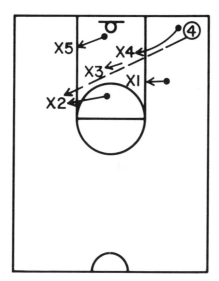

Figure 7.13. Defender X2 and the skip-pass threat.

Defensive Mistake

The receiver of the skip pass is guarded closely, player-player, by the alert X2, so the ball is reversed back to the top of the key in Figure 7.14. Player X3 advances to meet this threat, and the team shifts into a 3-2 or 1-2-2 zone formation.

An emphatic mistake occurs in Figure 7.15 when the defense allows an inside pass from the top of the key to an offensive cutter in the free throw lane. This is an example of exploitation of an inherent weakness in this zone defense and of a teammate's failure to aggressively compensate for the weakness. As the pass was made to cutter 4 in the seam, X1 and X3 were located out near the free throw line and X4 was defending near the low post block; X1, with back to the cutter, had no warning, so the defensive deficiency belongs to X4 (refer to X4's limits, Figure 7.10), who should have reacted to the intruder with ball-you-player tactics. At the same time, X4 should have called out for X1 to drop down and rotate as the replacement around the low post block.

The point is that this defense does not tolerate such a pass; X4, with individual player-player effort, must front and deny any pass to a cutter coming through her goose egg. Figures 7.20 through 7.26 outline ball-you-player situations and explanations.

Assume that the pass did get through and must be acted on. In Figure 7.15, player X4 guards the receiver in player-player fashion, to the limits of her goose egg. X1 slides down and rotates to the extreme limit of her

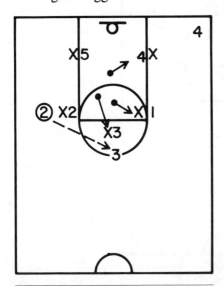

Figure 7.14. Open player, top of key.

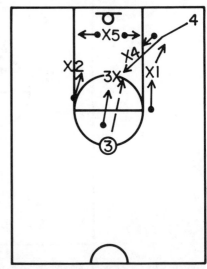

Figure 7.15. A pass gets inside.

zone. X2 and X3 drop down, and X5 is moving within her area of responsibility, preparing to accept the cutter, who is launching herself for a jump shot.

Pass to Corner

Suddenly, in trouble inside, cutter 4 spies an open teammate, 5, in the left corner periphery and dumps the ball over to him (Figure 7.16). Player X5 goes there to defend, as X4 did in Figure 7.12. Player X3 rotates down to the limit of his zone and replaces X5. Players X1 and X4 slide over into the key; X2, along the left side of the free throw lane, is on the alert for an interception. The team has adopted a formation that resembles both 1-2-2 and 2-1-2.

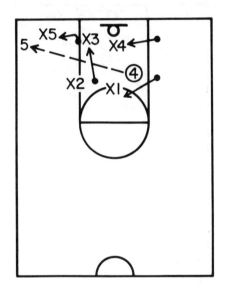

Figure 7.16. Open player in the corner.

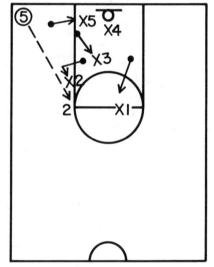

Figure 7.17. Pass back out to wing.

Action and Reaction, Pass From Corner

Player X2 tries to intercept the pass from corner to free throw line in Figure 7.17, fails, and recovers in time to check the receiver in player-player fashion out at the free throw line. Player X1 advances to the free throw line on her side. Player X3 comes up in the key, shutting off the passing lane to the low post. Player X5 releases from the corner, and returns to the low post block. Player X4 assumes under-basket responsibility.

Strong Defense Against Dribble-Drive

In Figure 7.18, player 2, the receiver of the pass from the corner, assumes the triple-threat stance, gives the head-shoulder fake, makes the cross-over step, and drives around X2 with a right-hand dribble. Player X2 releases from the dribbler, who is thwarted by both X3 and X4 in their respective goose eggs. Individual conversion from the zone stance to aggressive player-player action is an important key in this successful containment, as is teammate-to-teammate communication.

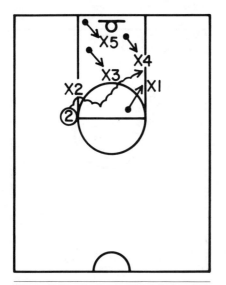 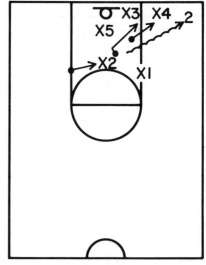

Figure 7.18. Defensing the dribble-drive.   **Figure 7.19.** Dribbler turned away.

Another Example of Rotation

Meeting good player-player defense inside by X3 and X4, the dribbler continues toward the corner in Figure 7.19, furnishing one more example of the helping, rotating aspects of the defense. Still within zone limits, X4 moves toward the corner with the dribbler, 2. Player X3's overlapping goose egg requires X3 to slide aggressively along the arrow and rotate down an arrow to defend X4's vacated low post area. X5 moves over to the limits of her own overlap, under the basket. X2 guards the inside of the key, and X1, again, is ready to make an interception if the dribbler makes an ill-advised pass out to the corner.

Ball-You-Player

There are four components in the *ball-you-player* aspect of this chapter's combination-type defense. They are (a) the basketball; (b) you, playing zone defense in your goose egg; (c) you, playing player-player defense in your goose egg; and (d) the offensive player, your responsibility of the moment, in your goose egg.

The ball-you-player tactic is best defined as the relationship the player establishes in situations involving all of the previously cited items; simply, the relationship of getting, or staying, between your opponent and the ball (when your opponent doesn't have it, of course) in your oval of responsibility. This relationship, mandatory in those portions of your goose egg area designated by the coach, is such that an imaginary triangle can be drawn, the flatter the better, with the three points of the triangle (Figure 7.20) signifying (a) the location of the ball, (b) you, and (c) the player you are guarding. The base of the triangle is the imaginary line between the player you are guarding and the ball. You are the apex of the triangle.

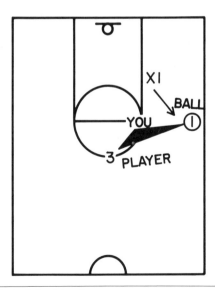

Figure 7.20. The desired flat triangle.

Example of Jump Toward the Ball

In Figure 7.21, player X3 is playing soft defense against 3, because 3 is just outside the three-point line at the top of the key. A pass is made from 3 to the wing, player 1. Acting correctly, X3 leaps toward the line of the pass, flattening the imaginary triangle which is shaded in Figure 7.20. When the passer, 3, makes the cut down the key asking for the return give-go pass in Figure 7.22, the leap toward the ball has placed X3 in the desired ball-you-player relationship. Player 1 cannot return the pass to the cutter.

It should be stated that when the jump toward the ball is made, X3's arms are moving and flailing, and his total defensive demeanor is one of hard-nosed, aggressive denial of a cutting or passing lane.

As mentioned before, X3 is denying the give-go pass from 1 to 3, which may raise a question about the possibility of a lob, or alley-oop pass, since 3 is *behind* X3. The answer is that X3's defensive teammates have moved over with the action, and no such pass is workable.

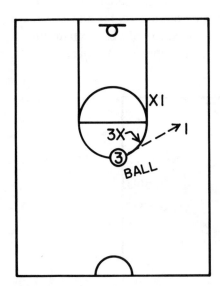

Figure 7.21. The pass, and jump toward the ball.

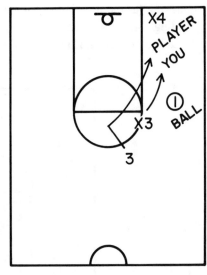

Figure 7.22. Ball-you-player relationship.

Adjustments of Teammates, Rotation of X3

During the action described for Figures 7.20 through 7.22, all defenders are making adjustments, completed in Figure 7.22A. Player X1 comes out to check 1, who has the ball at the wing; X3, at his zone limit, releases from 3; player X4 moves over quickly, to pick up 3; X2 and X5 slide into the key and lane, toward the action (Figure 7.22A).

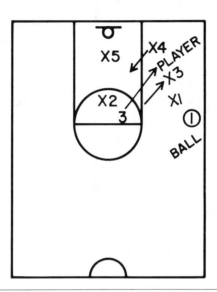

Figure 7.22A. Development of adjustments.

Unacceptable Ball-Player-You

Figures 7.23 and 7.24 depict unacceptable defensive action in 32Z operation. The pass from 3 is made to wing 1; X3 does *not* leap toward the line of the ball. After passing, 3 pushed a step ahead, causing X3 to retreat a step; 3 made a head-shoulder feint, pushed off his left leg in executing the V-cut, and flashed down the side of the lane, asking for and receiving the return give-go pass from 1. Behind him, X3 was in no position to deny the pass. Player X4 would have to pick up the cutter (Figure 7.24), and X3 would rotate to the bottom limit of his zone, near the vacated block. The unsatisfactory large triangle in Figure 7.24 (shaded) should be noted and compared with the one in Figure 7.20.

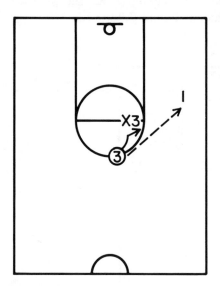

Figure 7.23. New sequence. X3 fails to jump.

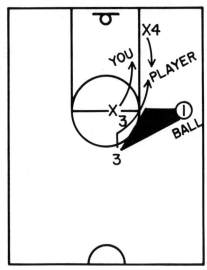

Figure 7.24. Result: unacceptable ball-player-you.

Defensive Reaction to Pass-and-Cut

Individual slides and team shift are shown in Figures 7.25 and 7.26 to demonstrate the reaction to a traditional pass-and-cut tactic that starts at the wing. Passes A and B swing the ball from wing 1 to wing 2 by way of the point. As the passes are made, the original passer, player 1, cuts diagonally for the basket, looking for a cross-key pass from 2.

Communication is important while defensive adjustments are made. X1, playing ball-you-player defense, goes with the cutter to the limits of his zone. X3 initially steps out toward the ball at the point, then slides over as the ball swings over to the left wing. X2 steps out to challenge that pass while, on the other side of the key, X4 advances to front and ball-you-player the cutter in Figure 7.25 as he enters X4's zone. X1 releases from the cutter, and X3's important slide is shown, in which he hurries down to the limits of his goose egg to shore up a vacated sector (Figure 7.26).

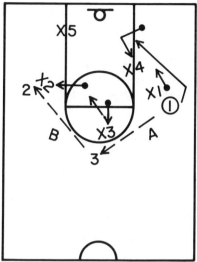

Figure 7.25. Cutter without ball. Player X4 fronts.

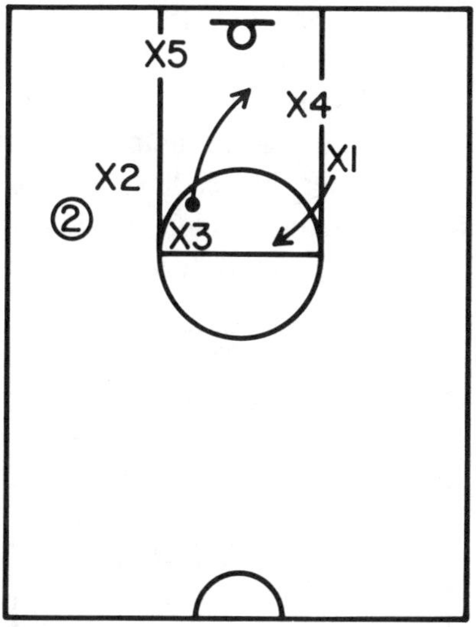

Figure 7.26. Adjustments. Player X3 rotates down.

Defensive Rebounding Plan

Since zone defenses do not have individually assigned player-player responsibilities, including those related to rebounding situations, a plan should be prepared for areal blockade of a portion of the floor under the basket.

At a coaches' clinic, coach John Wooden stated that "basketball is a game of triangles." This premise is especially valid in defensive rebounding. Areal blockage, necessarily utilized by a zone defense, is very effective if it forms a triangle under the basket.

In most situations, both player-player and zone, the rebounding plan is relatively simple. With a field-goal attempt in the air, X3, X4, and X5 are usually the players who transfer to the three points of a triangle under the basket (Figure 7.27). If defensing player-player, they find their opponents and block them out. If playing 32Z, players X3, X4, and X5 usually go to designated spots and block out a triangular area (Figure 7.27). In Figure 7.28, however, it is assumed that X4 has gone out to the limit of the arrow in the corner area (supposing an excellent shooter has the ball out there), and that X3 has rotated to X4's former location, around the block. If a shot goes up from the corner, X4 should not be expected (Figure 7.29) to retract to a rebounding spot. Player X2 drops down to form the triangle with X5 and X3, and X1 and X4 get into position to receive the outlet pass, and the lanes fill for Early Offense (Figure 7.29) or fast break.

The same plan would be in effect if the field-goal attempt was from the other corner. Player X5 would be out, defending in the corner area, and the rebounding triangle would be comprised of X4, X3, and X2. Players X1 and X5 would hurry to outlet-pass locations.

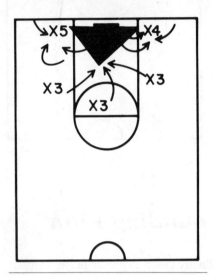

Figure 7.27. Customary triangle block-out.

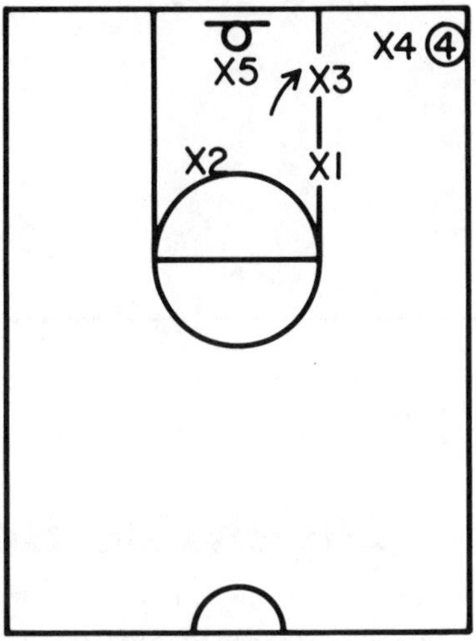

Figure 7.28. 32Z defense, shot from corner.

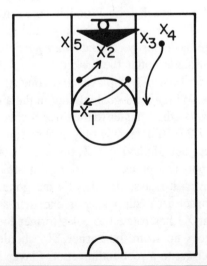

Figure 7.29. A triangle of X2, X3, and X5.

Selected Drills for Fundamentals

The following selected defensive drills are basic to the installation of this team defense. Players cannot be expected to go out on the floor and execute instinctively the maneuvers described so far in this chapter. There must be practice drills that develop basic skills pertaining specifically to the 32Z Goose Egg Defense and show individuals how to fit into the team plan.

The teaching objectives listed below should be considered:

* How to "open up to the ball"
* How to read and react to dribblers and cutters
* How to make the individual conversions from zone to player-player techniques in the goose eggs of this combination defense
* To learn the proper rotation processes of "releasing," "replacing," and "taking over" as dribblers and cutters go through
* To ascertain the importance of communication and, specifically, how and when to communicate
* To work out the basic techniques of fronting, ball-you-player, and denial coverage

The preceding diagrams in this chapter (Figures 7.1 through 7.29), and the accompanying text installing the defense, should provide substantial material for break-down drills. Combined with the following drills of fundamentals, a total workable plan for organizing and establishing the 32Z Goose Egg Defense is assured.

Shut Off the V-Cut

Figure 7.30 sets forth a simple, basic exercise involving offensive player 3, defensive X3, an assistant coach with the ball, and the coach. As the assistant coach passes to the coach, 3 fakes for the basket and then comes toward the ball. Not deceived, X3 leaps toward the line of the pass, opens up to the ball as necessary, and fronts all the way, including when 3 makes the V-pattern as a change of direction. Denial all the way! *Notes*: X1 and X3 change duties. For purposes of the drill, 3 may not deviate in the V-route. Play one-on-one, if a pass is successful.

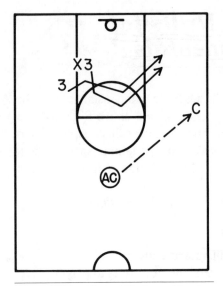

Figure 7.30. Player X3 shuts off cutter.

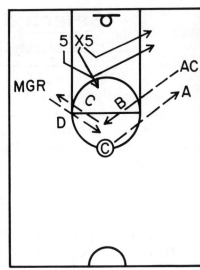

Figure 7.31. Tough "D" at low post.

Tough "D" at the Low Post

Personnel: the coach with ball, an assistant coach, a manager, 5, and X5. The drill in Figure 7.31 is a bit more detailed, in that 5 (offense) and X5 follow the swing passes, with 5 trying to get open at the low post blocks and in the key, while X5 fronts and denies during all of the side-to-side V-route maneuvering. When the coach, at the point, passes to the assistant coach, at the wing, X5 leaps toward the line of the pass and shuts off 5's attempt to receive a pass from the assistant coach. The ball swings from wing to point to wing until the sequence is terminated by the coach. X5 and 5 then change over. *Notes*: For purposes of the drill, 5 must not deviate from the general V-route. The coach is looking for tough defense from X5 and lots of effort by 5 to receive a pass somewhere in the V-route. If able to get open for a pass, 5 plays X5 one-on-one in the low post areas (Figure 7.31).

Action in the Back-Line Goose Eggs

In this game-situation drill, similar to Figure 7.31, X5 is joined by X4, and there are two goose eggs in operation. Player 5 moves from block to block in V-routes, trying to get open for the reception of a pass. Players X4 and X5 communicate in player-player operation when 5 is in their respective zones. The communication we want is along the lines of "Your Player!" "Take him!" "Here he comes!" "I've got him!" "Front him!" "Release!" Player 5 may not deviate from the V-route from block to block. *Note*: This drill is important, and the coach will be very critical and verbal. If 5 does receive a pass, he or she must play offense against both X4 and X5 down low (Figure 7.32).

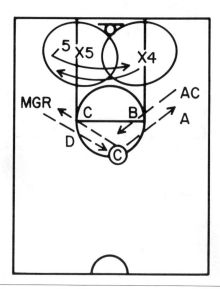

Figure 7.32. Drill for players X4, X5.

Slap-Away, Go for the Dribbler

Personnel: the coach, with two basketballs, one at her feet; player 1; low post player 5; and the defender, X. This drill begins in Figure 7.33, as X gives soft attention to passes A and B from the coach to 1 and from 1 to the coach. These passes are outside the three-point line. When the coach looks down at 5, preparatory to passing, X jumps into the passing lane just as the pass is made (Figure 7.33A) and slaps it away. The coach's pass should be for the teaching benefit of X's slap-away. Reaching down quickly for the ball at her feet, the coach passes the second ball to 1 (Figure 7.33B). Player X flashes over as 1 starts a dribble-drive and plays aggressive one-on-one against the dribbling 1. *Note*: X and 1 change duties after each sequence.

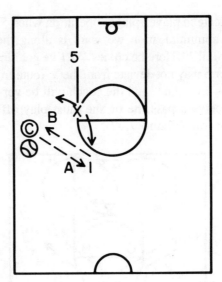

Figure 7.33. Drill starts.

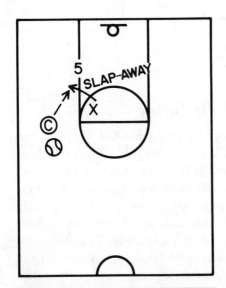

Figure 7.33A. Drill continues. Slap-away.

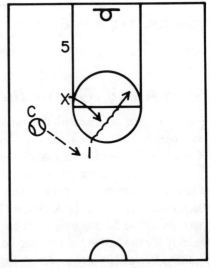

Figure 7.33B. Drill ends one-on-one.

Deny the Cutter Twice

Personnel: one offensive player (P) with a ball; one X, one assistant coach, and the coach, who has a second ball at his feet. Player P passes to the assistant coach and starts a cut through the lane (Figure 7.34). Sensing the cut, X leaps toward the line of the pass, flattening the triangle and utilizing ball-you-player. The assistant coach passes on to the coach, who, recognizing X's good ball-you-player defense, deliberately passes so that X can deflect and slap away the pass from P's hands.

In the key, P hooks back toward the free throw line in Figure 7.34A, as the coach picks up the second ball (from the floor) and swings it back out to the assistant coach. X responds to the "hook" by opening up to the ball and fronting P. The assistant coach, receiving the coach's pass, tries to pass to P as P "fish-hooks" and starts to post up. X, after opening up, slides with P and prevents (slaps away) the assistant coach's pass. If the pass is successful, P and X play one-on-one; if X does deflect the pass, he has played good defense and should be informed of that. *Note*: To open up, pivot on the foot nearest the basket, swing the arms out, get down in the boxer stance, and turn so that visual contact with the ball is never lost. Peripheral vision is important here, because X is defending and watching P while trying to keep in touch with the ball. X and P change over after the sequence.

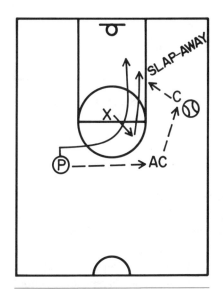

Figure 7.34. Drill starts, deny cutter.

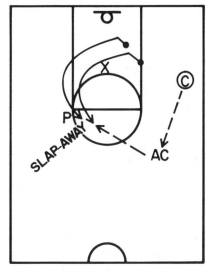

Figure 7.34A. Drill ends. Defend the post-up.

Cutting Through the Goose Eggs

This is a game-situation drill. It is the same drill as drawn in Figures 7.34 and 7.34A, except that X1, X2, and X3 participate against P (Figure 7.35). Again, P has a ball, and the coach has a second ball at her feet. X2 jumps toward the ball as the pass-and-cut is made by P. X2 fronts P to the limit of her zone and releases, and X1 takes over, denying the pass from the coach. When P hooks back, X3 takes over from X1, opening up if necessary, to slide with P and deny the second pass from the assistant coach. If the pass is made to P, P and X3 play one-on-one and change over after the sequence.

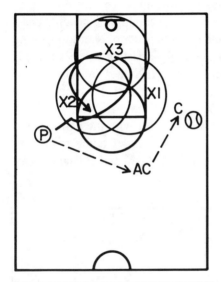

Figure 7.35. Same drill vs. three goose eggs.

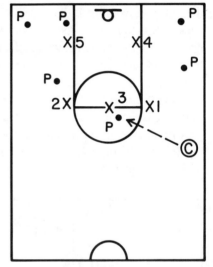

Figure 7.36. Shift with the ball.

Shift With the Ball

Personnel: coach, with basketball; five Xs; and players (Ps), each standing at each imaginary dot. The purpose of this drill is to practice defensive slides and shifts as the ball is passed from one "dot" to another. Players remain stationary, and pass to any dot they choose (Figure 7.36). Coach starts the drill with a pass. As each pass is made, the X person in the goose egg area occupied by the ball and receiver (P) goes into player-player action. The other Xs slide with the pass, forming a collective shift each time. Coach may halt this important drill at times to check fundamentals and make corrections. *Note*: This is also a good drill for the enhancement of passing skills; all types of passes should be used. Coach should demand communication, especially when the ball is passed inside.

Take the Charge

Personnel: coach with basketball, one offensive player (4), and one defensive player (X5). Coach passes to 4, who executes a cross-over step and left-hand dribble to the key and basket (Figure 7.37). X5 steps in to take the charge. *Note*: Players 4 and X5 change duties. Instructions to X5: "When 4 dribbles into the key, be in position; don't be moving; raise your arms straight up; and stick out your chest. The "principle of verticality" applies here. When you take the charge, "fall back, fall down, grunt loudly for the official, and get back up as fast as you can."

Take the Charge With Help

Personnel: coach with basketball, one offensive player (4), and two defenders (X5, X3). Same drill as in Figure 7.37, except that X5 is taught to yell "Help!" when moving over to take the charge, and X5 signals for X3 to slide down and cover his vacated position. X5 takes the charge, and X3 slides low, to the limits of his goose egg (Figure 7.38).

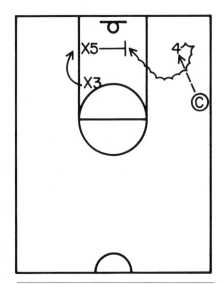

Figure 7.37. Take the charge!

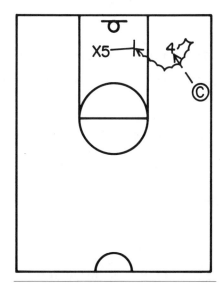

Figure 7.38. Take the charge with help.

Shuffle Off to Buffalo

Personnel: one defensive player, who doubles over, places the palms of both hands on the floor, and slide-steps as shown (Figure 7.39). Work fast, keep down, and make the feet, legs, and hands do the work in a crab-like slide and shuffle. *Note*: This is a good conditioner, as well as a slide-step drill.

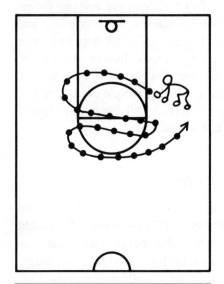

Figure 7.39. Shuffle off to Buffalo.

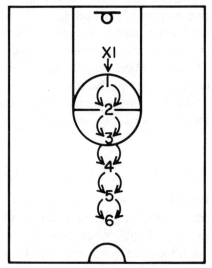

Figure 7.40. Backward obstacle course.

Backward Obstacle Course

Personnel: one X and six stationary players, all standing in line, in depth, facing each other's backs. Drill teaches X to "feel" for an obstacle or barrier, such as a screen, with her hands moving behind her, and checking an imaginary opponent, face to face, while moving backward. As stated, X has her back to the line of players (Figure 7.40). She is sent through the line in a boxer stance, with a backward slide-step. *Note*: Coach demands hard work, stressing aggressive backward slide-stepping. X becomes 6; 6 to 5, 5 to 4, 4 to 3, 3 to 2, 2 to 1, and 1 to X.

The Chair

X sits in the chair, ready to spring out in a boxer stance when 1, with the ball, starts his dribble (Figure 7.41). Maintaining the boxer stance imposed by the chair, X slide-steps and plays one-on-one against 1. Sequence ends when 1 gets a shot or commits a turn-over. *Note*: This must be an intense drill. It teaches basic boxer stance, slide-step, and basic player-player defense.

The following notes apply to teaching proper boxer stance:

- Knees flexed (do not bend at the waist).
- Butt down, back fairly straight (at an angle of about 45° with the floor).
- Forearms parallel with the floor, elbows above the knees, hands spread, palms up.
- Body in balance, feet about shoulder-width apart, one foot slightly in front of the other in a heel-toe relationship.

Summary

The 32Z Goose Egg Zone is a blend of the traditional 3-2 zone defense and an innovative concept that divides a portion of the floor into five over-lapping, oval-shaped sectors of defensive responsibility, within which both player-player and zone techniques are used.

This defense collaborates well with the 32Z Trap (chapter 8) during a game. One popular and effective strategy calls for the team to fall back into this 32Z Goose Egg Zone after an unsuccessful field goal or free throw

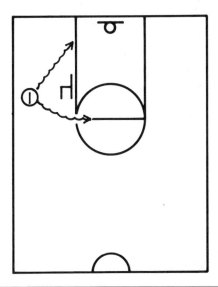

Figure 7.41. The chair.

attempt, and into the 32Z Trap after a successful field goal or free throw. This alternating method disrupts the opponent's offensive tempo and game plan.

The 32Z Goose Egg is relatively easy to teach and install. The players recognize the simplicity and effectiveness of this defense and accept it with enthusiasm as the team's basic defensive plan.

CHAPTER
8

Disrupting an Offense: The Trapping 32Z

This chapter presents a trapping, double-teaming scheme that operates within a limited area and at designated times during a game. Striking suddenly from an initial set that places three front players across the free throw line and two back players in the block area, the 32Z Inside Trap, harassing and aggravating the offense between the free throw line extended and the baseline, has the following objectives:

- To disrupt the movement, timing, and general efficiency of the opponent's inside game.
- To force mistakes and turnovers that result in repossession of the basketball and a likely fast-break opportunity.
- To change the tempo and momentum of the game.

Addition of the clock (both 30- and 45-second) and the three-point line has changed a lot of thinking in basketball, including increasing the emphasis on defensive trapping and double-teaming. Before the introduction of the clock, a team on defense and leading on the scoreboard could set up a lay-back zone formation, pack it in, and shut off the inside, promoting hurried, impatient, low-percentage outside shots as the opponent tried to get back in the game. Conversely, an offensive opponent in possession of the ball and the lead, and recognizing the compressed defensive alignment, could merely pass the ball around the perimeter, tease the inside a bit, and entice the defense to stretch and expand; through control and patience, the offense eventually would force the defense to abandon its lay-back ideas and come out for the ball, exposing open defensive seams.

The two rules seem to place the spotlight, and the burden, on the offense. First, the offense must *attack* the defense, no matter what kind, because the clock is ticking away. Second, because the three-point line is just a high-percentage distance away from the basket, the offense must concentrate more jump-shooting attention and effort along its border. (Concomitantly, players need to lighten up a bit on the old concept that to be successful, the ball must always go *inside!*)

By coincidence, in 32Z trapping major pressure is exerted along the curvature of the three-point line, aggressive attention is given to offensive threats all along the outside, and the inside areas are attended to, in like manner.

Personnel and General Responsibilities

The 32Z Trap requires players who possess and exhibit the mental (attitude) requisites of tenacity, perseverance, toughness, and a belief in the team concept. While these attributes may be somewhat intangible, it is not too difficult for them to be observed and evaluated on the practice floor and in games.

In physical aspects, the needs for the 32Z Trap are relatively modest. Figure 8.1 points out the initial location and formation of the five Xs in the 3-2 set. Each will be considered below.

The individual numbers shown in Figure 8.1 are applicable to both defense and the New Option Offense. Player X1 is traditionally the point guard, floor leader, and the coach on the floor on both defense and offense. From position in the critical place in the front line of the 3-2, X1 goes to contain and trap, mainly at the point, wing, and along the A-line (with X3). On offense, he or she is designated as 1.

Player X2 (2 in the New Option Offense) is, ideally, taller and stronger than X1, although X2's duties in the 32Z Trap are identical to those of X1 on the opposite side of the floor. He or she operates as a traditional "off guard" in the offense and also operates at Rotary wing; on defense X2 contains and traps at the point, wing, and along the A-line (with X3).

X3 is the center player in the front line as it sets in the 3-2 formation (Figure 8.1). In the New Option Offense, this player is 3, wing and high post player in Red and White, and wing player in Blue. X3 is ideally, a bigger player, highly mobile, with good defensive quickness and antici- pation (instinct) while roaming the A-line. Player X3's above-average size and defensive demeanor discourages inside movement and passes.

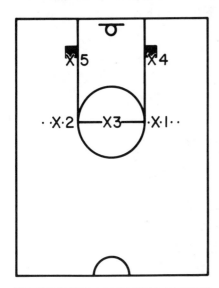

Figure 8.1. Initial set.

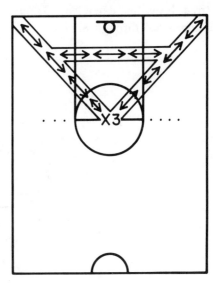

Figure 8.2. The A-line routes of X3; including the "A-bar."

Figure 8.2 gives special attention to the A-line of X3. Players X4 and X5 (4 and 5 as double-low-post players in the New Option Offense) are the two biggest, tallest, strongest players, yet they must possess natural agility and anticipatory instinct in getting out to the wing and corner areas quickly from the back line (the blocks on either side of the free throw lane).

Figure 8.3 displays the composite defensive plan for all team members. Responsibilities of each are represented as arrows projecting from the initial 3-2 set, with the arrows juxtaposing and overlapping to effectively demonstrate a team collage of defense and trapping. Figure 8.3 is more easily understood if each player's arrows of movement are examined one by one.

Note in Figure 8.3 that X1, X2, and X3 are expected to move out beyond the free throw line individually, one-on-one, in view of the threat imposed by jump shooters along the three-point line. (There is a brief discussion of the implications of the three-point line near the end of this chapter). Any one of X1, X2, or X3 may have to jump outside a step or two, if a ball handler is ready to shoot from the top of the key or the elbow area. If this happens, the other four defensive teammates are already in something of a box formation, and the original 3-2 resembles a 1-2-2 zone formation. Of course, when the ball crosses the designated trapping line (free throw line extended), 32Z is in effect, with reactions as shown in Figures 8.4 through 8.27.

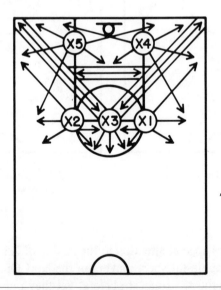

Figure 8.3. Responsibilities of X1, X2, X4, and X5.

Actions and Reactions; the Entry Pass

Offensive passing actions, and the defensive reactions to each, are illustrated in Figures 8.4 through 8.25. In Figure 8.4, the entry pass from point to wing is shown. Penetrating across the imaginary extension of the free throw line, the pass makes the receiver a target for the 32Z Trap. Figure 8.5 shows X5 blasting out from her block and X2 sliding over, forming a trapping duo. At the same time, X3 slides down the A-line, shutting off a possible pass to the low post, and the team shift is completed when X1 and X4 rotate toward the ball side.

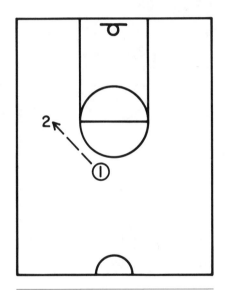

Figure 8.4. Ball to wing.

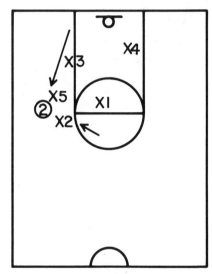

Figure 8.5. Reaction.

Wing-to-Corner Pass

Suppose the wing player was able, somehow, to overcome the trap pressure with a pass down to the corner in Figure 8.6. The 32Z reaction is drawn in Figure 8.7, as X3 sweeps down quickly along the A-line to the corner, joining the aggressive X5 to enclose the receiver in that critical area. Player X4 fires across the key, along the baseline, defensively responsible in case of any low post activity. Players X1 and X2 rotate toward the ball, away from the weak side.

A pass to a corner is viewed with great satisfaction by the 32Z-Trap team. No other place on the court is so vulnerable to defensive trapping action. Here, X3 and X5 are intimidating, crowding, and jumping, with arms windmilling and flailing, all the time denying the pass, dribble and shoot options. Additionally, the baseline acts as a "third" defensive player and the sideline acts as a "fourth."

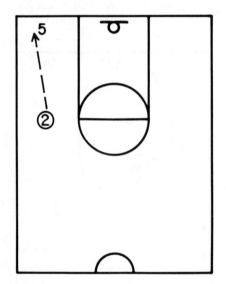

Figure 8.6. Ball to corner.

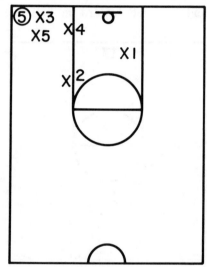

Figure 8.7. Reaction.

Low Post Threat

Unlike the requirements of its 32Z Goose Egg partner, the 32Z Trap should not expect X4 to front and deny a low post player in a Figure 8.7 situation. For one thing, a pass from the corner to a low post player is improbable and not permitted by the trapping pressures of X3 and X5; for another, a fronting, denial position by X4 opens up the weak side and leaves it too vulnerable and unguarded. Instead, with the ball in the corner, X4 should slide along the baseline across the key, set up on a low post player's hip, and try to negate any corner-to-low-post pass by extending an arm across the face and body of the low post player (Figure 8.8). If, somehow, a pass is made, X4 must force the opponent to put the ball on the floor and must get immediate help from X5, as depicted in Figure 8.9. X3 slides back toward the action via the A-line route, in case the pass is made. X4 releases from his defensive duties on X5's side as soon as possible and slides over to protect the weak-side under-basket area.

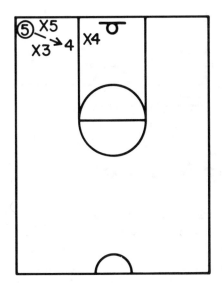

Figure 8.8. An improbable pass.

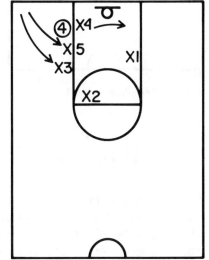

Figure 8.9. Reaction.

Low Post Passes Back Out

Examples continue in Figure 8.10 as the low post player is able to dump the ball back out to the strong-side wing. The trapping reaction in Figure 8.11 reveals X2 containing the receiver as X5 joins in the trapping action. X3 remains in his A-line between the ball and the basket. X4 and X1 rotate to critical close-in areas.

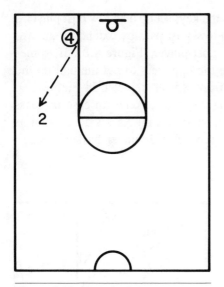

Figure 8.10. Pass back out.

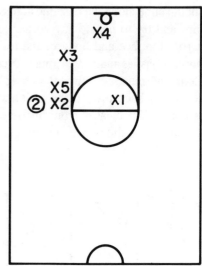

Figure 8.11. Reaction.

Wing-to-Wing Skip Pass

The wing player spots an open teammate on the weak side of the court and skip-passes (Figure 8.12). Because a horizontal skip pass is the quickest way to move the ball from side to side, the defense must respond promptly, whether trapping or not. X1 is closest to the receiver, and contains him as X4 flashes out to complete the trap in Figure 8.13. Here, we observe X3 "running the bar" in his A-line, as he takes the short cut across the key toward the ball. X2 and X5 move to their own new areas of responsibility.

A Note About Containment: Only in rare instances should we presume that two trappers will arrive simultaneously at a given point of pass reception (a "trapping place"). One of the two will get there first, mainly because of the proximity factor; he is the container, until joined by a teammate, with his job to impede and contain, one-on-one, for just an instant. This modus operandi, of course, calls for extensive teaching and drilling on the practice floor to enhance aggressive individual skills. The technique calls for the container to advance on the ball handler, shuffling and slide-stepping (sometimes from an erect stance, and sometimes from the chair or boxer-like stance), arms moving, pressing as closely as possible, shutting off driving and passing lanes, without fouling. He contains, even if just for an instant, until joined quickly by his trapping teammate. The two of them jump, kick, flail their arms, press closely, intimidate, and shut off all options until the ball handler is forced to a turnover or a desperation pass.

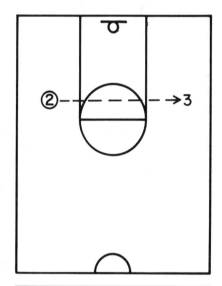

Figure 8.12. Skip pass.   **Figure 8.13.** Reaction of X3.

Another Wing-to-Corner Pass

In Figure 8.14, we have the wing-to-corner pass, with the reactions to it in Figure 8.15. Players X3 and X4 trap in the corner, and X5 moves over to defend against any low post action. Players X2 and X1 slide toward the ball. In this situation, a corner-to-low-post pass is a threat, although uncommon.

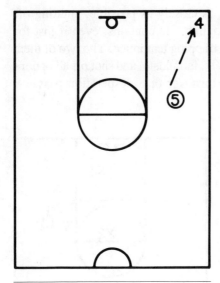

Figure 8.14. Ball to corner.

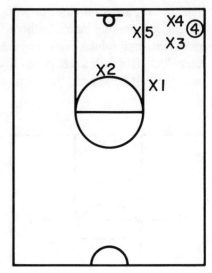

Figure 8.15. Reaction.

Defending the Low Post

The threat materializes in Figure 8.16. To combat the pass from this corner and the ensuing low post action, X5 should have set up on the low post player's *left* hip, and extended his or her *left* arm and hand across the low post player's body to discourage or deflect a pass (Figure 8.17). If the pass does get through, it will probably be to the post player's *right*, target hand. In such a probability, X5 must force the opponent to put the ball on the floor and must shut off the baseline and hope for immediate help from X4, as shown in Figure 8.17. Player X3 slides toward the action in his or her A-line, and X5 releases from the trap as soon as possible, aware of the weak-side vulnerability.

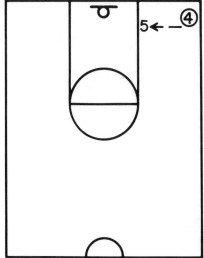 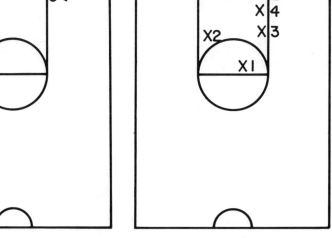

Figure 8.16. Pass from corner to low post.

Figure 8.17. Reaction.

Interception Possibilities

When the trapping action occurs in a corner, the defensive player out at the wing area (X2 in Figure 8.7, and X1 in Figure 8.15) should anticipate the probability of the desperation pass coming out of the corner to the wing area; *interception* should be uppermost in the minds of X2 and X1, culminating in a getaway fast-break basket at the other end.

For an additional example, assume that the corner player in Figure 8.16 could not pass in to the low post but did spot a teammate out at the point for a successful pass. Figure 8.18 shows this as a skip pass, and Figure 8.19 sets forth the trapping action of X1 and X3, with X1 containing the receiver until X3 hurries up the A-line to help out.

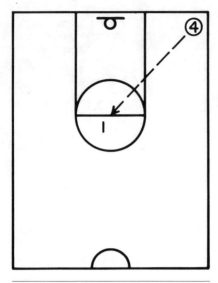 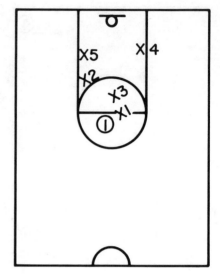

Figure 8.18. Skip pass out to the top.   **Figure 8.19.** Reaction.

Post to Wing

In Figure 8.20, player 1 passes to wing player 3. (Player 1 had been double-teamed in Figure 8.19.) The reaction to the pass is detailed in Figure 8.21 and shows X1 and X4 double-teaming and trapping. At the same time, X3 is shutting off the inside passing lane, and X2 and X5 are rotating toward the strong side.

Another Skip Pass

Examples continue with a skip pass from wing to wing in Figure 8.22. Players X5 and X2 go to trap in Figure 8.23, which also gives special attention to the short cut taken by X3 in her "A-bar" lane. Players X1 and X4 rotate to the strong side.

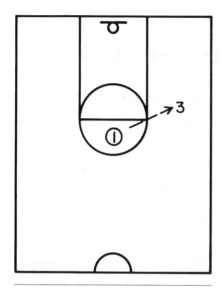

Figure 8.20. Point to wing.

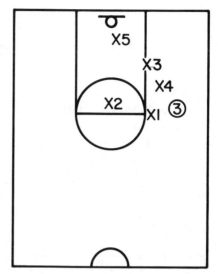

Figure 8.21. Reaction.

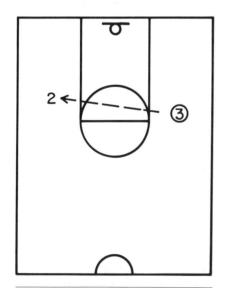

Figure 8.22. Skip pass.

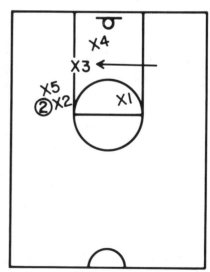

Figure 8.23. Player X3 runs the "A-bar."

Difficulty of
Wing-to-Low-Post Pass

Although a pass from wing to low post is emphatically improbable, if not impossible, such an unlikely act is included in Figure 8.24 to answer any conjecture about a pass getting through. The reaction to this pass in Figure 8.25 shows X4 containing the low post player and X5 backing up in a hurry, around teammate X3. An arrow in Figure 8.25 also illustrates the release by X4, which must always be a consideration. The weak side is vulnerable, and X5 must take individual defensive action against the low post player as soon as possible after the initial trapping pressure and allow X4 to release from it.

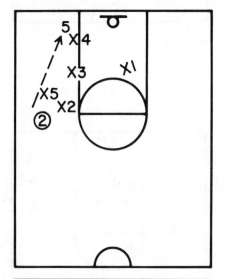
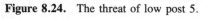

Figure 8.24. The threat of low post 5.

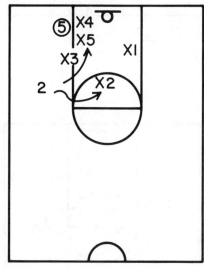

Figure 8.25. Reaction when pass is made.

Teaching Note: Low-Post Defense

Because the wing-to-low-post passing lane is so important to many, if not all, offenses, a note applicable to the 32Z Trap defense is in order here. With the ball at the left wing (Figure 8.24) and a low post player appearing as a threat, establishing himself, and asking for the ball, X4 should set up on the low post player's *left* hip, overplay him from the left, and try to deflect or deny the pass from the wing by extending his left arm and hand across his opponent's body. If a pass does get through (Figure 8.25), it will probably come to the low post player's right, target hand. X4 contains him momentarily, until X5 can get back and help (Figure 8.25). The small area of baseline under the basket must be shut off, and the low post player should be forced to put the ball on the floor.

Trapping the Dribbler-Penetrator

The 32Z Trap must be concerned about the dribbler-penetrator. Actions and reactions are illustrated in Figures 8.26, 8.26A, and 8.26B, where the dribbler is going to the left and in Figures 8.27, 8.27A, and 8.27B where the dribbler is going to the right.

Dribbling Toward the Left Side

A dribbler going to the left will be dribbling with the left (outside) hand in order to protect the ball with her body. The front X in Figure 8.26 channels the dribbler toward a side trap, harassing the *inside* shoulder all the way, denying *vertical* penetration.

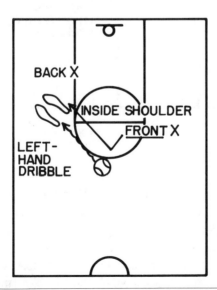

Figure 8.26. Dribble to the left.

Reaction

With arms waving, the back X runs directly at the dribbler, aiming at the shoulder on the side of the dribble, denying any more *horizontal* or *oblique* penetration.

The two Xs must not allow the dribbler to make a *splitting* move, in which she dribbles directly between them. They hope primarily that the dribbler will pick up her dribble; secondarily, they hope that she will try a reverse dribble. In Figures 8.26A and 8.26B, she does exactly the latter. Blocked by the back X, the dribbler pivots on her left foot, swings her right foot all the way around, changes to her right hand, and starts a new dribble in the reverse direction. Front X releases the dribbler to the back X, and moves to take a charging foul in Figure 8.26B. Even before that, the ball could have been "flicked away" by the back X in Figure 8.26A.

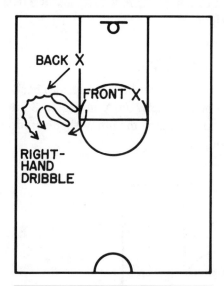

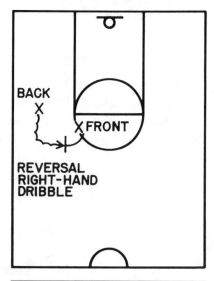

Figure 8.26A. Right-hand reverse dribble.

Figure 8.26B. Front X releases, steps in.

"Flicking": Rare and Much-Maligned

Although it is frowned upon by many coaches, some of whom cynically call it "matador defense," "flicking" does have a place in the teaching of trapping procedures. Too often, however, it is overzealously interpreted as a fouling violation by officials. In Figure 8.26A, the back X has an opportunity to flick, and the act should be practiced. As the dribbler reverses (remember, the back X has been the main reason for the reversal, with her aim at the shoulder, and her blockage of the original dribble), back X steps in the area right behind the dribbler's pivoting foot, stretches, extends her arm, and taps or slaps at the ball, flicking it to a teammate. If a teammate does recover the ball, she tosses it ahead of the flicker for a breakaway and lay-up at the other end of the court.

Figures 8.27, 8.27A and 8.27B depict action to the right. Because the responses of front X and back X are directly opposite those described for action to the left, they are self-explanatory.

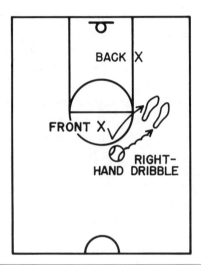

Figure 8.27. Dribble to the right.

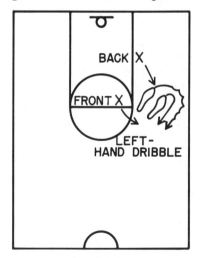

Figure 8.27A. Reversal and left-hand dribble..

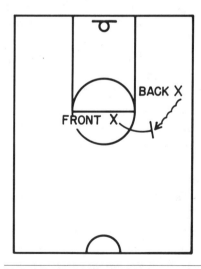

Figure 8.27B. Front X releases, steps in.

Advantages of the 32Z Trap

All schemes and methods have their strengths and weaknesses. The 32Z Trap is no exception, although its proficiencies far outweigh the shortcomings. This trap has been tested with excellent results, and it complements a team's primary, basic zone defense. Particular strengths and advantages of this defense include the following:

1. *Surprise.* When the opposing team brings the ball down the floor it is unaware that a trapping process is in the offing. The defense has rushed back into a lay-back 3-2 traditional set, drawn in Figure 8.1, with arms extended straight up above the head, or horizontally, shoulder-high, indicating zone. The trapping, double-teaming intent is not immediately apparent and comes without warning or signal, especially if being used in conjunction with a primary defensive system such as the 3-2 zone defense presented in chapter 7. The 32Z Trap goes into gear as a five-player, team effort when the ball progresses past the imaginary extension of the free throw line, symbolized by solid dots in Figure 8.1. Up to that time, one of the two guards, X1 or X2, might have been working outside and beyond that limit, pressuring the ball handler, but the paramount interest is to get down to the business of trapping.

2. *Simplicity.* The 32Z Trap is very easy to teach and uncomplicated in its planned operation. It features simplicity because the need for defensive improvisation and free-lancing is minimal. Each player, by numbered position, has distinct, explicit responsibilities that coalesce into a team coverage of a designated sector of the floor.

As one illustration of this trap's simplicity, Figure 8.2 shows the A-line, which X3 specifically traverses as the ball (and players) move from point to point. The sides of the A-line (the V) take X3 from the center of the free throw line to each corner; the bar in the "A" furnishes a short cut lane if a skip pass is made from side to side or if X3 must make a quick floor adjustment for some defensive reason. Simply enough, X3 must only memorize the routes of the A-line and understand its primary objective, which is to shut off inside passing lanes.

Detailed examples of the duties of other team members, and more about X3's role, have been described in this chapter (Actions and Reactions) and illustrated in Figures 8.4 through 8.25. By providing realistic game situations, the examples and accompanying diagrams support the claim that the 32Z Trap, as part of a total defensive system, stands out as a simply-taught, easily-learned trapping method.

3. _Denial of the inside game._ The 32Z Trap concentrates its main trapping energy at the top of the key, the wings, and the corners. Offensive players are taught that when they receive the ball at any one of these three general locations, they should aggressively square up, read the floor, and proceed into the pass, shoot, or dribble-drive of the triple-threat. If choosing the first alternative, the pass should be directed to an inside cutter, to a low post player, or to an open teammate in an inside seam. If harassed and double-teamed by the 32Z Trap, however, this player cannot effectively and completely read the floor and usually finds only two open spots for a hurried, perimeter-type pass: to the corner or back out. In the corner, the receiver in turn becomes subjected to double-teaming action when considering his own triple-threat options. If trying to shoot quickly if the trappers are arriving a bit late, the attempt is a low-percentage one, which most often rebounds out toward the top of the key, becoming the activator for a fast-break getaway by the defense. If double-teamed, the corner player has almost no chance of passing to the low post. A dribble-drive against two defenders should be considered an impossibility.

Returning to the wing player and the ball, we find this player still being harassed by trappers X1 and X4 (on one side) or X2 and X5 (on the other). If the wing tries to pass inside to the low post, he finds the passing lane closed and blocked by X3; if able, somehow, to see past the trappers, he also finds X3 dropping back just a bit to _front_ the low post player. These two negative and discouraging factors are abetted and compounded by a third: one of the two back players, X4, or X5, slides over, ready to defend behind the low post player, just in case.

If the wing player gives up and passes back out, the 32Z Trap is winning the battle because the offense is having to regroup and start over, the clock is ticking away, and the trap is preparing for a new onslaught.

The opportunities for the wing player to use the second triple-threat option, the dribble-drive, will be very restricted, if not shut off, by the two-player intimidation. The possibility that the wing can shoot (third option) from 15-18 feet is the one possible weakness in the 32Z Trap. The container, X1 or X2, must get to the wing quickly and aggressively, with a hand in the shooter's face or on the ball, while X4 (or X5) must be trained to flash out in double-quick time to act as the second helper in the double-team.

4. _Utilization._ The 32Z Trap is easily activated and managed. By prearrangement, it may be used in conjunction with the team's basic defense during a game. For example, prior to the game, at halftime, or during a time-out, the team can be instructed to alternate this trap with the regular

32Z Goose Egg Defense of chapter 7, with the alternation to occur after a successful field goal or free throw; if the field goal or free throw attempt is unsuccessful, the team would fall back into the regular defense. Another activating method is the hand signal from coach to quarterback. The 32Z Trap can also be used for designated periods of time as the sole defense.

Disadvantages of the 32Z Trap

A quick, smart penetrator, dribbling toward a wing area from outside the trapping zone, is a main problem. If he catches X5 or X4 (depending on the side of movement) midway in a dash out to the wing area to trap, the penetrator may dribble one-on-one against X1 or X2, jump high, and dump the ball down into a vacated, open, inside spot. This could also be a little bounce pass or hand-off to an open, inside player. Only an alert X3, running the A-line, and an active back player (X4 or X5) can thwart such a penetration move.

The main disadvantages of the 32Z Trap are the following:

1. *Jump shooter threat.* Quick release, accurate, close-in jump shooters in the wing and top-of-the-key areas pose a threat to the 32Z. Attempts from beyond 20–21 feet are not very seriously considered; the 32Z coach adamantly refuses to believe that *outside* shooting beyond 21 feet will defeat his team. At the same time, the coach, with good reason, fears high-percentage jump-shooting implications that accrue along the important three-point line. The area between the curving top of the key and the free throw line is especially critical. X1, X2, and X3 must be trained to jump out and jump back in the most aggressive manner.

2. *Overload triangle threat.* A triangular formation comprising high post, wing, corner, and low post players, with spirited passing and movement in the triangle, creates an overload situation that causes potential problems, especially if the shooters and passers operate in high-percentage areas and if the defenders lack aggressiveness. It should be remembered,

however, that a 3-2 zone, whether or not trapping, is inherently and traditionally strong against offensive action at the wings and top of the key.

3. *Skip-pass problem*. Skip passes, especially from wing to wing, cross-court, are troublesome. Only the upmost combative reaction by the defenders will counter the effect of these passes. X4 and X5, particularly, have a most difficult task in rotating and retracting from block to wing, wing to block, block to corner, and corner to block, as skip passes are made.

Coaching Points and Drills

Earlier in the chapter the statement was made that tenacity, perseverance, toughness, and a belief in the team concept are highly desirable characteristics for the success of the 32Z Trap. Two additional qualities are proposed in closing out this chapter: anticipation and reaction. A limited number of significant drills are included that develop and improve the specific skills that apply to the six qualities.

Although an individual's tenacity, perseverance, toughness, anticipation, reaction, and concept of team may very well be innate characteristics, all of these can be nurtured and polished through spirited drills on the practice floor. The limited number of drills which follow are augmented by certain of the drills in chapter 7.

Trap in the Circle

Passers are about 8 feet apart. Passers must pass two or more places away. The closest two Xs trap the receiver. The other X looks for the interception. If the ball touches any one of the Xs, the passer exchanges places with that X. Figure 8.28 shows the pass from 1 to 3, player 3X containing and joined by next closest X (1X) for the trap. Player 2X anticipates the interception, but Figure 8.28A indicates that the pass from 3 to 5 was successful, and 2X was not successful when he "shot the gap" for the interception. In Figure 8.28A, 2X becomes the container against X5, joined by X3, and X1 becomes the interceptor. Passes and action continues.

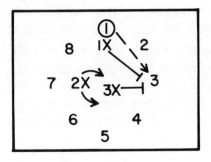

Figure 8.28. Trap in the circle.

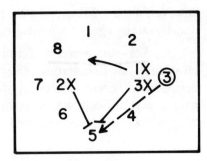

Figure 8.28A. Trap in the circle (cont.).

Coaching Points to 2X

Watch the feet and eyes of the passer, then use quick footwork to cut off the passing lane or to intercept in it. When two opponents are harassing, the passer will usually look directly toward the teammate he intends to pass to, with feet pointed in that direction; but you can't always depend on that, because a smart passer will "look one way, and pass another." In this drill, the passer will probably be jumping, so possibly you can interpret his intention from the jump.

Coaching Points to All Xs

Three-player *teamwork*, with communication and *talking* as the main elements, is absolutely necessary. Deflect passes by slapping the ball. Trappers are windmilling their arms, jumping, and denying. Hands and arms are active. Do not foul. If passer goes up with the ball, go up also, but don't be fooled by a vertical pump fake.

Coaching Points to Passers

Use the "Down the Well" technique to defeat the trappers, as follows: As you are being trapped, *push* the ball straight *up* to your full height (protect it as you do so, with both hands). Hold tight. This causes the trappers to jump. As they jump, you *pull* the ball *down*. Trappers will come down with their jump. As they do so, you go back up and pass off as they come down.

Shoot the Gap

The coach passes the ball to 1, who turns and faces the basket (Figure 8.29). Two Xs immediately trap, trying to force a telegraphed pass to 2 or 3. Defender X3 *anticipates* and goes for the interception. Player 1 may not dribble; she must pass or accept the tie-up by the trappers.

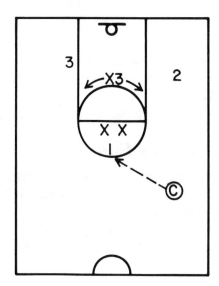

Figure 8.29. Player X3 intercepts.   **Figure 8.30.** Pressure!

Pressure

Both 1 and 2 have a basketball. One at a time, at the coach's signal, X1 and/or X2 put tight pressure on 1 and/or 2, respectively. Players 1 and/or 2 have to stay in place, with no dribbling. You may pivot as necessary and keep the ball swinging and moving, up and down, side to side, right to left, and left to right. No foul by X! X guards closely for four seconds (the coach counts); on the count of five, the ball is passed back to the coach (Figure 8.30).

Coaching Points to Xs

Pressure. No fouling. Move the feet. Windmilling arms. Nose on the ball. Narrow base. Body balance. Go up if the opponent goes up, but watch for the *pump fake*. SWARM all over the opponent. This is a *tight* trap, not a loose trap, because we assume the opponent has no dribble left and cannot pick up the pivot foot and put it back on the floor without a violation. Your narrow base allows only a possible bounce pass; the windmill waving of the arms is a distraction and restricts passing lanes.

Coaching Points to 1 and 2

Withstand pressure for four seconds. Pass back on fifth second. Pivot, go into triple-threat attack position, swing the ball, holding it tightly with both hands. Execute head-shoulder feints.

"Not Fair" Drill: Three Versus Four

Three Os on offense for a specified time (six minutes, for example) against four Xs, half-court (Figure 8.31). Keep score. Scoring for Os: Two points for made field goal; shoot one-and-one if fouled; and two points for offensive rebound, plus possession of the ball. Os can put the ball back up if the rebound is close-in, plus the two points for the rebound. Scoring for

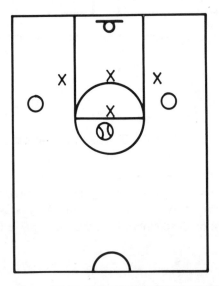

Figure 8.31. Extra man on "D."

Xs while on defense: +1 for every rebound (rebounds are returned to Os each time, however); +1 for every turnover by Os. Os keep possession of ball on turnovers.

One Versus One, Deny and Trap

The coach has the ball. When the coach slaps the ball, 1 tries to get open for an entry pass in the shaded area within four seconds (Figure 8.32). 1 tries to deny, player-player. If the pass is successful, X2 blasts over for a double-team, as 2 drives for the basket, looking for a pass from 1. If 1 can pass to 2, she has been successful. If 1 cannot receive the pass from the coach within four seconds, she has been unsuccessful.

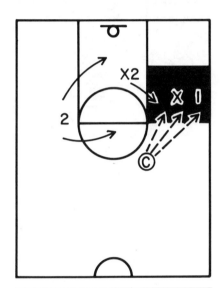

Figure 8.32. Deny the pass.

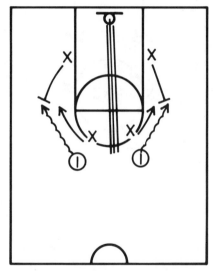

Figure 8.33. Trap the dribbler.

Practicing the Trap: Whole-Part Method

Figure 8.33 is an illustration of the *whole-part* method of teaching. The trap is broken down into a *part*, which is practiced until perfected. The two front Xs are X1 and X2; the two back Xs are X4 and X5.

The *overlearning* procedure is also a feature of this drill. Players practice this part over and over (overlearn) until it is performed to the coach's satisfaction and will operate properly when the *whole* (the 32Z Trap) is assembled, practiced and scrimmaged.

Other parts of the whole may similarly be worked on independently in drills and practice, using Figures 8.4 through 8.27 as guides.

The drill area in Figure 8.33 is divided by an imaginary line, as shown. One offensive player, with a basketball, and two defensive Xs work on each side of the division. Player 1 starts a dribble to the right (or left), channeled and guided by the front X. As 1 crosses the free throw line extended, his dribble is used up and suspended by the double-team action of the two Xs.

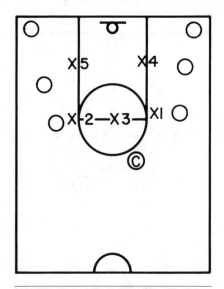

Figure 8.34. Setting up the drill.

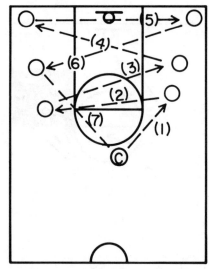

Figure 8.34A. Skip-passing and team reactions.

Skip-Pass Reaction Drill

Figures 8.34 and 8.34A end the special drills for this 32Z Trap chapter. The purpose of this exercise is to improve the team's reaction when it must shift as a unit and accomplish individual responsibilities. Figure 8.34 sets up the formation, with the Xs in place, seven stationary Os comprising the offense, and the ball out at the point. Figure 8.34A starts with the entry pass (1) from point to wing and continues with six subsequent passes, numbered (2) through (7). The Os stand in place as they receive and pass, while the Xs shift into traps and respond properly in all defensive aspects of the 32Z Trap. The coach controls the action, stopping it as necessary for corrections and instructions. Passes are of the overhead variety, which makes the drill doubly valuable in teaching and practicing this relatively difficult offensive passing technique.

The coach may want to control the drill development to the extent of permitting a pass only at her whistle signal, thus furnishing the trappers, interceptors and other defensive players a full load of work, and giving the passers the opportunity to practice "Down the Well" (refer to page 146) and other evasive techniques.

Rules for a Firing Line

This chapter concludes with general and specific comments regarding the rules for and ramifications of the three-point line and the manner in which the 32Z Trap adapts to the addition of this line.

At present, there are differing rules for this line's distance from the basket. Scholastic and college rules in the United States, for both men and women, set the three-point line arcuture at a constant of 19 feet 9 inches from the basket. An International Rule, applied to World-Wide Service play and tournaments, to international and Olympic competition, to certain AAU play, and largely to Canadian competition, sets the line at 20 feet 6 inches. Pro-Am and professional NBA teams operate with a three-point line at 23 feet 9 inches.

Possible Rationale for the
19 Foot–9 Inch Three-Point Line

Without much doubt, adoption of the 19 foot–9 inch three-point line in United States play derived from the feeling that the game had to be opened up. The offensive inside game had become clogged up by zone defenses, which forced offenses to rely on an outside game; the 45-second clock, in this situation, also became an ally of the defense to an inappropriate degree. Giving three points to the offense for a successful outside attempt (instead of the long-established two) forces the defense to expand, and to go out and engage the offense to a greater degree. The three-pointer also put a premium on the art and beauty of jump-shooting, adds excitement to the game, demands more tactical and strategical thinking, opens up the inside, and whets the appetites of high-percentage jump shooters everywhere. Very few coaches are screaming "No, no!" at gunners during normal times of a game, now; certainly, the three-point line at 19 feet 9 inches encourages a shot that fits well into the New Option Offense!

The Three-Pointer and the 32Z Trap

The 32Z Trap does not fit the NBA and Pro-Am rules, which include player-player defense, the 24-second clock, and the 23 foot–9 inch line for three points. On the other hand, the implications of the 19 foot–9 inch and 20 foot–6 inch three-point lines for the 32Z Trap are considerable. Except for the area at the top of the key, either of these two curving border lines are perfect markers for wing, deep wing, and corner trappers, and both have a conformity to the A-line actions of X3. Expectant jump-shooters all along the borders of 19 feet 9 inches and 20 feet 6 inches will always find an aggressive, hand-in-the-face, tight-checking defensive opponent waiting (on the strong side), soon to be joined by a trapping, harassing teammate. The field goal attempt becomes much less than a high-percentage one, and the inside area is restricted because X3 is on the A-line and the weak-side back X has shifted over to defend against any low post activity.

Danger Points

The 32Z Trap will be very concerned about three-pointers at the top of the key and at the elbows formed by the curving borders on either side of the free throw line. The areas are slightly outside the trapping limits, so there must be individual, aggressive defensive effort. As illustrated in Figures 8.35 and 8.36, defender X1 or X2 will jump out to check a jump-shooter, one-on-one, while X3 (Figure 8.37) must step out to defend against a shooter, one-on-one, at the top of the key.

Temporary Shifts to 1-2-2

These adjusting movements will shift the initial 3-2 set into a temporary 1-2-2, but the effectiveness of 32Z trapping will not suffer in the designated areas (wing, deep wing, corner, and low post). Practically all the areas inside the new three-point border, from free throw line extended to the baseline, fit the limits of the 32Z Trap like a glove.

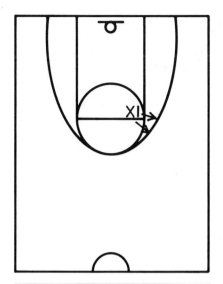

Figure 8.35. Player X1 jumps out.

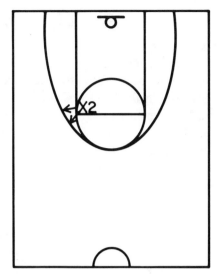

Figure 8.36. Player X2 jumps out.

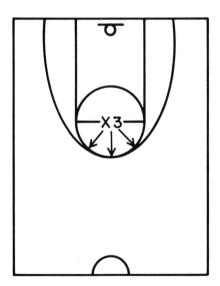

Figure 8.37. Player X3 vs a jumper.

An Optimistic Note

Introduced and put in practice during recent seasons in competition under 30-second clock rules for men and women, and in other competition governed by the 45-second clock, the 32Z Trap has been "tested in battle." As has been emphasized, its efficacy will be in direct ratio to the players' display of the qualities *tenacity, perseverance, toughness, team concept, anticipation,* and *reaction.*

A War
at the Window:
Rebounding
Action

George Raveling, a foremost advocate of the importance of rebounding and its basic skills, stated at a Medalist Basketball Clinic that "rebounding is 75 percent desire and 25 percent ability." Many other well-known coaches agree, interpreting *desire* as competitive spirit, courage, and aggressiveness; calling *courage* the most important aspect, by far; and pointing out that offensive and defensive rebounding is the "blood and guts" of basketball. Coach Raveling adds that "rebounders must be hostile."

Desire (or intensity, if you will) stands out as an important element in all four essentials of both offensive and defensive rebounding: (a) anticipating (preparing for movement), (b) timing (movement), (c) reacting (movement), and (d) positioning (a result of movement).

Positioning is usually deemed the most important component in defensive rebounding; movement, with its elements of anticipating, timing, and reacting, is considered the major factor in offensive rebounding. Many coaches feel that practice time spent on the fundamentals and techniques of positioning and movement is more valuable, and yields a bigger return, than time spent on drills for jumping and similar skills. This brings to mind the rebounding success, both offensive and defensive, of Wes Unseld and Paul Silas, former professional players in the National Basketball Association. These two were board dominators in spite of their limitations in height, jumping ability, and natural agility. In practice after practice, drill after drill, they must have worked exceptionally hard to master the fundamentals of positioning (boxing out, blocking out, cutting out) in defensive rebounding. In offensive rebounding drills they became proficient in the hard-nosed, aggressive movement details of anticipating, timing, and reacting.

It is refreshing that in a team sport so dominated by individual creativity, improvisation, and innate physical abilities, there is room for those who are competitive mainly because of practice and hard work in established basic fundamentals and intelligent application of learned skills.

Defensive Rebounding: A Rule to Remember

Perhaps the cardinal principle in defensive rebounding is to check your opponent *before* concentrating on the rebound. That is, don't turn your head to follow the ball the instant it is released for the basket. *Watch your opponent* first! Read her intention. If your opponent indicates a move to the board, *cut her off* from the board *before* you even look for the ball. Five players doing this on every shot establish a defensive no-man's-land around the basket, ensuring control of the board.

Footwork: Front Pivot Action

The basis for good defensive rebounding is the boxing-out action (sometimes called blocking out, or cutting out) and the footwork that goes with it. Footwork is the key. In Figure 9.1, the defensive man, with his back to the hoop, must use a staggered stance (one foot ahead of the other) to establish a strong, wide, balanced base. As the ball goes up in Figures 9.1 and 9.1A, the defensive player, with his back to the basket, adjusts his feet and starts turning his body to meet the opponent's assault against his side and back. He will feel the body contact as he goes into his front-pivot action, pivoting on his right foot (#1 in the diagram) and swinging his left foot (#2 in the diagrams) around toward the hoop (Figure 9.1B).

It is obvious that the swinging of the forward foot (#2, left) is crucial in setting up the barrier. As the defender boxes out, he must maintain solid contact using his side and back. With the advantage of starting in an inside position, he can (without fouling) hold out his opponent, the offensive rebounder, until the ball contacts the rim or board, is rebounded, or strikes the floor (Figure 9.1C).

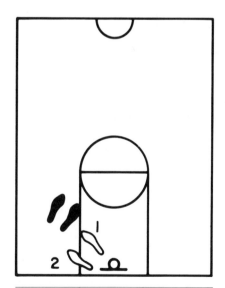

Figure 9.1. Getting set.

Figure 9.1A. Start of pivot.

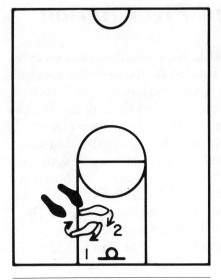 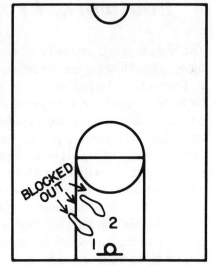

Figure 9.1B. Pivot-turn.　　　　**Figure 9.1C.** Shut off.

Rear Pivot Action

Figures 9.2 through 9.2B show the offensive player trying a different tack. He pivots to face the basket, gives a head-shoulder fake, and tries to slide by and over the back of the defender. To block this, the defender must now pivot on his front foot (#2) and sweep back the other foot and leg (#1). This is rear-pivot action, intended as continuous movement in the three diagrams. The offensive player is boxed out in Figure 9.2B.

"One Thousand One, One Thousand Two . . ."

At a coaches' clinic in Bellevue, Washington, Coach Digger Phelps demonstrated the efficacy of this footwork in a defensive rebounding drill that deployed eight players (four versus four) in a perimeter set-up around the rebounding area. He launched the drill with a shot from the perimeter,

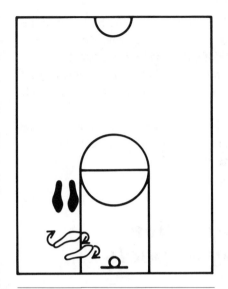

Figure 9.2. Starting a box out.

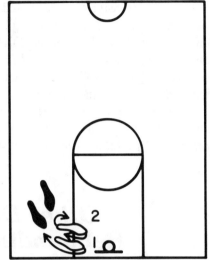

Figure 9.2A. The pivot-turn.

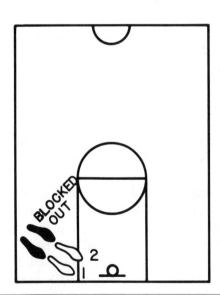

Figure 9.2B. Offensive player is boxed out.

as the four defensive players started blocking out. As the ball neared the rim, Coach Phelps started counting "one thousand one, one thousand two, one thousand three." He wanted the defenders to box out for three seconds, and he wanted the ball to *strike the floor*. That would denote a good boxing-out job; the offensive rebounders would be shut off from the ball, the perimeter, and the baseline.

Coach Phelps also instructed his rebounders (defensive) not to worry about committing fouls as they boxed out. "Play rough," he advised. "The referees will tolerate a lot around the basket."

Other Defensive Rebounding Aspects

Up to this point, the discussion has been concerned with boxing-out and defensive footwork procedures. Now we turn to the concomitant rebounding techniques of body positioning, pivoting, and the outlet pass.

Assume that, with the ball in the air and a rebound coming up, the defender has taken care of the aforementioned footwork. We expect his body to be low, tail down, with the knees slightly bent in a kind of crouch. He is facing the basket, with his opponent blocked out. The body must be in balance, with the feet spread a little wider than the width of the shoulders, elbows out and away from the body, and forearms raised to about shoulder level.

While in this position, the defender must anticipate the rebounding angle. If the ball is shot from the left side of the floor, it will tend to rebound to the right side of the hoop. If shot from the right side, percentages suggest that the ball will come down on the left side. On shots from the corner, many rebounds will bounce from the rim straight out toward the free throw line.

With the ball rebounding on the left side (Figure 9.3), the defensive rebounder, facing the basket, his opponent boxed out behind him, should go up and gather the ball at the top of his jump, then pull straight down—like pulling on a rope—to about chest level. He should come down spread-eagle, legs jackknifing, landing on the balls of both feet, and pivoting to the left on the ball of the left foot (Figure 9.3). In the same motion, he swings the right foot and leg completely around in the new direction (foot B in Figure 9.3). Holding the ball securely as he *turns away* from his opponent, the defensive rebounder looks for an outlet receiver, who is, preferably, making himself available on the left side of the court.

The ultimate rebounding objective here is to make a strong, accurate pass to teammate 2 that will launch a fast break. This pass is shown as the last action in Figure 9.3.

Figure 9.4 demonstrates the identical rebounding action on the other side of the hoop, with the outlet pass being made to the outlet, player 1. Again, the rebounder swivels around, and *away from*, the opponent behind him, by pivoting on the left foot, swinging the right leg around, and facing the outlet teammate on the right side. The pass to the outlet person is shown in Figure 9.4.

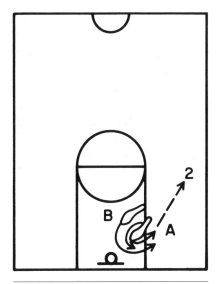

Figure 9.3. Rebounding and outlet passing left side.

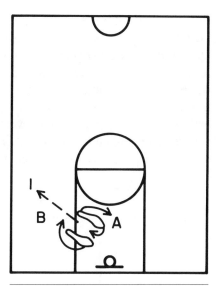

Figure 9.4. Rebounding and outlet passing, right side.

The Outlet Pass

Some coaches want the outlet pass to be made while the rebounder's body is turning on the way down, before the feet strike the floor. I disagree. Most young players do not have the coordination, agility, and strength for such acrobatics, and the action itself is unessential to either the rebound or the fast break.

The outlet pass should be either a baseball pass, a two-handed chest pass, or a two-handed overhead pass, made during the pivot-turn. An outlet player must not drift away or run away from the pass. If anything, she should *come to meet it*, as she can not expect the rebounder, under duress, to accurately throw an unusually long pass.

As the rebounder turns and looks for the outlet receiver along the sideline, she must think *pass; directly, accurately*, and *timely*. She should avoid putting the ball on the floor in a wasteful dribble.

Once the ball is in the hands of the outlet player, she looks for teammates filling the other two lanes (center and other side) for the fast break.

The Triangle

Figure 9.5 illustrates a good collective effort in defensive rebounding as the three big players, (forwards and centers) automatically move and set up in a defensive triangle when the shot goes up. Setting a triangle is the ideal defensive rebounding strategy. At least three offensive rebounders will be trying to infiltrate the triangle, and the three defenders (X3, X4, X5), in their favorable inside positions, must box them out and go after the ball on the rebound. They must work hard to keep their backs in contact with their individual opponents when the shot is on its way to the basket, maintain the integrity of the triangle, and keep the triangle expanded.

Figure 9.5. The triangle.

Going to the Window
Offensively

Most of the principles and basic techniques of defensive rebounding apply to offensive rebounding as well. Footwork, anticipation, timing, and reaction are of paramount importance to both. In offensive rebounding, however, natural ability definitely takes a back seat to skills that are learned and honed in practice sessions. The offensive rebounder has to work unusually hard and at a disadvantage: The defense claims the inside area as a territorial right, and a typical game official watches closely, it seems, for illegal offensive moves such as pushing off the back of the defender, swinging the elbows, and charging over the top. The offensive rebounder must operate as if every shot is going to miss. He or she must use more finesse and guile than strength.

Carom-and-Loop to the Right

In Figure 9.6, the defender has established a rebounding position and, with the ball in the air, is pivoting and turning to box out the offensive player. In this instance, the right foot is pivoting in place, and the left (forward)

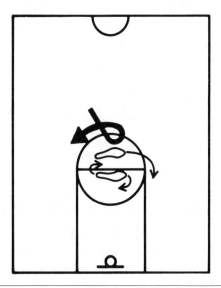

Figure 9.6. Carom-and-loop to the right.

foot and leg are swinging around. With finesse, the offensive rebounder drives in, establishes light contact (without charging), caroms off the back, and does a spin-and-roll (loop) toward the hoop. The defender ends up with *nobody* fixed on his back because he misread the carom-and-loop.

Carom-and-Loop to the Left

Figure 9.7 shows the offensive rebounder executing the carom-and-loop in another direction, and the defender's positioning and reaction. In this diagram the defender misreads again; she pivots on her left foot with the ball in the air and swings the right leg back and around in an ineffective sweep. She has not fixed the opponent on her back in this situation, and the path to the basket is open and clear.

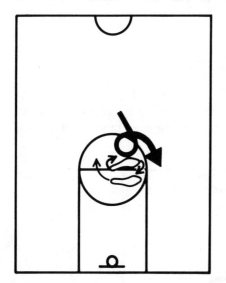
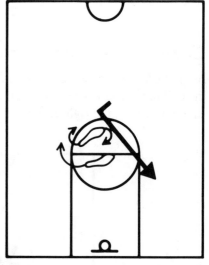

Figure 9.7. Carom-and-loop to the left. **Figure 9.8.** Brush-and-oblique to the right.

Brush-and-Oblique Move to the Left

Another attempt is shown in Figure 9.8 as the player breaks for the hoop, establishes light "brush" contact with the back of the defender without fouling, pushes hard off the right leg, and changes direction to his left oblique. Turning, with the ball in the air, the defender attempts unsuccessfully to block out, with a pivot on the left foot and a rearward sweep by the right foot and leg. He ends up with nothing on his back, and the attacker has a clear path to the basket and the rebound.

Brush-and-Oblique to the Right

The brush-and-oblique move can be made to either the right or the left and is set up with a head-shoulder-body fake by the attacker. Figure 9.9 shows the change of direction to the right oblique and the defender's boxing-out reaction. The defender pivots on the right foot and swings the left foot and leg around, hoping to stop the offensive player; however, in this example, she has again misread the intent. The attacker slides and slips by, free, open and clear for the basket and the rebound.

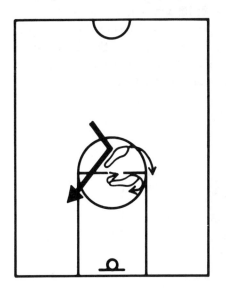

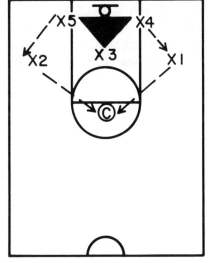

Figure 9.9. Brush-and-oblique to the right.

Figure 9.10. Rebound and outlet pass.

Drill Program:
Drill #1. Rebound and Outlet Pass

Figure 9.10, the first illustration in the drills program for rebounding, is a defensive rebounding and outlet-passing exercise. With a rebounding insert in the basket, Coach (C) puts up a shot from anywhere on the perimeter. Players X3, X4, and X5, in the triangle, rebound and then outlet-pass to X1 or X2, who passes it back to the coach, and the drill continues. Player X5 outlet-passes to X2, player X4 out to X1, and X3 out to either X2 or X1. Because the players in the triangle are unopposed, the coach can spend all of his time on instruction and criticism. This is a very important drill for basics and fundamentals.

Drill #2. Triangle Block-Out

In Figure 9.11, the ball is placed on the floor and surrounded by the defensive rebounders (X3, X4, X5) and respective opponents (3, 4, 5). Individual opponents face one another, the Xs with their backs to the ball and the Os facing the ball.

When the coach (on the outside) blows his whistle, the Xs go into their box-out positions, while the Os try to get inside the triangle, using the moves described for Figures 9.6 through 9.9. Some illegalities should be expected, but the drill should not be allowed to degenerate into a shoving contest. It should be spirited and marked with aggressiveness.

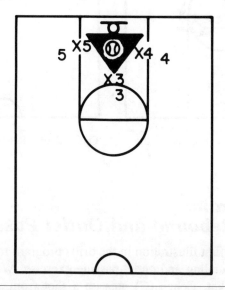

Figure 9.11. Triangle block-out.

Discovering Routes

Figures 9.12 through 9.15 show drills that are designed for the bigger players, with the rebound insert in the hoop. The coach shoots from various spots around the perimeter in all four of the drills. The two waiting *offensive* rebounders simultaneously start for the rebound, each practicing the carom-and-loop and brush-and-oblique moves. Defenders are not used in any of the drills.

The routes are self-explanatory. Drills for carom-and-loop practice are drawn in Figures 9.12 and 9.13. Drills for brush-and-oblique are drawn in Figures 9.14 and 9.15. The coach announces the required specific move as the ball goes up, and the rebounder goes in and rebounds with one of the following:

- A tip-in (into the insert).
- A rebound, coming back down with the ball under control and then going back up to lay the ball into the insert.
- A simulated three-pointer: come down with the ball, fake going back up (pump), draw the simulated foul, then go back up for the second time and put the ball in the insert.
- A jump shot; or work for a jump shot if the ball rebounds some distance from the basket.
- A "rebound-and-hook" (see below).

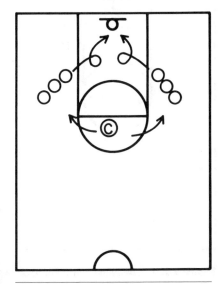

Figure 9.12. Discovering a route #1.

Figure 9.13. Discovering a route #2.

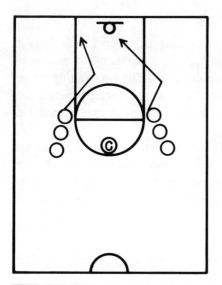

Figure 9.14. Discovering a route #3.

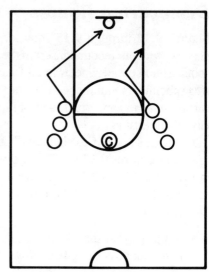

Figure 9.15. Discovering a route #4.

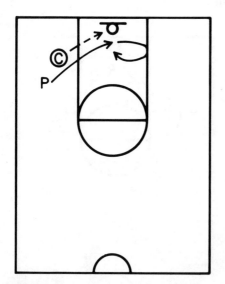

Figure 9.16. Rebound and hook back right.

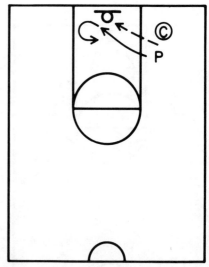

Figure 9.16A. Rebound and hook back left.

Rebound-and-Hook Drill

Rebound-and-hook is depicted in two parts in Figures 9.16 and 9.16A. This is an offensive rebounding drill, with the coach tossing the ball high *across* the top of the window and the offensive player hustling across the key to rebound. She fakes putting the ball back up, then pivots around to her right for a left-handed hook shot. The coach then secures the basketball and moves quickly to the right side with the player, where the procedure is repeated with the player now taking a right-handed hook shot. The drill continues from one side of the basket to the other.

Combo Drill

Many obvious offensive and defensive procedures are involved in Figure 9.17, comprising the Combo drill. The perimeter players swing the ball "around the horn" while the low post player works from side to side, asking for the ball in the lane and at the blocks. Players 1, 2, 3, and 4 remain rather stationary while executing good bounce, chest, and overhead passes. The Xs guarding 1, 2, 3, and 4 do not particularly try to

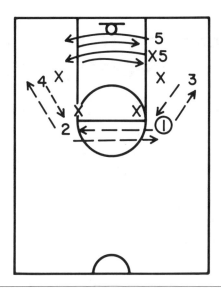

Figure 9.17. Combo.

prevent the passes down to 5. The weak-side Xs drop back to help out against 5 when he receives the ball; this teaches 5 how to operate at the low post against double-team pressure.

Upon receiving the ball, 5 may work for a low post shot or dump the ball back out. The players outside (1, 2, 3, and 4) take jump shots (no insert is in the basket for this drill). The Xs box out defensively, and the outside players go for offensive rebounds. The teams rotate on offense and defense, depending upon ball possession or time limits set by the coach.

Side-to-Side Drill

A player sets up at the side of the window with a ball in her hands. She jumps high and pushes (not throws) the ball across the top of the window with both hands and then dashes across the key to rebound the ball on the other side—without allowing the ball to touch the floor. Jumping back up, she pushes the ball back across the top, other side, and the drill continues from side to side until terminated by the coach's whistle. This is an excellent conditioning exercise, as well as a rebounding drill; the player has to move fast from side to side, just as long as the coach wants her to work.

Teaching Reminders: Defensive Rebounding

The following are important to remember when teaching rebounding.

1. A defensive player hoping to counter the brush-and-oblique moves and the carom-and-loop tactics must use peripheral vision, work on reading the individual opponent, be aggressive in an interpretation of the attacker's intention, and react with the most appropriate footwork. For example, the defender in Figure 9.8 would have been more successful had he used the footwork drawn in Figure 9.9; for the particular action in Figure 9.9, a better defensive maneuver would have been that detailed in Figure 9.8!
2. Setting up a defensive box-out triangle (Figure 9.5), with the ball in the air, is very important for a team using a zone defense. Three players (X4, X5, X3) should rush to a specific area of responsibility.

Their positionings ideally form a triangle, and they block out *any* offensive infiltrator entering their locations. It must be remembered, however, that some zone defense plans may call for one of the three to slide out to the corner to defend against a shot from that area; in such a situation, his temporary place in the triangle must be assumed by a sliding, shifting teammate. For clarification, refer to Figures 7.27-7.29, chapter 7.

3. A player-player defensive team may not always be capable of shifting into the ideal triangle. With the ball in the air, the *primary* function of player-player defenders is to *find, fix,* and *box out* their own individual opponents. If the resulting three-person configuration is a triangle (and it usually will be), so much the better.

Summary

Coaches increasingly feel that rebounding skills are acquired in practices, where hard work and attention to basic details are predominant.

The four major components of rebounding are anticipating, timing, reacting, and positioning. *Desire* (aggressiveness) is a necessary ingredient in all four.

To the statistician, the capture of the basketball by way of a rebound is important because it represents a *possession*, which according to the traditional calculation should always be worth one point. For example, the statistician expects a team that is operating efficiently to score at least eighty points if it acquires the ball (in various ways) eighty times. Capturing rebounds is one element of operating with efficiency. A defensive team must expect to acquire the rebound at least 80 percent of the time.

Practicing: Option Offense Drills

The material in this chapter is a reflection of the *whole-part* method as it expedites the development of the New Option Offense. Preferably early in the season, but after the players are to some extent oriented to the total offensive framework (chapters 2, 3, and 4), practice sessions will feature the formation of two-, three-, and four-player units for becoming skilled at *parts* of the total system. An overlearning, repetitious approach is emphasized, and the drills feature running individual routes properly, over and over, along with a concern for enhancement of skills that are especially significant to the success of the New Option Offense. As practices continue and the parts are perfected, the coach will begin to focus progressively on the *whole* aspect, and the worksheet on her daily practice clipboard will emphazise drills that apply to the five-player options of chapters 2, 3, and 4.

As the season goes on, however, the coach will go back and spend practice time on both parts and whole. The general skills drills of chapter 11 will also augment the programming plans.

The objective in preparing the material in this chapter has been achieved if it lends a hand to the planning of practices and alleviates some problems in the operation of the New Option Offense.,

Clear the Side to High Post

Dribble entry for Red Series. Players 1 and 3 make a natural screen as 1 dribbles down and 3 clears out to the high post. Suspending her dribble, 1 pivots and turns to pass out to 3. As 1 turns away from the defensive player, she makes either an across-the-chest bounce pass or a jumping, one-hand (lefty) baseball pass (hook pass). After receiving the pass, 3 goes into triple-threat stance, with necessary footwork for a jump shot or dribble-drive. For the drill, 3 rebounds her own shot and passes out to new 1 (no rotation). This drill applies to the Red Series (Figure 10.1).

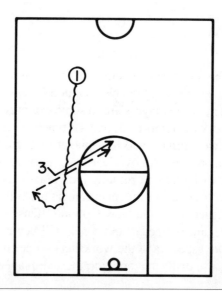

Figure 10.1. Clear the side to the high post.

Passing Options of Playmaker 1

This figure shows dribble entry for Red Series by 1 and his options of passing over to 5 (skip pass) and/or to 4 in the key. Players 4 and 5 execute screening action as 1 faces them. Coach varies the types of passes, designates the types of shots, and alternates passes to 4 and 5 (Figure 10.2). *Note*: *Timing* is important.

Figure 10.2. Passing options of playmaker 1.

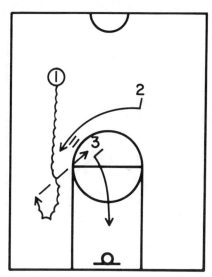

Figure 10.3. Hand-back over the top. Red.

Over the Top

Participants: 1, 2, and 3. This drill pertains to the Red Series. After entry dribble and 3's clear-out of the side (not drawn), 1 passes back out to 3 at the high post. Player 2 cuts over the top to receive the hand-off from 3. Player 2 sets a barrier-screen as she passes, and rolls to the basket. Player 2 takes a jump shot. For the drill, 3 rebounds and passes out to 1 line (Figure 10.3). *Note*: The V-cut by 2 before going over the top is important. Players 1 and 2 rotate. Work extensively on the pick-roll technique.

One Refusal,
Three More Options

Participants: 1, 2, 3, and 4. Player 3 has the ball at the high post, facing the basket, and dribbles back, signaling 4 to pop out (Figure 10.4). Player 3 passes to 4, who turns to refuse 1 going back-door. In Figure 10.4A (related to both Red and White series), 1 flashes on through the key, and 3 follows his pass to go over the top; 2 replaces 3, and 1 replaces 2. Player 4 has options: to 1, to 2, or to 3. Here, he passes to 2 for a jump shot.

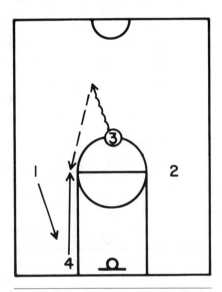

Figure 10.4. Back door is refused.

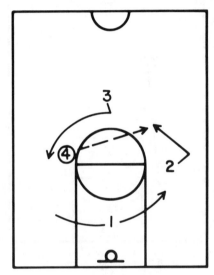

Figure 10.4A. Three options.

Hit the Open Player
From the High Post

Player 1 makes the entry pass dribble for the Red Series, and 3 clears to the high post. Player 1 turns, passes back out to 3, and then runs her usual route to the other wing, looking for a pass all the way. Player 2 moves over the top, adding to 3's options: pass to 1, hand back to 2, or use one of her own triple-threat options. *Note*: Coach varies the options.

Players 1 and 2 rotate. The option pass from 3 to 1 is an excellent probability for a three-point shot, especially against a zone defense (Figure 10.5).

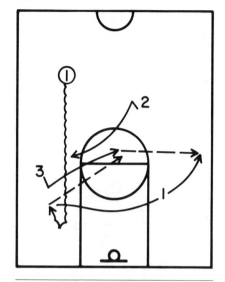 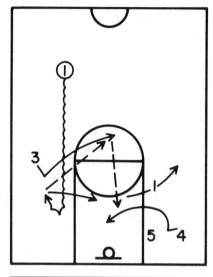

Figure 10.5. Hit the open wing.   **Figure 10.6.** High-low pass option.

High-Low Pass Option

Player 1 makes the entry dribble as 3 clears the side for the high post. Player 1 turns and passes out to 3. Player 4 cuts over 5's screen to receive high-low pass from 3. Player 1 runs his usual route to the opposite wing. *Note*: High-low pass from 3 to 4 must be worked on extensively. Also, 5 must set a good screen for 4. Players 4 and 5 rotate. Related to Red Series (Figure 10.6).

Another High-Low Pass Option

Player 1 makes the Red Series entry dribble as 3 clears the side and goes to the high post. Player 1 turns and passes out to 3; 4 cuts over 5's screen but is not open, so 3 passes to 5. *Note*: 4 will be shut off many times when proper defensive switching takes place; therefore, 3 must look for 5, whose new defensive opponent (on a switch) will be behind. Player 5 must give a target hand for the pass, and 3 must read the floor down low with intelligence and aggressiveness. Players 4 and 5 rotate duties (Figure 10.7).

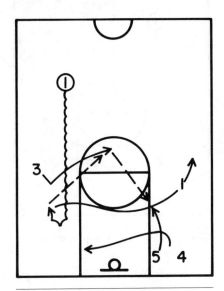

Figure 10.7. Another high-low pass option.

Figure 10.8. Low-post-exchange drill.

Low Post Exchange Drill

The low post exchange is important to the Rotary phase in both Red and White. Here, 3 has the ball at the high post and passes to the wing. He then chooses one of the two Rotary option routes from the point, as shown: cutting down the key, asking for the give-go pass, and emerging on the other side, becoming the new wing. Player 1 refuses 3 and passes down to 5, who has exchanged blocks with 4. *Notes*: 5 uses various close-in shooting options, unguarded. Player 1 uses various passes to 5. Player 1 does not stand still after his pass, but instead tries to get open for a return pass from 5 for a jump shot. Players 1 and 3 rotate (Figure 10.8).

Pass and Screen
Opposite Option, Rotary

In this Rotary drill, 3 again passes over to wing 1 but chooses the *second* Rotary option from the point, hustling over to set a screen for 2 at the opposite wing. Player 2 either flares out to the top of the key to receive a pass from 1 for a jump shot (pass B), or else swings a pass on over to 3 (pass C). *Note:* This is bread-and-butter in the Rotary and must be presented in that light by the coach. V-cuts are absolutely necessary, as are passes to the outside, target hand. Coach sets up rotations and shooting options (Figure 10.9).

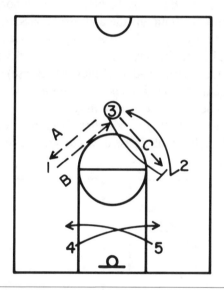

Figure 10.9. Pass-and-screen-opposite option, Rotary.

Back Door Drill (Rotary)

This drill emphasizes a Rotary feature, so it must be practiced extensively. Timing and surprise are keys to success. In this drill, coach passes to 3 at the high post. As a signal, 3 dribbles back a step or two, and 5 flashes out, receiving the pass from 3. Player 2 shifts gears to go back-door. *Notes*: Coach varies the options, with the most attention given to timing and passing. If 2 is refused when she dashes back door, she runs her usual route to the opposite wing. Drill should be run on the other side, with 4 and 1 replacing 5 and 2 (Figure 10.10).

Low Post Lateral Drill

The low post players are very important to the inside Rotary part of both Red and White. This drill develops the block-to-block horizontal exchange movement and improves both outside and inside passing techniques. For this drill, the point player passes to the wings *without* cutting down the key to run the usual route; he stays in place with 2 and 3 and concentrates on passing. *Note*: Coach may add an X player (defense) against 4. Wings 2 and 3 always square up quickly and read the low post area when they receive the pass. The back-door move *may* be made a part of this drill, if desired. (See Figure 10.10.) As another variation, point 1 may fake a pass to a wing before dropping a pass down to 4 in the key (Figure 10.11).

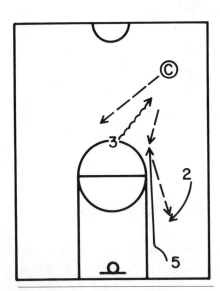

Figure 10.10. Back-door drill.

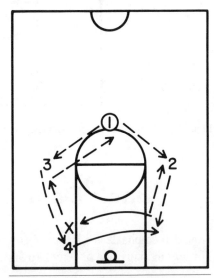

Figure 10.11. Low post lateral drill.

Low Post Pick-Roll

This two-player free-lance may occur at any time during the Rotary of Red and White and is signaled when the wing puts the ball on the floor for a dribble towards the corner. Player 5 comes out to screen, 2 dribbles over the top heading for the basket, and 5 rolls for the hoop. Player 2 may take a jump shot at the top of the screen, drive in, or pass to 5 as he rolls for the basket (Figure 10.12). *Note*: Run the same drill on the other side, with 1, 3 and 4. Point and wing players rotate.

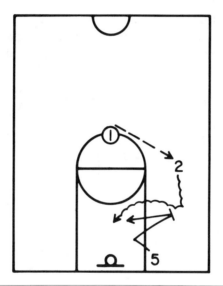

Figure 10.12. Low post pick-roll.

Swing the Ball

Figures 10.13 and 10.13A describe a drill that improves the execution of Rotary in both Red and White series. The wheeling of the outside players and the block-to-block exchanging of low post players calls for the participation of all five teammates; thus, it is a *whole* of the whole-part method of instruction. The two diagrams are self-exaplanatory and are a specific part of the Rotary. Point player passes to a wing, cuts down the key, and goes to the opposite wing, who takes over at the point. If possible, the ball is passed to the low post by the wing. For purposes of the drill, the low post player passes out to the new point player, the ball is reversed to the other wing, 2, and the ball is again passed down to a low post player who has exchanged blocks with the swinging of the ball. *Note*: To practice the fundamentals involved in the routes, and the pattern itself, this drill may go without the interruption of a shot by having the low post player pass back out to the point or to the wings. If back-door is included in the drill (and it may be), the cutter dribbles out from under the basket (no shot) and passes back out, for drill continuity. This drill has been called "passing game drill" and has included the low post pick-roll in its continuity. Notice that the two options were exercised in the two diagrams by the point players: pass and cut down the key, and pass-and-screen opposite. Both diagrams are also examples of "outside-in, inside-out" passing techniques.

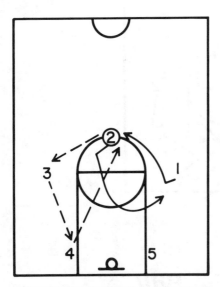
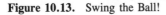

Figure 10.13. Swing the Ball!

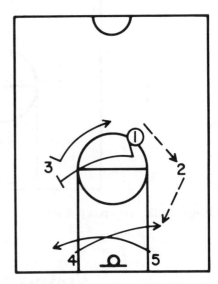

Figure 10.13A. Rotary development.

White Series, First Option

This is the basic White Series entry and first option. Player 1 dribbles down and passes back to 2, the off-guard. Player 3 flashes out to the high post, clearing the side and receiving a pass from 2 as 1 goes back door.

Player 3 passes to 1 for the lay-up. *Note*: Players 1 and 2 rotate. Timing is important. Player 1 practices the surprise shifting of speed. A variety of passes by 3 to 1 is recommended (Figure 10.14).

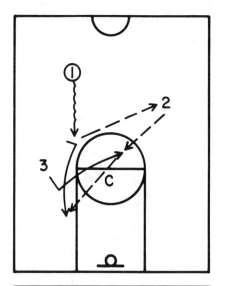

Figure 10.14. First White option: back-door.

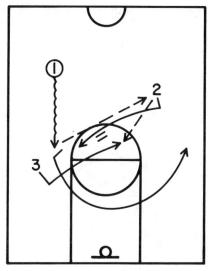

Figure 10.15. Over the top: second option.

Jump Shots at High Post

This drill is conducted as a separate one, but really is a continuation from the first option to the second one in the White Series. The same initial moves are made by 1, 2, and 3, as drawn in preceding Figure 10.14, but 3 refuses the back door cut by 1, holds the ball, and hands it off to 2 as she comes over the top. When she passes to 2, 3 must turn and set a screen for her. For this drill, 2 takes a jump shot. Player 1 continues to the other wing. *Note*: Have 3 rebound the jump shot. Players 1 and 2 rotate (Figure 10.15).

Surprise Skip Pass, White

This is one of the most important and mandatory drills because of its pertinence against zone defenses. It features an alley-oop skip pass and adds dimension to the deception and finesse of the White Series. When 3 clears the side and blasts out to the high post, 2 is given the choices of passing to him, or passing over his head (skip pass) to 1 in the cleared area. The latter is an excellent option against zone defenses. *Note*: 3 rebounds 1's short jump shot (or lay-up). Players 1 and 2 rotate (Figure 10.16).

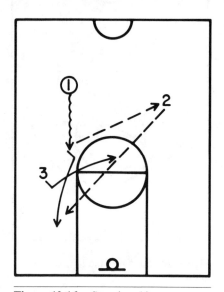 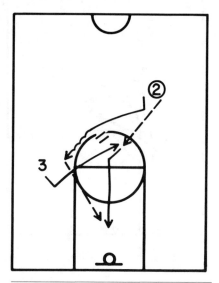

Figure 10.16. Surprise skip pass, White.

Figure 10.17. Pick-roll at the high post.

Pick-Roll at High Post

This drill adds to the skills of the high post player. Receiving the pass from 2, 3 waits for 2 to follow her pass and come over the top. Player 3 gives the ball back to 2, screens for her, and rolls for the basket, receiving the return pass for a lay-up. *Note*: No rotation. This is an example of a two-player game, so important to the total New Option Offense (Figure 10.17).

High Post Jumper or Drive

Figure 10.18 illustrates another drill for high post proficiency within the White Series, mainly in the mechanics of receiving a pass, assuming a triple-threat stance, and using the jump-shooting option from the top of the key. Player 3 receives the pass from 2 for the jump shot, which, if applicable, may be a three-pointer. *Note*: Coach may vary by permitting 3 to practice free-lance moves, primarily dribble-driving right and left after receiving the ball. Players 1, 2, 4, and 5 practice the continuation of their routes, as shown in Figure 10.19.

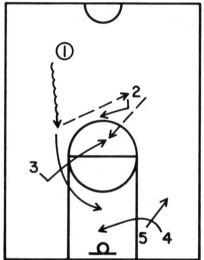

Figure 10.18. High post jumper or drive.

Figure 10.19. Pass on down.

Pass On Down

Except for the culminating option, this drill duplicates the one for 10.18. This is an important *inside* White Series option, in which 3 refuses everybody and dumps the ball down to 4, who benefits from 5's screen. Figure 10.19 shows the routes of 1 and 2 to the wings. *Note*: Like 10.18, this drill involves all five players, the *whole* in the whole-part method, and at least two salient points must be stressed: (a) the importance of proper execution of all passes and route movements, and (b) the timing and execution of 5's screening action. No rotations in this drill; the coach will have five replacements, as designated for each position, waiting and ready. Outside-in passing skill is improved in this drill.

5 Rebounds 4's Shot, and Passes Back Out to the New 1

In Figure 10.20, the drill for Figures 10.18 and 10.19 culminates with the coach commenting on the pattern efficiency. This diagram does not represent a drill. The ball has ended up in the hands of 4, who has made his field goal; 1 and 2 are at their new wing positions, and 5 has moved back to his low post block. It is time for some evaluation by the coach!

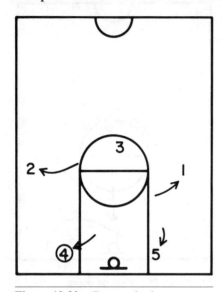

Figure 10.20. Routes check.   **Figure 10.21.** Reading the floor inside.

Reading the Inside

The purpose of the drill drawn in Figure 10.21 is to teach 3 to read the low *inside* as she turns to face the backet with the ball. In the illustrated read, she catches the player-player defense in a poor switching action, with the result that 5 is open (instead of 4, as in preceding Figure 10.19). Player 3 has refused 1 and 2, and looked down the key. The high-low pass is an excellent option, one to be practiced extensively, and the pass will usually be to 5's right hand, her outside, target hand. For the drill, 4 rebounds and passes out to the new 1. No rotation. As in Figure 10.20, all players end up in the set for Rotary.

Split the High Post, Blue

This drill represents the first part of the Blue Series, and therefore it is important that players become proficient at it in practice. This is right side action; identical action for the left side will follow. Player 1 passes to 3, who passes to 5 moving diagonally to the high post elbow. Players 1 and 3 split the post, and 5 hands off to 3 for a jump shot. *Note*: 5 rebounds the jump shot. No rotations (Figure 10.22).

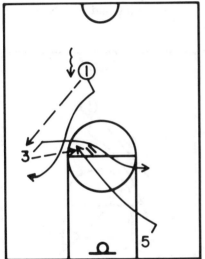

Figure 10.22. Split the high post, Blue.   **Figure 10.23.** Hand-off option, Blue.

Another Hand-Off at the High Post, Blue

This drill gives the high post player the option of handing off to the second cutter in the splitting action over the top. Player 1 passes to 3, who passes to 5 moving diagonally to the high post elbow. Player 5 refuses 3 and hands off to 1 for a jump shot. *Note*: 5 rebounds the jump shot and passes out to the new 1 as the drill continues. No rotations (Figure 10.23).

Give to the Corner and Go, Blue

This drill teaches that 3, the wing, has an option of passing to the corner instead of to the high post. As 1 passes to the wing, 4 goes to the corner, and 5 moves out diagonally to the high post. Player 3 passes down to 4 (pass B) and cuts through the key, receiving the return pass (pass C). Player 1 had followed his pass and moved over the top of 5 to replace 3 at the wing. *Note*: Player 4 rebounds the lay-up and passes out to the new 1. Head-shoulder fake by 3 is important. Stress timing and V-cuts (Figure 10.24).

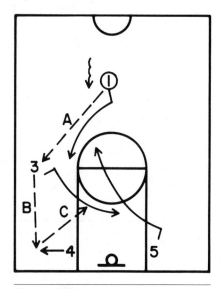

Figure 10.24. Blue give-and-go.

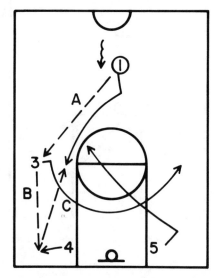

Figure 10.25. Open cutter coming over the top.

Open Cutter Coming Over the Top

This drill is the same as that drawn in Figure 10.24, except that 4 uses the option of passing to 1 for a jump shot as 1 comes over the top of the high post (pass C). Player 4 had refused 3. *Note*: This drill teaches open-player basketball as players run their designated routes, and the coach stresses the importance of doing this properly. Player 4 rebounds the jump shot and passes out to the new 1. No rotations (Figure 10.25).

High Post Slides Down, Blue

This drill teaches the slide-down requirement of the high post player in the sequence of the Blue Series. Drill starts with the ball at the wing. Player 3 passes down to 4 and cuts across the key, asking for the ball. Player 2 cuts over the top of the high post, asking for the ball. Player 4 refuses both, which signals 5 (high post) to vacate and post up at the low post block. When she does so, 4 passes to her, and for this drill 5 is required to use various low post techniques for a close-in shot (Figure 10.26). *Note*: Coach may vary the drill by having 4 and 5 play a two-player game or by having 5 pass out to an open teammate (as in Figure 10.27). Player 4 rebounds. No rotations.

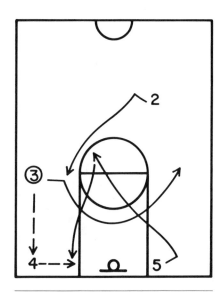

Figure 10.26. High post slides down, Blue.

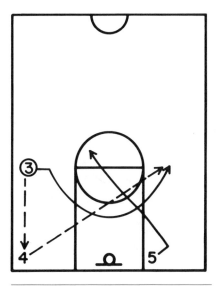

Figure 10.27. Skip pass drill, corner to wing.

Skip Pass Drill,
Corner to Wing

Only 3, 4, and 5 are required for this drill, which reemphasizes the importance of the open-player concept. Player 3 passes down to 4 in the corner, as 5 moves out to the high post. Player 3 cuts through the key, asking for the ball; refused, he goes on to the wing, always looking back for a delay pass. Player 4 finds 3 open and skip-passes over to him for a jump shot. *Notes*: This could be an excellent three-point possibility, since 3 takes position at about the three-point line. No rotations. Player 4 rebounds the jump shot and passes back out to a new 3 as the drill continues.

Left-Side Drills, High Post

In Figures 10.28 through 10.33 we go to the left side of the court for the selected drills that apply to Blue.

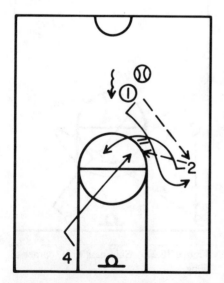

Figure 10.28. High post blue, left side.

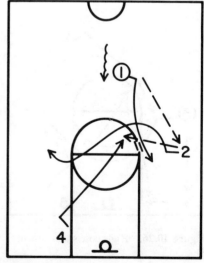

Figure 10.29. More left side, high post.

High Post, Left Side

Except for designated personnel (numbered positions), the drills are identical to those of the right side. Player 1 entry-passes to the left wing, 2, who makes the short pass to 4 at the high post. The splitting action by point and wing follows, with 4 handing off to 2 in Figure 10.28 and to player 1 in Figure 10.29. In both drills, 4 rebounds and passes out to the new 1. No rotations.

Blue Give-Go, Left Side

As in the identical right-side drill, three passes are made (A, B, and C), from 1 to 2 to 5 and back to 2 as she moves through the key. Player 4 had moved to her high post but had been refused by 2. Player 5 rebounds the ball, and passes out to the new 1. No rotations (Figure 10.30).

Coming Over the Top, Left Side

As in Figure 10.30, this drill gives 5 (corner player) the option of passing out to 1 as he comes over the top of 4 for a jump shot. Player 2 continues to the other wing, in his route. Player 5 rebounds and passes out to the new 1. No rotations (Figure 10.31).

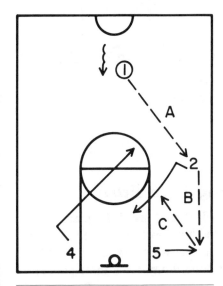

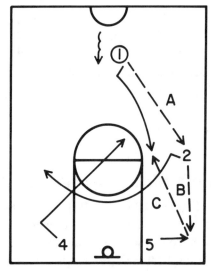

Figure 10.30. Blue give-go, left side.

Figure 10.31. Coming over the top, left side.

Left Side, High Post Slides Down

This drill involves the slide-down action of 4 from high post to low post, as illustrated earlier in Figure 10.26 for player 5 on the other side. Movements and options are identical to those described for Figure 10.26; player 4 may work for her own close-in shot. or she may look for the open teammate; player 1 out at the elbow, player 2 across the key, or player 5 in the corner. Player 5 or 4 rebounds in this drill and passes out to the new 1. No rotations (Figure 10.32).

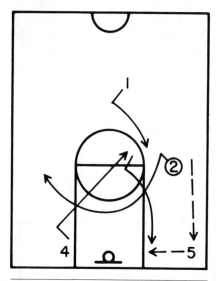

Figure 10.32. Left side, high post slides down.

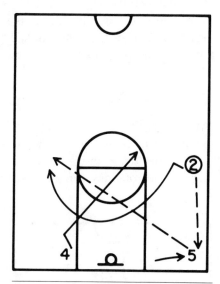

Figure 10.33. Left side, corner-to-wing skip pass.

Left Side, Corner-to-Wing Skip Pass

In Figure 10.33 the drill starts with the ball at the wing, 2. He passes down to 5 in the corner, after refusing 4 at the high post, and receives a skip pass from 5 while coming out at the opposite wing. As in Figure 10.27 for the right side, this is an excellent opportunity for a three-pointer.

Continuity Drill for 4 and 5, Blue

Figures in this sequence combine to illustrate a nonshooting, nonstop drill designed to teach the fundamental diagonal, corner-to-high-post movements of 4 and 5 in the Blue Series. The ball swings around on the *outside only*, in this drill. Figure 10.34 begins the drill, with 1's pass to wing 2; player 4 flashes out to the elbow, and 5 goes to the corner. In Figure 10.34A, player 2 refuses both 4 and 5 and swings the ball back to the point, and 1 rotates the ball on to the other wing, 3. Player 4 goes to the strong-side corner, and 5 comes out to the strong-side elbow. Continuing the drill in Figure 10.34B, player 3 passes back to point 1; 1's pass to wing 2 maintains the continuation. *Note*: Coach stresses that 4 and 5 are always looking for a surprise pass during their diagonal movements. When they arrive at the elbow (and even before arriving), they are asking for the ball with both hands, in good body balance. This is a five-person drill; thus, it is one of the *whole* drills that assemble the *parts* into the team pattern. No rotation. No movement, only passing, by outside players 1 and 2. There are other nonstop, nonshooting ideas that the coach will want to use.

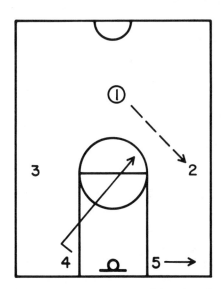

Figure 10.34. Continuity drill begins.

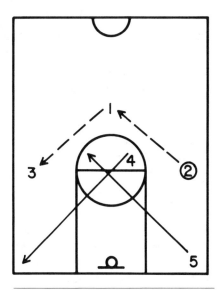

Figure 10.34A. Continuity, 4 and 5. Reverse pass.

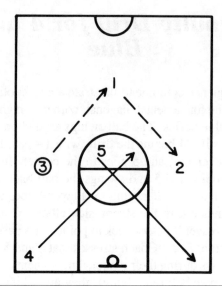

Figure 10.34B. Drill continues, side to side.

Summary

Since time is always an element, and a problem, in coaching, this chapter aids the busy coach. Any part of it may be used verbatim and transferred to the worksheet for practice sessions; used as a reference, with additions and deletions; or used and/or altered in any way to fit needs, as the early organization and refinement of the New Option Offense progresses.

The formation into two-, three-, and four-player units makes individual players feel that they are being very closely observed, evaluated, and appreciated. The result is that players show excellent effort, spirit, and morale throughout.

The concept of teamwork and team-pattern discipline begins here. Players gain confidence in themselves, in their teammates, and in the New Option Offense system; this feeling pays off when the five-player units are assembled and the drills and options of chapters 2, 3, and 4 are included.

The assistant coach responds to this part of the program with a best effort. With the break-down of the whole into parts, the assistant has an opportunity to gain varsity instructional experience and to demonstrate coaching expertise on the practice floor. The coach-assistant coach relationship is favorably enhanced.

Improving Offensive Skills

The purpose of this chapter is to provide drills for the improvement of basic offensive skills. Passing, shooting, dribbling and footwork will be discussed.

Passing

The primary objective of this first portion of this chapter is to present special passing drills, with coaching points, that are related to the New Option Offense and will have a bearing on its success. The secondary goal is to include drills that promote general passing proficiency. A random pot-pourri of drills is not intended. An asterisk with the title of the drill in the text indicates that it is directly related to the New Option Offense.

Passing is one of the most important features of the New Option Offense, if not the most important. It is true that the basketball scoreboard does not give credit to the exciting art of passing and that points are recorded only when the ball goes in the basket; however, the success of this offensive system depends greatly upon purposeful, skilled passing that culminates in a good pass leading up to a high-percentage shot.

The scope of instructional material in this chapter segment touches upon the following passing techniques:

- Two-hand chest pass
- Bounce pass
- Two-hand over-the-head pass
- Across-the-chest pass
- Skip pass
- Shovel pass
- Baseball pass

Coaching reminders are included at the end of these passing drills.

Cross-Court Skip-Passing

Lines of players stand along each sideline, facing each other. Each player in one line has a ball. He skip-passes cross-court to his partner and receives a return skip pass. Back-and-forth passing continues as each player remains stationary, concentrating on proper skip-passing techniques (Figure 11.1).

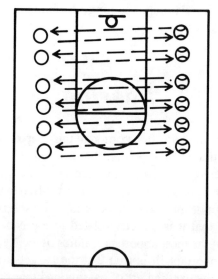

Figure 11.1 Cross-court skip pass.

Skip-Passing to Moving Players *

As 1, 2, 3, and 4 move counterclockwise to four designated spots, stationary 5 skip-passes to each place. Players 1, 2, 3, and 4 return the passes and rotate continuously, concentrating on improvement of passing techniques. Player 5 is replaced from time to time, as desired by the coach. This drill is related to the Blue Series (Figure 11.2).

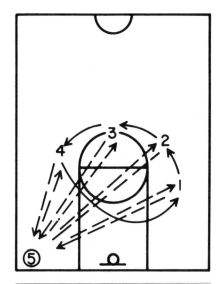

Figure 11.2. Skip-pass and move.

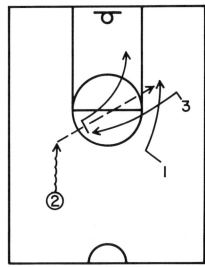

Figure 11.3. Skip over the top.

Skip Over the Top *

Player 2 dribbles down and 3 pops out to the high post from her initial wing set. With a head-shoulder fake and jab step, 1 shifts gears to go backdoor. The expectation is that 2 will pass to 3; instead, she makes a skip pass over the head of 3, to 1. Alternate the jump shots and dribble-drives. Player 3 always rolls to the basket, and 1 may pass to her, for variation. Players 1, 2, and 3 rotate after each shot: 1 to 2, 2 to 3, and 3 to 1. This drill represents the skip-pass entry option in the White Series (Figure 11.3).

Two Skip Passes and an Open Player

Player 2 dribbles down as 3 pops out to high post. Player 2 skip-passes over 3 to 1, who, it is assumed, meets defensive pressure. Spotting the *open player*, 1 makes a second skip pass over to 2, who is moving without the ball and free-lancing down the opposite side. Jump shot by 2. Player 3 rolls for the basket. For variation, 2 may pass to him. Rotation: 1 to 2, 2 to 3, and 3 to 1 after each shot (Figure 11.4).

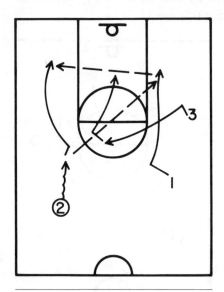

Figure 11.4. Skip pass to open player.

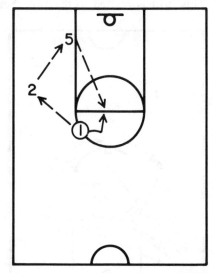

Figure 11.5. Triangle and jump shot.

Overload Triangle and Jumper *

Triangle overload simulation. Player 1 to 2 to 5, skip pass out to 1 for a jump shot around the top of the key. Player 1 might go for a three-pointer, and this could be a part of the drill. Coach stresses bounce passes for 1 and 2; for 5, the overhead skip pass. Player 5 must raise her target hand to receive the pass from 2. Only 5 and 4 play low post; 1 and 2 rotate. This triangular three-player action is an example of inside-out play in the New Option Offense (Figure 11.5).

Three Skips and a Jumper

Skip passes from 3 to 2 to 1 to 3 (passes A, B, and C in Figure 11.6). Player 3 moves for a jump shot at end of Pass C. Player 3, the shooter, rebounds his own shot, throws back out to new 3, then goes to his new place (at 2). After 3's shot, rotate: 3 to 2, 2 to 1, 1 to 3. This is a good drill for teaching the inside-out passing concept.

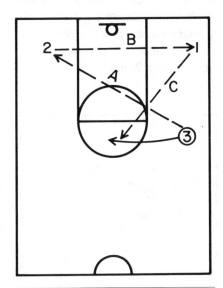

Figure 11.6. Three skips and a jumper.

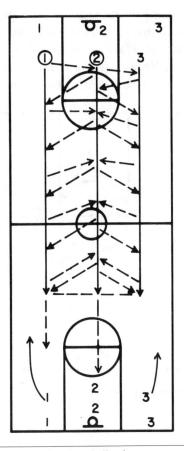

Figure 11.7. Two-ball salvo.

Two-Ball Salvo

Player 2 is the busy worker in the middle. Three lines, two balls, full speed ahead, chest or bounce passes, no dribble unless absolutely necessary to prevent "traveling" infraction. Go full court; at about the top of the key, players pass the two balls to two of the new 1, 2, and 3 players, who continue the drill toward the other end. Have three-player lines ready at each end. This is a great drill for coordination, intensity, and conditioning (Figure 11.7).

Push, Pull, Pass

Assume that a defensive opponent is overplaying 2 to prevent the entry pass from 1 to 2. Player 1 "pushes" with the full extension of her arms in faking the two-handed chest pass, pulls the ball straight back when she senses that her pass would be intercepted, and then passes to 2 on the backdoor cut. Player 2 can go either behind or in front of her imaginary opponent. Vary by inserting an actual defender against 2 and have 2 dribble-drive for the lay-up, one-on-one. Players 1 and 2 rotate (Figure 11.8).

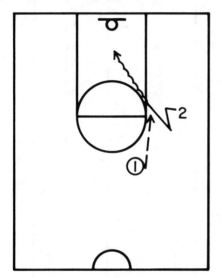

Figure 11.8. Reaction to overplay.

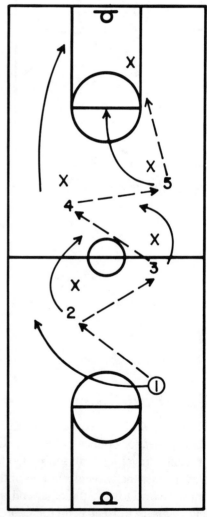

Figure 11.9. Full court, no dribble.

Full Court, No Dribble

Five-against-five, full court scrimmage. *No dribble.* If there is an inadvertent dribble, violator runs a lap, which creates a four-on-five situation until the fifth player returns from the run. Maximum of two dribbles is allowed if driving in for a lay-up. Passes are examples only. Arrows of movement are also examples. This is free-lance passing and moving, no dribble (Figure 11.9).

Two-Ball Passing Drill

The line of five players is about 15 feet from player 1, and facing him. He has his back to the basket. Start with a ball at 1 and a ball at 6. Player 1 passes to 2 as 6 passes in to 1. Player 2 passes back in to 1 as 1 passes out to 5. The two balls move continuously from 1 to the line of five players. Chest passes, bounce passes, and across-the-chest passes are recommended (Figure 11.10).

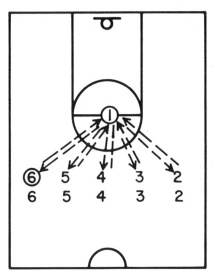

Figure 11.10. Two-ball pepper.

Run and Pick 'Em Up

Two balls, coach rolls them on the floor one after another, in different directions. Player P retrieves, passes one back, goes to the other rolling ball, passes it back before it goes out of bounds, passes it back, and the exercise continues for the one player until terminated by the coach. A new player comes out. P must stop, plant her feet, and pass out properly, with chest, bounce, or overhead passes. Coach may need an assistant to receive the passes and hand over the balls. This is an excellent conditioner, in addition to being a good fast-passing drill (Figure 11.11).

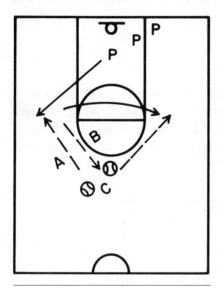

Figure 11.11. Run and pick "em up."

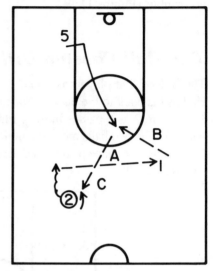

Figure 11.12. High post triangle.

High Post Triangle *

Triangle is maintained at 15-18 feet distance apart for players 1, 2, and 3. Coach insists on all types of fundamentally sound passes. Player 5 indicates a target hand when he comes out, and must give head-shoulder fake and jab step as he starts. Player 5 receives pass B, reads the floor quickly with his back to the basket, and passes back out to 1 (pass C). Player 5 returns to the end line, and a new 5 comes out. Players 1 and 2 rotate (Figure 11.12).

Low Post Triangle *

This is the classic point-wing-low-post passing game: 2 to 1 to 4, who must indicate a target hand. Coach varies the passes and demands proper techniques of chest, bounce, overhead, and across-the-chest bounce passes. Drill is also designed to have 4 work on the turn-around jumper, driving the baseline for a lay-up, driving across the key, right-hand hook, and left-hand hook. No defense (Figure 11.13).

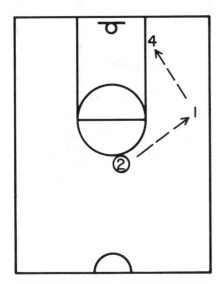

Figure 11.13. Low post triangle.

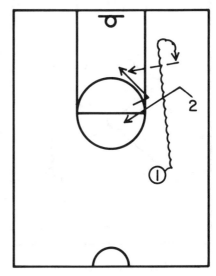

Figure 11.14. Back-door reaction.

Back-Door Reaction Passes *

When using the Red Series, the team must always be aware of defensive overplay and "cheating" against player 2.

Player 1 dribble-penetrates, stops, and turns to pass out to 2. Suddenly, she sees that 2 is being overplayed, so she executes "Push, Pull, Pass" (See Figure 11.8, this chapter) as 2 V-cuts and flashes back-door for the delay pass and lay-up. Bounce pass and across-the-chest bounce pass should be featured here. Players 1 and 2 rotate (Figure 11.14).

Passing in a Pair of Triangles

Keep 2 busy! He must use peripheral vision, and pivot-turn properly. Two balls as shown. Player 1 passes to 2, turns to pass to 3, and 3 passes out to 1. As 2 pivots back, he receives a pass from 4 and passes on to 5.

Player 5 passes out to 4. Thus, the pass sequence for one triangle is 1 to 2 to 3 to 1; for the other triangle, 4 to 2 to 5 to 4. Vary the types of passes. No rotations (Figure 11.15).

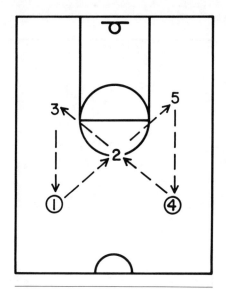

Figure 11.15. Passing in a pair of triangles.

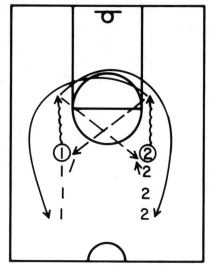

Figure 11.16. Penetrate and pass back.

Penetrate and Pass Back

Two balls, as shown. Players 2 and 1 dribble down, stop, pivot-turn, and make one-handed hook (baseball) out to next players in line. Player 1's pass will be left-handed; player 2's will be right-handed. Dribbler may prefer to pass at the top of a jump, and that is acceptable. Drill may be varied with a two-handed overhead pass. Player 1 rotates outside to go to the rear of line 2. Player 2 rotates outside to the rear of line 1. Distance is somewhat shorter than usual for a baseball pass, so it could be defined as a hook pass (Figure 11.16).

Overloading Triangles; Pass and Shoot *

Two balls. Two triangles. In one triangle, passes go from 1 to 4 to 2 to 1, and 1 shoots; simultaneously, in the other triangle, passes go from

6 to 5 to 3 to 6, and 6 shoots. Coach rotates as he or she desires, but only 5's and 4's play low post. Players 5 and 4 make outlet passes to 6 and 1 as they rebound each shot. All types of passes: bounce, across-the-chest bounce, short overhead, and chest passes. Players 5 and 4 give a target hand. Do not telegraph passes. These are inside-out passes which result in high-percentage jump shots (Figure 11.17).

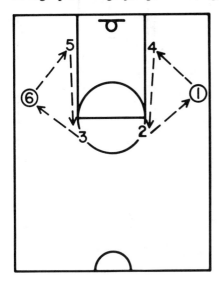

Figure 11.17. Overload, pass and shoot.

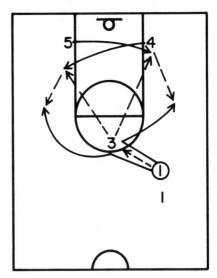

Figure 11.18. High to low and back out.

High to Low and Back Out

Player 1 passes to high post 3, who turns, squares up, reads the floor, and passes down low to either 4 or 5. They exchange blocks as 3 turns. Player 1 moves to the side of the pass, gets a pass from 4 or 5, and takes a jump shot. Vary the shooter as desired; pass back out to 3 for a shot, or have 4 and 5 apply their low post moves for a shot. When the ball goes in the basket, have 4 or 5 pull it out of the net, step out of bounds quickly, and make a baseball pass out to the new 1. Teach them to run the baseline as they look for 1 (Figure 11.18).

Pass and Surprise *

In Figure 11.19, players 1, 2, and 5 are passing in their triangle. Judging that 2's defensive opponent (simulated) is becoming anxious and overplaying, 1 backs up with a dribble in Figure 11.19A, 5 pops out for a pass, and 2 goes back-door. Player 5 turns to pass to him. Lay-ups and jump shots by 2; 1s and 2s rotate. Only 5s and 4s play low post.

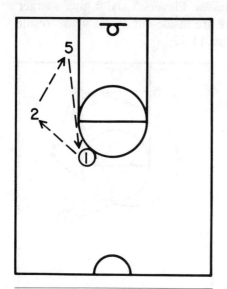 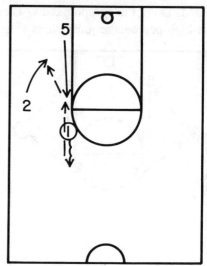

Figure 11.19. Triangle passing.   **Figure 11.19A.** Surprise!

Four-Against-Four, Keep Score

Half-court, four vs. four. Four players operate on offense for a given number of minutes, four on defense, then change over. Both offense and defense get points, as follows:

Offense:
- Scores only on two-point field goal.
- Offensive rebound. Put the ball back up if possible; if not, take it back out without interruption.

Defense:
- If rebounding defensively, pass the ball back out past midcourt against transition pressure.
- If offense makes a turnover, defense gets to shoot one-and-one free throws.

- If defense fouls, violator runs to the sideline for a five-second count, creating a four versus three situation until the violator returns (Figure 11.20).

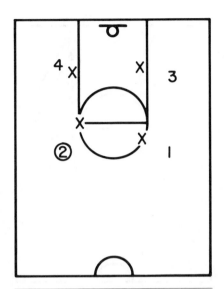

Figure 11.20. Four-against-four, keep score.

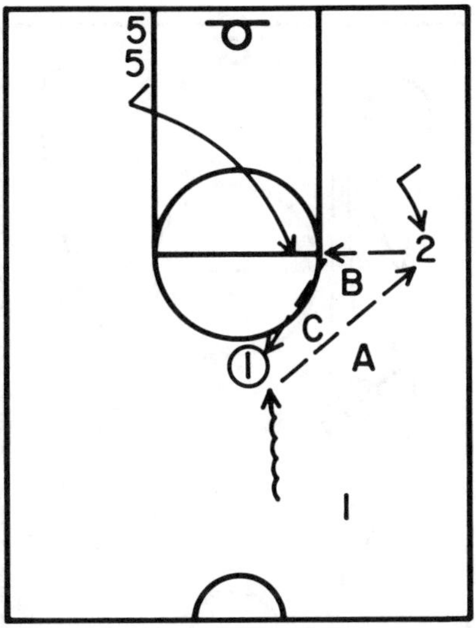

Figure 11.21. Wing-to-high post mini-pass.

Wing-to-High Post Mini-Pass *

Drill is related to the Blue Series. Player 5 comes out to receive the short pass from 2 and 5 passes back out to new 1, as the drill continues with a new 5. No shooting, only triangular passing, with main attention focused on the 2-to-5 short pass. Do not telegraph the pass. Players 1 and 2 may rotate (Figure 11.21).

Pass and Follow

Use bounce and chest passes. Player 1 passes to 4 and cuts properly (in this case, to the outside) and to the rear of that line. Player 4 passes to the next player in line 1, and moves to the rear of that line. At the same time, 2 passes to 3, cuts to the outside, and goes to the rear of line 3.

Player 3 passes to the next player in line 2 and moves to the rear of that line. Do not run in a straight line or travel in a "banana" route. Meet the pass, don't wait for it. Don't telegraph the pass (Figure 11.22).

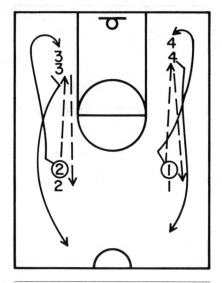

Figure 11.22. Pass and follow.

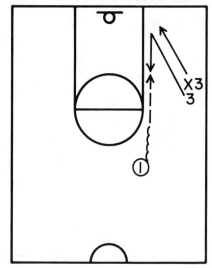

Figure 11.23. Cut and come back.

Cut and Come Back

For this drill, 3 is guarded by X3, and cuts straight for basket as 1 dribbles in toward him. Suddenly, 3 cuts back down low to receive the pass from 1 and plays one-on-one against X3 on that side of the floor. Bounce or chest pass from 1 is required (Figure 11.23).

Two V-Cuts and Come Back

Having a rough time with the overplaying X3 at the wing, 3 makes a V-cut, cuts hard for the basket, stops, executes another V-cut, and comes back to receive the pass from 1. She may then play one-against-one with X3 on that side of the floor (Figure 11.24).

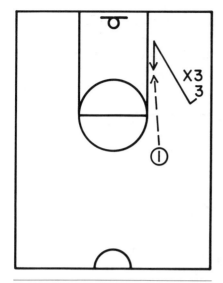 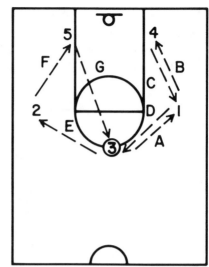

Figure 11.24. Two V-cuts, come back. **Figure 11.25.** Windshield wiper.

Windshield Wiper *

Players 1, 2, and 3 are stationary passers. Players 4 and 5 exchange from block to block as the passes rotate from side to side. Passes A through G are drawn, although the drill actually continues in this general manner until the coach's terminating whistle. This is important around-the-horn passing, which always considers the low post player. The low post player may, at times, skip-pass out to the point with an overhead pass. Wings and point always square up quickly and read quickly, upon receiving the pass. Chest, bounce, overhead, and across-the-chest passes are required. No rotation. Drill teaches reading the floor and inside-out passing techniques (Figure 11.25).

Running Baseball Pass

Coach stands under the basket with the ball, facing 1, who will make the running baseball pass along the baseline. Coach passes to 1 as he runs.

Player 1 leaps in the air and makes a long, baseball pass to 2; 2 completes a baseball pass to 3, who dribbles in for a lay-up, rebounds, and rolls the ball the length of the floor to the coach. The drill continues with a new trio. Rotation: 3 to 2, 2 to 1, and 1 to 3 (Figure 11.26).

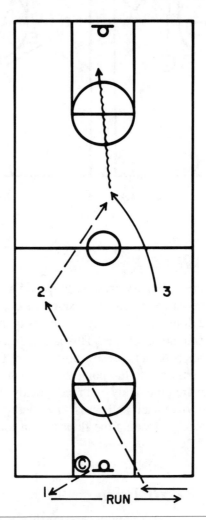

Figure 11.26. Running baseball pass.

Get Open!

Five-against-five, half-court. One team stays on offense a designated number of minutes, then changes over. Offense may run either the established offensive system or improvised patterns. Coach calls out (for example) ''Seven passes, Jones,'' designating the shooter on the seventh pass. Two points are given if Jones gets open on ''seven'' but misses; three points if she makes it on ''seven''; and one point if she makes a basket between ''one'' and ''ten.'' (The drill sequence goes up to ''ten.'') If offense makes a turnover, or fails to get player Jones a shot within ''ten,'' the *defense* gets two points. If defense fouls, give offense two points (and do not shoot free throws) (Figure 11.27).

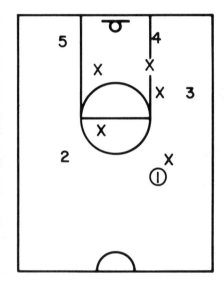

Figure 11.27. Get open!

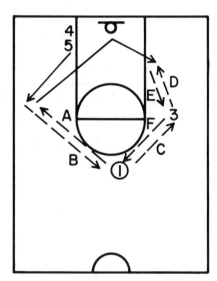

Figure 11.28. Passing and moving, 5s and 4s.

Pass and Move, 5s and 4s

Low post player 5 comes out from the block to the low wing area to receive a pass from 1. After returning the pass, 5 cuts diagonally down the key, completes a V-cut, and comes out to meet pass D from player 3. (Player 1 had passed to 3.) Upon receiving pass D, player 5 returns the pass to 3 and returns to the rear of the line. Player 3 returns the ball to the point, 1, and a new 5 or 4 continues the drill. There is a total of six passes (A, B, C, D, E, F), of all types, including chest, bounce, overhead, lob, and across-the-chest bounce passes. Coach should concentrate on the agility, quickness and hard work of 5 and 4 (Figure 11.28).

Pass for Points!

Five-against-five, half-court. Either run the team's established offense or improvise patterns. No shooting, *no dribbling*. If offense completes nine consecutive passes in the half-court, it gets one point, and a new sequence is started. Players call out the number of passes during a sequence. If defense intercepts or causes a turnover before "nine," it gets one point. If defense fouls, offense gets a point. Do not shoot free throws. If offense fouls, the defense gets a point. After a given number of minutes, teams change over on offense and defense. Keep score! This is as much an intense, aggressive drill for defense as it is a passing exercise. Offense *passes* and *moves* (Figure 11.29).

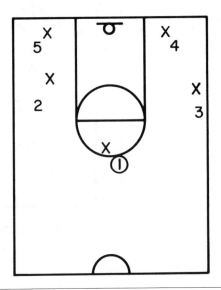

Figure 11.29. Pass for points!

High-Low Pass *

This drill of three passes (A, B, C) touches on the techniques of guard-guard passing, entry passing to the high post, and the notable high-low pass, all related to the New Option Offense. Getting open for the pass, meeting the pass, pivoting at the high post, and under-basket shooting are byproducts of the drill, which is designed primarily for specific passing.

Player 1 dribbles down and makes a back pass to 2, who passes to 4 at the high post. Player 4 pivots, turns, looks down, and passes to 5 cutting into the key. Player 5 rebounds his own shot passes out to new 1. Players 1 and 2 rotate, and 4 and 5 rotate. Vary the types of passes and under-basket attempts (Figure 11.30).

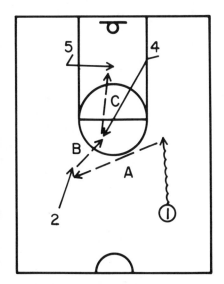

Figure 11.30. High-low pass.

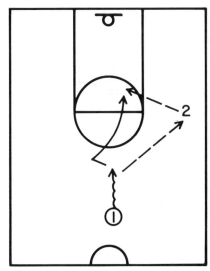

Figure 11.31. Give-and-go.

Give-and-Go *

This depicts the classic give-go pass. It is encouraged in the New Option Offense as an improvised surprise tactic, and is a part of Red and White Rotary as well. Player 1 dribbles, passes to 2 at the wing, gets open with a V-cut and head-shoulder fake, and receives the return pass down the key. Players 1 and 2 rotate and vary the types of shots (Figure 11.31).

High Post Pass to Cutters

This is an excellent practice for improvised cutting and passing situations during a game. Player 1 passes to high post 3, who turns and pivots to read the cutters in the key. Players 2 and 4 cut as shown, and 1 follows her pass and goes over the top, using 3 as a screen if she gets a hand-back. No rotation. Lay-ups, jump shots, and all other types of passes are practiced. This drill enhances the outside-in, high-low passing technique (Figure 11.32).

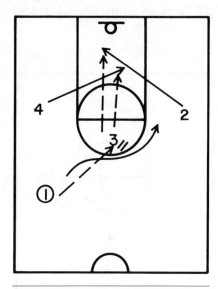

Figure 11.32. High post pass to cutters.

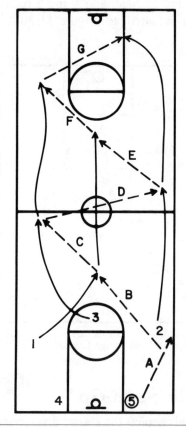

Figure 11.33. Full-court and return, no dribble.

Full Court and Return

This is *not* a fast-break drill. Players may free-lance all the way, and passes A, B, C, D, E, F, and G are shown only as examples of five players passing the ball full-court and returning, *without a dribble*. Pass and move! Players 4 and 5 are trailers; they catch up and get in the offense as the ball crosses the center line. Any one of the five may jump shoot or go in for a lay-up, but the ball may not touch the floor. Don't hurry. Set up an offense. The five players return with the same procedure, and a new team of five players carries on (Figure 11.33).

Full-Court, Two Players Passing

Player 1 makes a baseball pass (A) to 2 and follows the pass, as shown. Player 2 dribbles for a jump shot, rebounds, completes an outlet pass (B) to 1, and runs down-court on the opposite side, to the rear ot 1's line. Receiving the pass, 1 turns, dribbles back down court, stops, and delivers a chest pass to new player in line 1 (C). Player 1 runs to the end of 2's line. Drill continues with a waiting line of 1s and 2s. Baseball passes, chest passes, bounce passes, and outlet (overhead) passes are practiced (Figure 11.34).

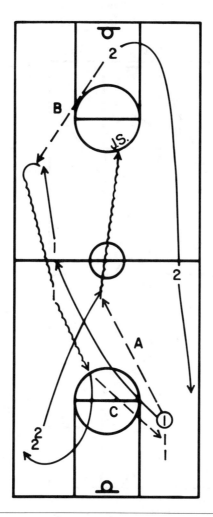

Figure 11.34. Full-court, two players passing.

Six Baseball Passes

The baseball pass is usually used for longer distances, although it may be used for shorter distances when the passer jumps while releasing the ball. A one-hand jump pass may be called a hook pass. The one-hand baseball pass is a quick pass, and the passing motion is somewhat like that of a baseball catcher throwing to second base. Coach (C) passes in to 1, pass A. Player 1 makes a baseball pass to 2, and 2 passes to 3, who shoots a jump shot or dribbles in for a lay-up. Player 4 rebounds, passes to 5, 5 to 6, and 6 to C. Rotation after each pass: all players follow their passes to new positions. No side-arm throwing. As in most other drills, have a waiting line at each location (Figure 11.35).

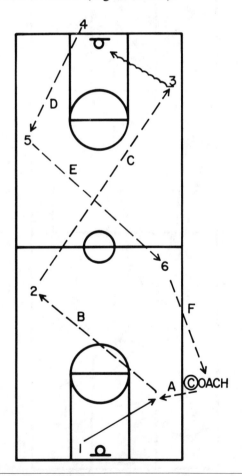

Figure 11.35. Six baseball passes.

Coaching Notes: Passing

The following coaching notes and reminders for this section are unusual in that they intentionally touch on the most basic fundamentals. Thus, they are significant as a prepared aid to coaches at all levels and stages of instruction: those who are teaching basics in introductory situations and those who are reviewing at all levels. Some of the coaching points may be used verbatim, coach to player.

Two-Hand Chest Pass

This is the most fundamental, conventional, and familiar pass in basketball. The ball is held with both hands in front of the chest, fingers spread on the sides of the ball, which is not in contact with the palms. Elbows are bent, with the insides of the elbows close to the body. As the ball is released, a step forward is taken, adding impetus; the arms are pushed straight out, and the wrists snap as the ball is released. Thumbs and fingers give spin to the pass, which is always directed toward the target hand of the receiver, usually away from the defender. The passers must not telegraph the pass, and their eyes do not necessarily follow the pass. They make "soft" passes that are catchable, with the ball rotating and spinning. Ideal passing distance is 15 to 18 feet.

Bounce Pass

The delivery is similar to the chest pass. The bounce on the floor is closer to the receiver than the passer, and the receiver wants to catch it in a low position, about knee-high. A step forward gives impetus and direction to the pass, and there is backward spin and rotation as the fingers and wrists operate as they do with the chest pass.

Overhead Pass

Hold the ball over the head, hands slightly behind, fingers pointing straight up, thumbs fairly close together, and elbows bent. The hands drop back and down as the fingers rotate backward with the ball. The hands and wrists go forward, the fingers rotate downward, and the ball is released from over the top of the head. Follow through, assuring a soft, catchable spin on the ball. This is the most acceptable outlet pass after a defensive rebound and is the key to the fast break. It is also an excellent pass from low post out to jump shooters or out to the top of the key. In this case, it is sometimes called a "fan" pass.

Skip Pass

This is usually the two-hand over-the-head pass; however, sometimes the ball may initially be held a bit farther behind the head, and some players like to jump as they pass. The skip pass provides the quickest and most direct means for moving the ball from one side of the court to the other. Since it bypasses an intervening player and eliminates at least one pass, the skip pass also cuts down on ball-handling errors. Used against zone defenses, it exploits the weak side very effectively, finding an open player there for a jump shot before the zone can react and shift over. Taking a step in the direction of the pass adds strength and impetus to the pass. The ball should be held firmly with both hands prior to delivery, slightly behind the head. Watch the tendency for the ball to be brought back too far behind the head. A skip pass should not be lobbed. The coach defines his or her own preferences as to the parabola and speed of the pass.

Baseball Pass

These instructions are for a right-hand passer, who first plants the right foot for power, then brings the ball back over the right shoulder, with both hands holding it at ear level. The left knee bends, the weight goes to the right foot, and there is a step forward with the left foot, shifting the weight on that foot (left) as the ball is released. The left hand comes off the ball, the passing hand stays behind, and the fingers move under the ball, giving it rotation. Throw overhand, not sidearm; throwing sidearm sometimes causes the ball to curve. The baseball pass is used many times by the inbounds passer, who either steps out of bounds quickly and passes down the floor to a getaway player or passes while running the baseline after an opponent's made shot.

In many ways, the *hook pass* could be defined as a shorter baseball pass. It is a one-hand pass, similar in technique to both the baseball pass and the close-in hook shot. The ball is held in a wide-spread hand, with the passer's body between the opponent and the passing hand. The passing arm is extended, and there is a sweeping motion as the ball is brought over the head toward the receiver (or basket). Like the baseball pass, the weight of the body shifts from right foot to left foot as the ball is released over the head. A jump usually accompanies the pass.

Across-the-Chest Pass

Knees are slightly flexed. With both hands, bring the ball up to one side of the head; at the *same time*, bend the head down, lean slightly to that side, and execute a cross-over, oblique step with the opposite foot as the ball is released. This turns the body, and a bounce pass is made by bringing the arms and ball in a diagonal, swinging motion across the chest to the opposite side of the body. Follow through! This is an increasingly popular pass from wing to low post, when a direct pass can not be made and when a penetrator stops, turns, and feeds back out to a receiver. Sometimes a "look away" technique is helpful (for deception), in which, in this particular situation, the passer doesn't look directly at the receiver at the time of the pass.

Hand-Back (Shovel) Pass

This pass is most popular in hand-off situations, as when the high post player feeds players who are slicing over the top as they scissors or split the post. Screening action by the passer usually accompanies the handoff. The passer holds the ball firmly with both hands, in strong body balance and with feet wide apart, and delivers a short pass with a shoveling motion as a teammate goes by. The passer does not flip the ball and does not stick the ball in the receiver's stomach. Instead, this is a very short pass, with a kind of underhand sweeping motion of hands and arms. To complete the action, the passer turns while passing, presenting a screen-barrier with his or her body, rubbing off the cutter's defender.

Shooting

The three-point field goal, which was discussed at some length near the end of chapter 8, has complicated coaches' thinking about the role of offensive effort and concentration along the parameters of the three-point line. Strategies have to be readjusted, with emphasis on the need to maintain shooting accuracy at new places on the floor. Three points on the scoreboard look better than two! In the past, there was an established offensive truism that "the ball must go inside;" now, although that axiom remains largely valid and important, its acceptance is tempered by the thought that, in an increasing number of cases, the ball should be made available to the high-percentage shooters along the three-point arcuture.

A stand-out coach of a popular team in a major college conference stated that his basic offensive philosophy would be adjusted immediately following the legislation of the three-point rule and the close-in placement of its border line: in the future, the entire length of that avenue arc would become the region for planned routes and movement leading to optimum sites for three-point field goal attempts. His statement was reflected in his team's offensive pattern and tendency the following season, featuring three-player weaves and screens all along the line and inside-out passes, in which the ball was delivered to the inside post players and then kicked back out to the outside three-point gunners.

The distance between the three-point line and the basket is not at all forbidding to college jump shooters, nor is it beyond the authentic shooting range of high school players. When high school rules are universally adjusted to a three-point line, players at that level will be shooting and working along a comparable, imaginary line in practice and games, knowing full-well that proficiency along that border must be developed in preparation for future college play.

The general shooting drills in this chapter focus on (a) teaching (through drilling) the importance of shot selection, including some attention to the three-point line (imaginary or not), and (b) the importance of practicing shots that commonly occur at the pace and speed of an actual game. Shooting drills relating specifically to the New Option Offense are in chapter 10.

Jump Shot, No Basket

Proper shooting techniques should be presented at the first turnout, no matter what the level of play. In most cases, of course, this instruction serves as a review for shooters. Daily shooting drills, involving those of a general nature as well as those of the established offensive system, are conducted only after the initial shooting instruction. Figure 11.36 presents a drill for the opening offensive turnout. Two lines face each other, 10–12 feet apart. All members of one line have balls. They take "jump shots," with the ball being caught by the opposite teammates, and returned by them with "jump shots." This is the basic place for instruction and review on shooting. After listening to the coach's orientation and instructional remarks, and as the drill continues, the players will become knowledgeable enough to be encouraged to point out teammates' flaws in a constructive way (Figure 11.36).

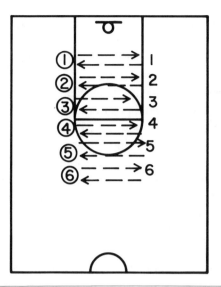

Figure 11.36. Jump shot, no basket.

Teaching Points and Orientation

A coach must be prepared to teach, advise, and observe critically as players develop and maintain shooting skills during practices and games. The following points help in teaching proper fundamentals and also apply when veteran players experience shooting problems and slumps during the season.

1. To start, the ball is held above the head, centered near the right eye (right-hand shooter).
2. The elbow of the shooting arm is *in*, against the right side of the body. Eyes are fixed on the target.
3. The shooter's arm from shoulder to elbow is straight out from the body and parallel to the floor. The forearm is at a right angle to the upper arm. The wrist is cocked at a right angle to the forearm. This correct configuration of upper arm, forearm, and wrist (Figure 11.37) causes the skin of the wrist to wrinkle, and the ball is resting on the fingers. The elbow is under the ball, and the ball

will be released naturally at the top of the jump, with important backspin.

4. Legs are slightly bent, ready to generate power, and the head is *still*, in the center of the stance.
5. The left hand is held lightly on the side of the ball, for control only.
6. With the ball in a cocked position, the shooter's legs and feet provide the impetus for the power push and the launch straight up from the floor. The player imagines that he or she is jumping in a phone booth, straight up. (The phone booth is open at the top.)
7. At the very top of the jump, *pause* just before releasing the ball, and *snap* the wrist forward sharply, giving spin to the ball. The forearm moves *forward* as the ball is released, and the shooter comes down landing on the exact spot of the *launch* (Figure 11.37).

The release of the ball (after the slight pause) is the salient feature of all great shooters. As the wrist snaps, the fingers and hand *flex downward* in a kind of exaggerated "bye-bye" wave. This flex emphasis of hand and fingers (the downward wave of bye-bye) gives additional backward rotation, or backspin. In the practice gym, notice how a successful jump shot by a great shooter comes out of the net and rotates and rolls back toward the point of release.

The elbow *must* be under the ball. This is the second mark of a great shooter. Conversely, the shooter who goes up with the elbow sticking out ("crooked elbow") is a poor shooter.

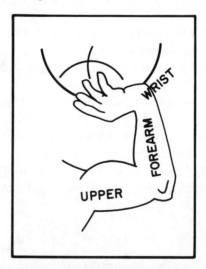

Figure 11.37. U-shaped arm configuration.

Run, Gun, and Run

Any number of basketballs (five here) *placed on the floor* at shooting points around the perimeter, a rebounder (R) at each spot, and one shooter (S) standing under the basket, waiting for the signal to go to the R1 spot for her first shot. How many baskets can she make in a designated time, usually 45 seconds? Use stopwatch. S goes to the ball, picks it up, squares up, and shoots; R1 rebounds and brings the ball back to her spot, as S goes on to shoot at R2, R3, R4, and R5. After the time limit, the rotation is S to R1, R1 to 2, 2 to 3, 3 to 4, 4 to 5, and 5 to S. This is a very competitive drill, and players like to encourage the shooter by clapping hands as she goes to each spot (Figure 11.38).

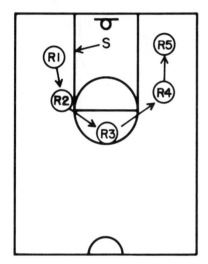

Figure 11.38. Run, gun, and run.

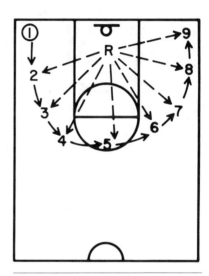

Figure 11.39. Shoot against time.

Shoot Against Time

One ball, one shooter, one rebounder. The shooter starts the drill with a shot from the corner area and moves to the next place on the perimeter, while the ball is rebounded and passed out to him. Work fast. Quick-release jump shooting is emphasized. The rebounder and shooter rotate on the coach's whistle. Keep score, for the sake of competition, as the shooter moves around the shooting perimeter. The coach may want to have a three-point designation at a place or two. Good outlet passes from the rebounder are encouraged (Figure 11.39).

Hand-in-the-Face

Two balls, two rebounders, one shooter. Close-in jumpers. Shooter (S) starts with a jumper; rebounder (R1) passes back out to S after each shot up to the fifth, and also *follows each shot out*, to get a hand in S's face. On the fifth shot, R2 takes over as rebounder and hand-in-the face checker. Keep score, announce score, and rotate on the coach's whistle (Figure 11.40).

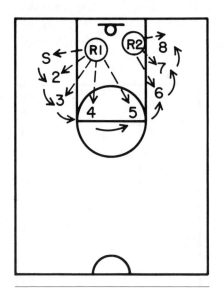

Figure 11.40. Hand-in-the-face.

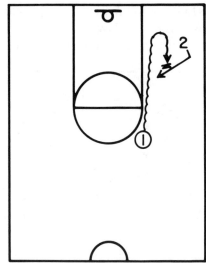

Figure 11.41. Dribble, screen, and jump shot.

Two-Player Dribble, Screen, and Jump Shot

Player 1 dribbles down the side. Player 2 is playing at deep wing. Player 1 turns to her right with the dribble, comes back a dribble or two, stops with firm possession of the ball, and sets in a post position with her back to the basket. Player 2, sensing the screening possibilities, comes over the top, receives the shovel pass from 1, uses the screen, and takes a jump shot. Player 1 rebounds and outlet-passes to new 1. As in most other drills, have waiting lines; 1 and 2 rotate to rear of the lines (Figure 11.41).

High Post Triple-Threat, and Jump Shot

Player 1 slaps the ball as a signal. Player 2 makes a V-cut (jab), head-shoulder fake, flares out to the free throw line, receives the pass, turns, squares up in the triple-threat position, and takes a jump shot. Player 1 rebounds and outlet-passes to the new 1. Players 1 and 2 rotate (Figure 11.42).

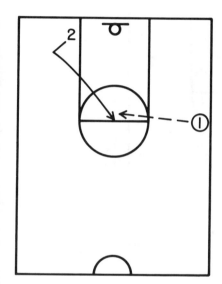

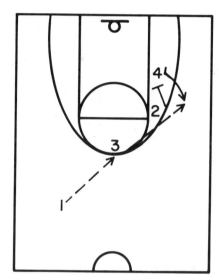

Figure 11.42. High post triple-threat and jump shot.

Figure 11.43. A three-point shot.

A Three-Point Shot *

This is a four-player drill. Player 1 passes to high post 3. Player 2 slides down to set a screen for 4, who moves to the three-point line to receive a pass from 3. Player 4 turns, squares up, and takes the three-point shot. Player 2 rebounds and outlet-passes (baseball pass) to the new 1. Rotation: 1 to 2, 2 to 4, and 4 to 1 (Figure 11.43).

Get a Shot Off the Two-Player Game *

Player 1 dribbles down the side as 5 sets into a low post offensive position. Using chest, bounce, across-the-chest, and overhead passes, 1 gets the ball in to the low post, then maneuvers for an open shot. The two-player game works here as 5 makes 1 maneuver to get open for the jump shot. Player 5 rebounds and outlet-passes to new player 1 in line (Figure 11.44).

Figure 11.44. Two-player game.

Jump-Shooting Game

Jump-shooting competition takes place between two "teams" who have formed shooting perimeters. Basketballs are at 1 and 7. The coach stands at midcourt, and statisticians at each end. Set the clock for six minutes. On signal, players 1 and 7 take their shots, and the sequence of shooting follows at each end, in order from 1 through 6, and 7 through 12. For each successful shot, give two points and assess no penalty if the ball touches the floor after it goes through the net. If the shot is unsuccessful, the ball must be rebounded by the shooter before it touches the floor. If it is not rebounded before, one point is subtracted. In either case, the shooter passes out to next teammate in the perimeter, and the drill continues (Figure 11.45). What is the score after six minutes?

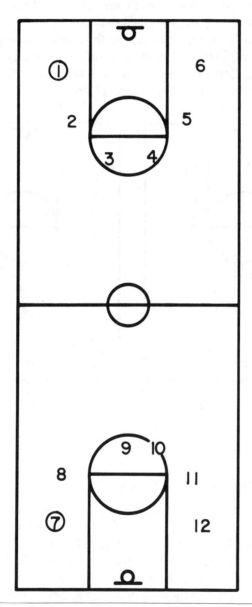

Figure 11.45. Jump-shooting game.

Come Back for a Jumper

The coach, with the ball, stands outside the top of the key and slaps the ball as a signal to start. Player 1 flashes down the side, stops, turns, reverses back, and receives the pass from the coach for a jump shot. Player 5 or 4 rebounds and delivers an outlet pass to the coach, who repeats the procedure for player 2. The drill continues, on both sides, and competition is recommended. Count the made baskets. As in most drills, have a waiting line of players at each site (Figure 11.46).

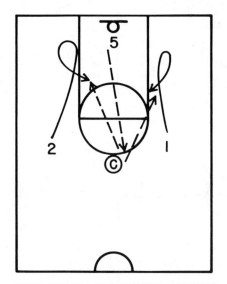

Figure 11.46. Come back for a jumper.

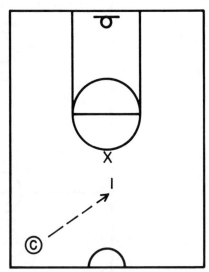

Figure 11.47. Coach passes to player 1.

Jab, Jump Shot

It is necessary to include certain drills that combine shooting with the skills of footwork. Figures 11.47, 11.47A, and 11.47B furnish illustrations of one such exercise. The action begins in Figure 11.47 when the coach passes the ball to player 1, who faces the basket to meet the challenge of defensive X. Giving a head-shoulder fake, 1 swings the ball from side to side, leans forward a bit in strong body balance, and brings the ball back on the right hip for protection, holding it firmly. Hoping now that X is guessing because no dribble has been used, 1 takes a short step to the right oblique with the right foot, as the left foot pivots (shown in Figure 11.47A). This is a jab step. As X steps back in defensive posture, 1's right foot recovers quickly (Figure 11.47B), and in the same "rocking" movement, a quick-release jump shot is taken. For purposes of the drill, X does not play too aggressively and allows the jump shot, although X does put a hand in the shooter's face.

No diagrams are drawn for the left jab step. The footwork is merely reversed: The right foot pivots, a step is taken to the left oblique with the left foot, the recovery is made, and a jump shot is attempted during the jabbing, rocking movement.

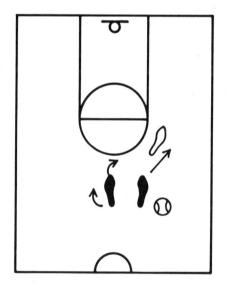

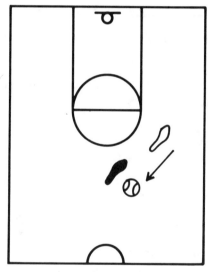

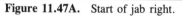

Figure 11.47A. Start of jab right.   **Figure 11.47B.** Recover, jump shot.

Move Without the Ball for a Shot *

Player 3 uses various types of passes in to low post 4, who delivers an over-head, fan pass out to 2 for a jump shot. Player 2 had made a V-cut to get open. Player 4 rebounds out to the 3 line. Players 2 and 3 rotate,

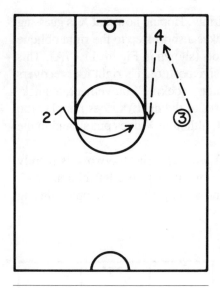

Figure 11.48. Move without the ball.

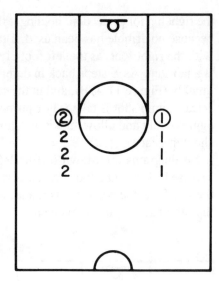

Figure 11.49. Follow the leader.

and 4 stays in place. Game-like situation; excellent three-player game (Figure 11.48).

Two Lines, Follow the Leader

Two lines, two balls. Players in line 1 do the following: (a) dribble in for a right-hand lay-up; (b) rebound, dribble back out, turn, and take a jump shot, (c) rebound, dribble back out, reverse dribble, and drive with hard dribble for a left-hand lay-up and (d) rebound, outlet-pass to the next player in line 1, and go to rear of line 2 (Figure 11.49).

Players in line 2 execute the same drill at the same time as the players in line 1. Their first shots, however, are left-hand lay-ups, and their third shots are right-hand lay-ups. They go to rear of line 1. All players in the lines make the same rotations.

Shoot Along the Baseline*

This drill is designed to improve the art of baseline shooting. The coach passes to 3 at the high post. This signals 2 to cut across the key, using the baseline and getting screens from 4 and 5 along the way. Player 1 passes down to 2 along the baseline, as shown. Player 2 stops, turns, squares up, and takes the shot. Players 5 and/or 4 rebound and outlet-pass (either baseball pass or over-head) to the coach as the drill continues. Players 1 and 2 rotate. Players 3, 4, and 5 stay (Figure 11.50).

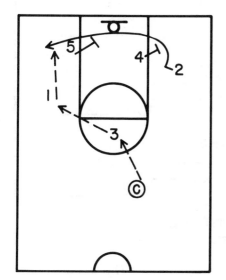

Figure 11.50. Shoot along the baseline.

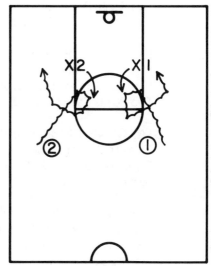

Figure 11.51. Off the glass only.

Off the Glass Only

Player 1 (with a ball) and defender X1 play on one side of the court; 2 (with a ball) and defender X2 play on the other. Players 1 and 2 dribble in on X1 and X2, respectively, and are met just below the free throw line. Forced to reverse-dribble and spin off, 1 dribbles, finally, to her left and takes a jumper off the glass. With the same problem against X2, player 2 makes the same move, goes to her right with a dribble, and also shoots off the glass. Players X1 and X2 play soft defense after forcing the reverse-dribble, but do get a hand in the face. They rebound, outlet-pass to the new 1 and 2 in line, and then go to the end of lines 1 and 2. Shooters 1 and 2 become the new defensive Xs (Figure 11.51).

SCORE CARD

Name: _____

STATION #1: TURN-AROUND JUMPERS
Five, Left Pivot, Jumper   (Made) _____
Five, Right Pivot, Jumper   (Made) _____
Two Points Each (Total 20)   TOTAL _____

STATION #2: DRIBBLE, HOOK SHOT
Five, Right-Hand Hook, Made _____
Five, Left-Hand Hook, Made _____
Two Points Each (Total 20)   TOTAL _____

STATION #3: DRIBBLE, JUMP SHOT
Five, To the Right, Made _____
Five, To the Left, Made _____
Two Points Each (Total 20)   TOTAL _____

STATION #4: SHOOT AGAINST TIME
Two Minutes on the Perimeter
Two Points for Each Made
Made: _____   TOTAL _____

STATION #5: MAKE A TRIPLE AND GO
Two Minutes on the 19'9" Line
Three Points for Each Made
Made: _____   TOTAL _____

STATION #6: SHOOT FREE THROWS
Fifteen Free Throws
One Point for Each Made
Made: _____   TOTAL _____

GRAND TOTAL _____

Figure 11.52. Model score card; Shooting at the County Fair.

Shooting at the County Fair

Furnishing a break in the inevitable monotony of daily practice sessions, a "County Fair" is suggested, one that is popular with players and features competitive shooting. It is made up of six stations, one at each basket in the gym, with managers, coaches and statisticians in charge.

Six stations are described and illustrated below, with equipment, personnel, and procedures. A model score card is included, which will be carried from station to station by each participant (Figure 11.52). The coach will summarize each card, a winner will be announced, and he or she will receive a prize from the coach. An ice-cold can of juice is always appreciated at the end of practice!

Station #1. Turn-Around Jumper

Equipment, Personnel: Scorer-passer (SP) with ball. Player P pops out from under-basket area to receive passes, as shown. He gets 10 turn-around jump shots near the top of the key, five to his left (pivot and turn on the left foot) and five to his right (pivot and turn on the right foot). After each shot, P rebounds and passes the ball back out to the scorer. After 10 shots, player moves to next station, with score recorded on his score card. There are 20 possible points (Figure 11.53).

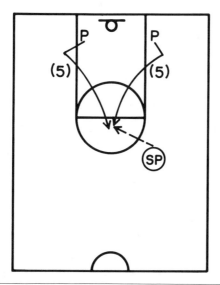

Figure 11.53. Station #1. Turn-around jumper.

Station #2. Dribble, Hook Shot

Equipment, Personnel: Scorer-passer (SP) with ball. Player P meets the pass as indicated, dribbles with her right hand down the right side of the key, makes a spin-off dribble move to her right, changes to a left-hand dribble, and powers into the key for a left-hand hook shot. Five such shots are taken, then the action moves down the left side of the key for five right-hand hooks. In the left-side action, the player dribbles down with the left hand, spins off to her left, changes to a right-hand dribble, and powers into the key for a right-hand hook shot. The player rebounds her shot and passes out to the scorer-passer. After the total of 10 shots, she moves to next station with her score recorded on her score card (Figure 11.54). There are 20 possible points.

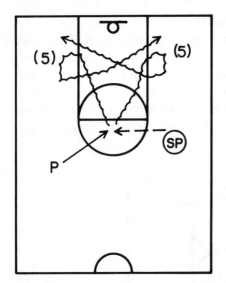

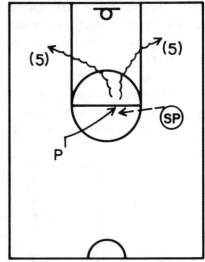

Figure 11.54. Station #2. Dribble, hook shot.

Figure 11.55. Station #3. Dribble, jump shot.

Station #3. Dribble, Jump Shot

Equipment, Personnel: Scorer-passer (SP), with ball. Player P meets pass, as shown, for the dribble and jump shot to the right; then, he repeats the action to the left. Five jump shots are taken on the right, and five on the left. The player must use a right-hand dribble when going to the right and a left-hand dribble for the action to the left, and must square up properly and face the basket with good shooting basics. After the total of 10 shots, he moves to next station with his score recorded (Figure 11.55). There are 20 possible points.

Station #4. Shoot Against Time

Equipment, Personnel: One scorer-rebounder (SR), one ball, and one timekeeper (TK) with a stop watch. *Inside* the three-point line, player P takes her first two-point jump shot; successful or not, she moves to the next shooting site (there are eight, symbolized by dots in Figure 11.56) to receive the rebounder's pass. She continues around the horn and back, receiving passes and taking jump shots at each designated site, until time (say, two minutes) runs out. The timekeeper designates start and finish. Two points for each successful shot; score is recorded, and the player moves on to the next station.

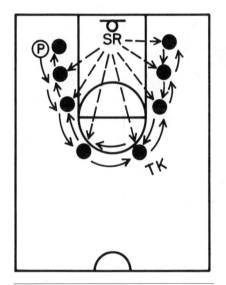

Figure 11.56. Station #4. Shoot against time.

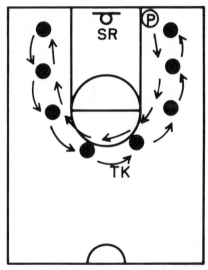

Figure 11.57. Station #5. Hit a triple and go.

Station #5. Hit a Triple and Go

Equipment, Personnel: Scorer-rebounder (SR), one ball, and timekeeper (TK), with stop watch. *Along* the three-point line, player P shoots from each of the eight designated sites. Given two minutes, he moves around the perimeter receiving passes from the scorer-rebounder at each place. Three points for each successful shot; two minutes of play. Score is recorded, and the player moves to the next station (Figure 11.57).

Station #6. Shoot for a Bonus

Equipment, Personnel: Scorer-rebounder (SR), and one ball. This station requires 15 free throws, with possible additional bonus attempts. Game conditions are simulated. One point for each successful free throw. Any player who makes 12 of the 15 attempts gets a bonus of 3 additional attempts. Total possible score: 18 points. Score is recorded and player moves to another station, if he or she has not completed the tour (Figure 11.58).

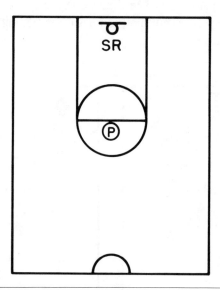

Figure 11.58. Station #6. 15 free throws.

Free Throws, "Four Up"

This is a competitive free-throw shooting drill. The players will feel the pressure of competition and respond with their best efforts. Six players (or half the team) line up at each of the two free throw lines, as shown. Coach stands at midcourt and calls out the score during the drill. *Procedure*: Players of each team shoot alternately. Player #1 for Team A shoots a free throw and moves to the rear of his or her line. If the shot was successful, the coach calls out, "One Up," and holds up one finger. Player #1 (Team B) shoots the answering free throw and moves to the end of that line. If unsuccessful, the coach stands with the one finger extended; if successful, he or she calls out, "Even up," and makes a fist, indicating an even score. Player #2 of Team A steps up for a try. If #2 misses, there is no change, and the fist remains in the air. Player #2 of Team B tries, and is successful. The coach points to Team B and calls out, "One up," extending a finger in the air. Shooting and scoring continue in this manner until one team or the other reaches "four up." Managers (M) act as ball retrievers during the drill and pass the ball out to shooters (Figure 11.59).

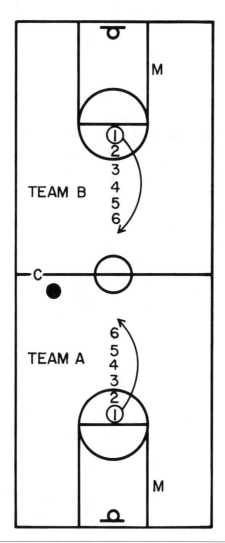

Figure 11.59. Free throws, four-up.

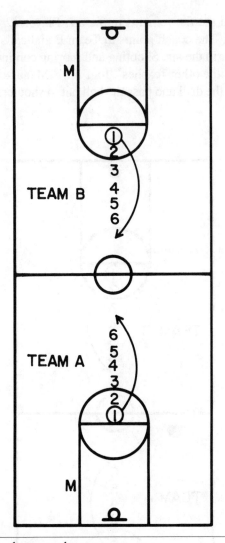

Figure 11.60. Free throws, under pressure.

Free Throws Under Pressure

The drill in Figure 11.60 enhances free-throw shooting proficiency, with a built-in pressure factor. The competitive objective is for one team to finish before the other, with the six players on each team setting up properly, preparing, and shooting free throws alternately. In line, the shooters may not move forward for the attempt until the player in front has made a successful shot. An unsuccessful shooter, receiving the rebound of the attempt from the manager, must stand at the line with the ball under his or her arm, for a five-second count, before trying again. The delay gives the opposing team, at the other end, a time advantage in the alternating process. Each sequence ("game"), with a winning team, will transpire rather quickly, and the coach should be prepared for that by keeping the drill moving, announcing the winner, and announcing the cumulative number of wins after each sequence.

Dribbling and Footwork

Dribbling is vital to the success of the New Option Offense, although the rule persists: "If you have a choice, pass the basketball instead of dribbling."

There is much more to dribbling than just bouncing the ball up and down on the floor. Like so many other skills, it is a *learned* skill, the proficiency of which is gained through proper instructional help and hard work on the practice floor.

The main objectives of the dribbler, in line with the role he or she plays in the offensive system, are as follows:

- To escape or evade defensive double-team
- To help retain the ball in "run out the clock" situations
- To aid in defeating the designs of a full-court press
- To penetrate the defense *inside*, and pass off to an open teammate
- To dribble-drive from the wing, the top of the key, or along the baseline, for a lay-up or jump shot
- To dribble in an improvised way, *if the path leads to the basket*
- To move the ball from one place on the floor to a better offensive place, if a pass is not possible or feasible
- To play one's part in the pick-roll offensive technique
- To be a part, if not the most important one, of the fast break, or Early Offense

The following presentation of dribbling tasks includes comments and notes with a number of the drills. Note that dribbling, and the enhancement of the skills involved, is often combined with other basketball abilities, such as shooting and footwork, in the composition of the drills. The inclusion of *footwork*, with teaching notes and reminders, is important because, without proper, basic footwork skill, there is no valid opportunity for a dribble-drive from the wing or top of the key. Too often, offensive players try to illegally power-charge their way or commit traveling violations as they shift their feet improperly. Modern officials seem only too eager to call footwork violations related to a dribble.

Catch Up and Go

Three balls and three lines are necessary for the drill. The players at the front of the lines each toss a ball high, with back spin, out to the free throw line. They catch up to the ball while it is bouncing, dribble on, full-court, for a lay-up. After the lay-up, they rebound, dribble back, pass to the next player in line, and go to the rear of the line. Among the skills enhanced by this drill are (a) going for the ball aggressively; (b) securing the ball; (c) dribble-driving, with head up; (d) making a lay-up; and (e) getting the ball out of the net quickly. This is a fast-moving drill, and it can become competitive, if the coach desires (Figure 11.61).

Basic Dribbling and Conditioning

Two dribblers at a time, as shown. Change hands during dribble route. Practice reverse, spin-off dribble and behind-the-back techniques as well as regular dribble. Make lay-up at the other end, return, pass to new person in line, and go to rear of line. Conditioning aspects are obvious. *Teaching notes.* Use finger tips to dribble. Do not use the palms. A skilled basketball player doesn't like "dirty palms." The forearm is parallel to the floor; don't slap at the ball. Wrist action controls the dribble. The weight of the body is forward, with the body in perfect balance. The dribble should be low in this drill, with the highest dribble not much above the knees. HEAD UP. A dribble is a *push down* of the ball, not a slap (Figure 11.62).

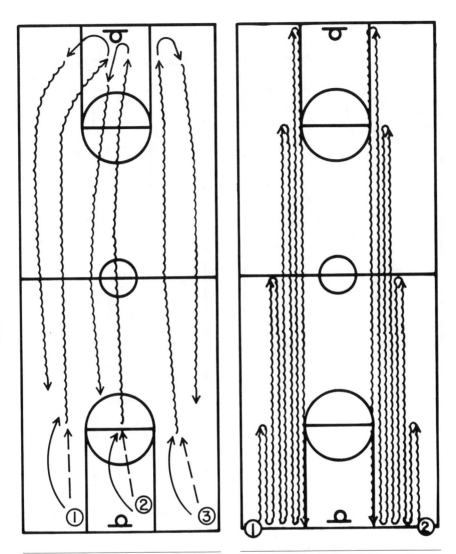

Figure 11.61. Catch up and go.

Figure 11.62. Basic dribbling and conditioning.

Call the Number

With his back to the basket, and facing the dribbler, the coach (C) holds up finger(s) at various times during the drill. The dribbler (D), calls out the number of fingers being raised during her dribbling route. Vary the drill by putting a defensive player on the dribbler, at least part of the way. This drill teaches the dribbler to keep her head up (Figure 11.63).

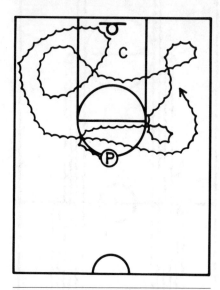

Figure 11.63. Call the number.

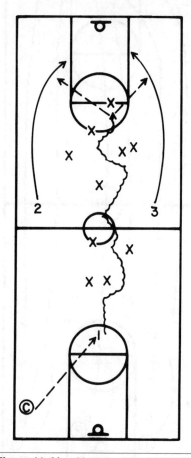

Figure 11.64. Obstacles in a fast break.

Dribbling in Traffic

This is a full-court drill. Stationary teammates act as "obstacles." The dribbler, 1, receives a pass from the coach and negotiates through and around the obstacles at a fast break pace. Players 2 and 3 fill the wings just beyond the center line, and the dribbler culminates the drill with a pass to either one for a fast-break lay-up. Obstacles may reach, extend their arms, and flick at the ball, but must remain stationary. The coach designates the rotation procedure (Figure 11.64).

Shut Off the Driver

This is a combined defense-offense drill. On signal, player 1 flashes out with dribble-drive. At a disadvantageous floor position, X moves quickly to shut him off. Don't foul! Player X has done a good job if he makes player 1 reverse-dribble. Action continues until there is a made field goal, made free throw, or turnover; then rotate (Figure 11.65).

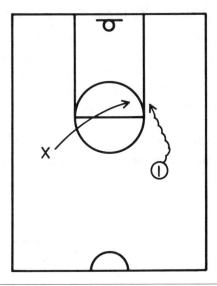

Figure 11.65. Shutting off the driver.

Power Invasion in the Key

The penetrate-and-pass-off maneuver down the key area from the top of the key continues as an important weapon at all levels. The first act is to deceive the defensive player and make him *commit* himself *before* putting the ball on the floor. Too many players try to force themselves on the defensive player instead of using the initial finesse. One remembers Gail Goodrich, particularly, who was the playmaker for John Wooden's UCLA teams of some years ago and later for NBA professional teams. Bending over low, protecting the ball, in good body balance, swinging the ball from side to side, and faking with eyes and upper body, Goodrich enticed his opponent into an overeager, committed mistake. The key to success was to get the opponent moving, leaning, and off-balance; then, using the footwork of *jab step*, *rocker step*, or *cross-over*, Goodrich put the ball on the floor with a driving dribble and headed for the basket. To reemphasize, the sequence is fakery, finesse, footwork; then power dribble, shoot, and/or pass off.

Penetrate, Pass, Perimeter Points

Player 1 dribbles hard into the middle of the key, stops and turns in the air to dump a pass to 3, who has followed along down the side. Player 3 takes a jump shot from any one of the four designated spots, as drawn. Player 1 rebounds, and outlet-passes to new 1, who repeats the action for 2's jump shot on the other side. Rotation: 1 to 2, 2 to 3, and 3 to 1 (Figure 11.66).

Figure 11.66 illustrates an infiltration pass-off drill. A discussion of the jab step can be found in the Shooting section.

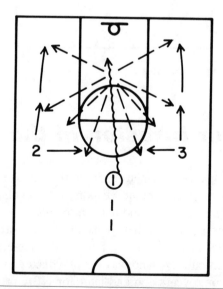

Figure 11.66. Penetrate, pass off, perimeter points.

The Rocker Step

The rocker step is brought into play when the player is probing for a defensive weakness, in which case he will drive to the basket with a dribble, or, with his defensive opponent "rocking" and leaning the wrong way, take a quick-release jump shot. In either case, his maneuver begins with a jab, in this example to the right (Figure 11.67). As his opponent steps back in a defensive reaction, the player recovers (step 2 in Figure 11.67A), and then takes a further step backward (step 3 in Figure 11.67A). Step 4 in Figure 11.67B shows recovery to the original position. The left foot remains in place as the pivot foot. With head-shoulder fakery and the ball on the right hip, the player hopes for a surprise jump shot, or he may execute a left cross-over step (see Figure 11.70B) for a dribble-drive to the basket.

A drill (not drawn in a diagram) for this sequence would have the coach passing a ball to the offensive players at both wings and the top of the key, with ensuing rocker-step practice against a teammate playing soft defense.

Figure 11.67. Jab right.

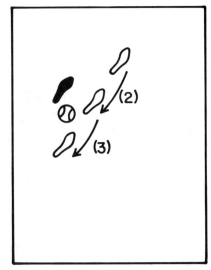

Figure 11.67A. Recover, rock back a step.

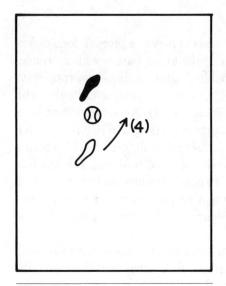

Figure 11.67B. Recover.

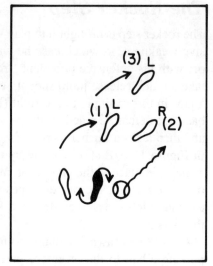

Figure 11.68. Cross-over right.

Cross-Over Right

A new sequence is illustrated in Figure 11.68 for the cross-over move. The player again hopes to go to her right with the ball. She executes a head-shoulder fake, swings the ball to get the opponent moving, pivots on the ball of her right foot, and simultaneously steps across her body with the left leg and foot (step 1 in Figure 11.68). The right-hand dribble starts, the right foot steps up past the left (step 2 in Figure 11.68), the left foot steps up past the right (step 3 in Figure 11.68), and the dribble-drive is in full gear for a lay-up. The swing of the left foot and leg across the body, as it turns, protects the dribble.

Zig-Zag

This is a combination drill of dribbling and individual player-player pressure defense. One X against dribbler 1; one X against dribbler 2, full-court. *Defense*: Xs defend with hands clasped behind back, in a boxer stance, executing a slide step all the way and applying constant pressure with the body. This develops proper stance and slide-step movement, as X tries to stop the forward dribble and force the dribbler to turn and reverse-dribble. *Dribbler*: Keep your head up, protect the ball and dribble with your body, change hands as necessary, use behind-the-back dribble, do not try to force the forward dribble, and reverse-dribble only if you have no other alternative. Defensive Xs and dribblers exchange duties for return full-court trip (Figure 11.69).

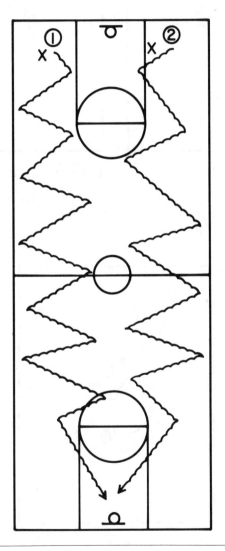

Figure 11.69. Zigzag.

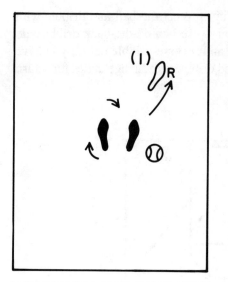

Figure 11.70. The jab.

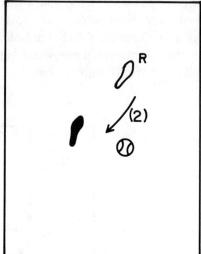

Figure 11.70A. Recover.

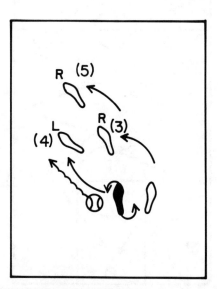

Figure 11.70B. Cross-over left after jab right.

Jab and Cross-Over Combined

Figures 11.70, 11.70A, and 11.70B illustrate a player starting to his right with a jab, being shut off, recovering, and changing to a cross-over step, which takes him to his left for a dribble-drive. In Figure 11.70, he jabs to his right; in 11.70A, the defense stops his move, so he recovers; Figure 11.70B shows the *cross-over left* after the recovery, and dribble continuity. Notice that the left foot remains the pivot foot in all diagrams, so there is no illegality when the jab becomes a cross-over. This is an excellent combination of basic moves. In Figure 11.70B, the left foot pivots to the left, the right leg and foot swing across the body (step 3), the dribble begins with the left hand, the left foot is planted (step 4), followed by the right foot (step 5), and the dribbler heads for the basket, protected by the body all the way.

A drill (not drawn) for teaching and reviewing the combined jab and cross-over would have the coach passing the ball to a player standing at the top of the key and facing the basket, with an X player in defensive stance challenging him and playing soft defense as he jabs, crosses over, and dribble-drives for the basket. This drill would even be more applicable if started from a wing position, because the dribble-drive from there has always been the trademark of the great power forwards in basketball. Modern players who exemplify this exciting power move are Terry Cummings and Mark Aguirre, NBA professional players. The past master of some years ago, Elgin Baylor, executed the same driving move, with more finesse than power.

The same drill should be run on the other side of the floor (at the wing). Footwork is merely reversed; the same techniques are involved.

Hearing Footsteps

This drill combines dribble, lay-up, defensive pressure from behind the dribble, denial of inbounds pass, and two-against-one full-court.

Player 1 dribbles full-court for a lay-up. Player 2 allows 1 to have a lead at first, then tries to catch her. Player 3 races downcourt behind both 1 and 2. After 1's lay-up, 2 takes the ball out of the net, steps out of bounds, and tries to pass in to 1, who has moved, as shown, after her lay-up; player 3 tries to deny the inbounds pass to 1. When the ball is inbounded to 1, she and 2 return offensively, full-court, against the defense

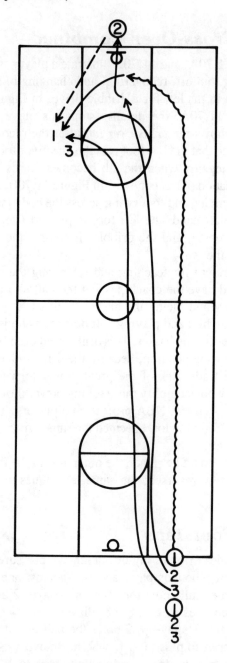

Figure 11.71. Hearing footsteps.

of player 3. Three new players (new 1, 2, and 3, player 1 with second ball) start as 1, 2, and 3 return (Figure 11.71).

Weak-Hand Basketball, No Figure

Three players on offense against three on defense. Half-court. If right-handed, a player must use only his left hand for dribbling. If left-handed, he must use his right hand for dribbling. Offensive and defensive players exchange roles after five minutes. Keep score. Only offense can get points. Scoring: +2 for a made field goal; +1 when defense makes a foul (don't shoot free throws); -1 if defense gets a rebound (defense gives the ball back); and -1 if offense makes a turnover (offense keeps the ball).

High and Low Post Skills

The following material, illustrated in Figures 11.72 through 11.83A, carries on with the development of high post and low post players' skills. Proficiency at these positions is of singular importance to the operation of the New Option Offense, as demonstrated by the scope of drills for those positions in chapters 2, 3, and 4. While each drill in those chapters is specifically related to the New Option Offense and demonstrates how the learned skills fit into the offensive plan, the high post and low post work here in chapter 11 is more general in nature. The blending of *specifics* and *generalities* in the total program will produce a more versatile and well-rounded offensive player, one who is capable of free-lancing from post positions when an opening occurs as well as being skillfull and disciplined when the offense team patterns are in progress.

Some of the drills combine defensive and offensive work, affording opportunity for the coaching staff to give time-saving attention to both aspects of instruction.

Hit the Post Five Times

This drill involves three-against-three, half-court. One trio is on offense for a designated time, then players exchange duties. Each trio should have a playmaker, one wing player, and one 4 or 5 player. The offense may not attempt a field goal until it has passed in to the post player at least five times. Passes may be either to low post locations or to high post. Clock rules (24, 30, or 45) apply. Scoring: +2 for a made field goal, and +2 if the defense commits a foul (do not shoot free throws). If the offense fouls or makes a turnover, the violator drops out and runs to the sideline for a five-second count, creating a two-against-three situation while out. If the defense rebounds a shot, the ball is passed back out to the offense, and play continues. Keep *offense* score for each team (Figure 11.72).

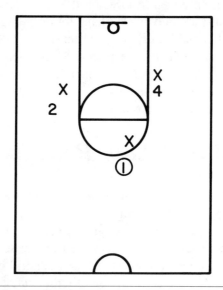

Figure 11.72. Hit the post five times.

Low Post Power *

The coach passes in to 5, on the move in both diagrams. In Figure 11.73, player 5 flashes across the key to receive the pass and executes one of the four basic low post moves: (a) *Muscle shot and jump fake* (a head-shoulder fake, footwork, one power dribble, muscle in, pump fake one to three times, and put it up), (b) *Pivot and jump shot* (pivot on foot nearest the baseline, head-shoulder fake, go up, and shoot off the glass from an angle), (c) *Drop step, pivot and hook shot* (pivot on foot nearest the baseline, toward either the key or the baseline, then take a long, driving step into either the key or the baseline approach, and take a hook shot, using the glass if at an angle), or (d) *Step through and lay it up* (pivot to the baseline, pump fake, step through, dip the shoulder as necessary, and take a close-in hook shot or lay-up). *Note*: Always look baseline upon receiving a pass at low post. This must be a habit (reading the baseline). Same procedure in Figure 11.73A, other side. Player should execute all four moves at each side. Coach may vary by adding a defensive player against 5.

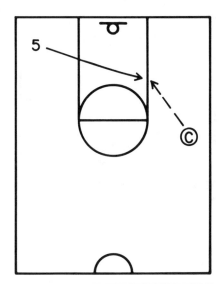

Figure 11.73. Pass to 5.

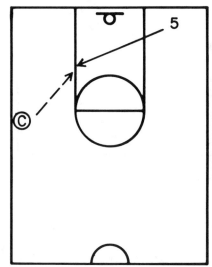

Figure 11.73A. Pass to 5 from other side.

Three-Player Low Post Drill *

Point, wing and low post engage in a three-player game in the triangle. Player 1 passes to 2, 2 to 5, and 5 back out to 1; after this pass (C), 5 maneuvers for position, simulates a hip trap on a simulated defensive man, and drops in to the low key area to receive pass D from 1. *Note*: No rotations. Practice all kinds of passes. Check chapter 3, Figure 3.22, "Fronting the low post." Player 5 rebounds on his own shot, passes back out to 1 as the drill continues (Figure 11.74).

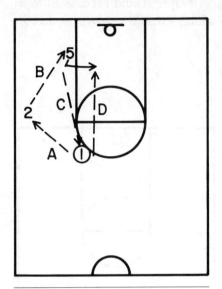

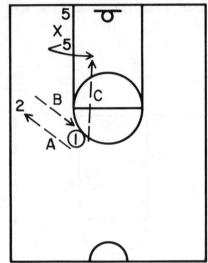

Figure 11.74. Three-player low post drill.

Figure 11.75. Three-player low post drill #2.

Three-Player Low Post Drill #2 *

Passes A, B, and C find player 5 maneuvering against X5 for an inside shot in the paint. Player 2 must look inside and fake a pass or two to 5 before making the pass. Player 5 may hip-trap defensive X (chapter 3, Figure 3.22) or give a head-shoulder fake, followed by a quick reversal into the paint for reception of a pass at a "sweet spot." *Note*: No rotations. Player 5 rebounds his own shot (or X5 may do the rebounding) and passes out to 1 as the drill continues. After a time, the coach may want to have X5 and 5 exchange duties (Figure 11.75).

Dribble and High Post Pick-Roll *

This drill exemplifies free-lance play and how informal communication between two players can lead to success. Player 1 starts to dribble down the side of the key, signals to 3 for a screen, continues to dribble over the screen for a high-percentage jump shot, or passes to 3 on her roll to the basket. *Note*: Coach may vary by having 3 set only a flash-and-go screen (Figure 11.76).

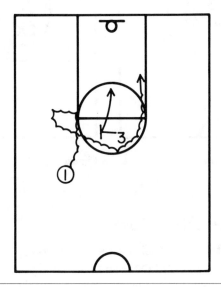

Figure 11.76. Dribble, high post pick-roll.

Beating the High Post Sag *

Three players are involved on offense, two on defense. The sagging shut-off of highpost play by X2 and X3 is shown in Figure 11.77. Player 1 has the ball, X2 sags away from 2, fronting 3 as much as possible, and X3 overplays 3 on the ball side. In Figure 11.77A, players 1, 2, and 3 react to the sag. Player 1 fakes a pass to 3 and dribbles to the inside of 2, as 3 sets a screen on X2. Player 1 suspends his dribble, spins, and hands off to 2 as he comes over 3's screen. Player 2 goes on with a dribble-drive or jump shot. Player 3 rolls for the basket, and 1 tries to get open on the other side. *Note*: Rotate players.

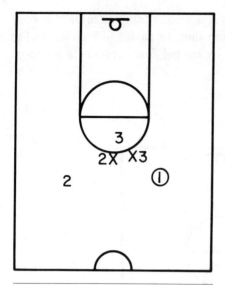

Figure 11.77. Sagging at the high post.

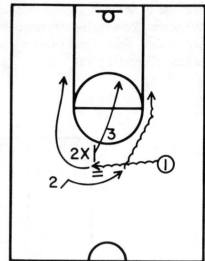

Figure 11.77A. Reacting to the sag.

One-on-One Plus Post

Players 1 and 2 stand with their backs to 3, who has the ball at the high post. She rolls the ball toward the center circle and yells, "Go!". Players 1 and 2 sprint for possession of the rolling ball, and the retriever goes one-on-one against the other, in the half-court area. Player 3 becomes the high post or low post player, depending on the location of the ball at various times. The player with the ball may pass to the post or use her as a screen, but 3 may not shoot, dribble, or rebound. Start over after each made field goal. On unsuccessful field goal attempts, rebounding determines possession. If the player with the ball is fouled, she gets an automatic point, keeps possession, and starts over on offense; if she commits a turnover, she gives up the ball. Two points are awarded for a made field goal. Keep score (Figure 11.78).

Spin and Receive at the Low Post *

Player 4, with her back to teammate 1, faces X. Player 1 has the ball at the wing. Suddenly, 4 steps toward defensive X, then spins around to receive the pass from 1. Player 4 makes any low post move to get a shot in a sweet spot around the low post block, while X plays tough defense.

Note: Players 4 and X rotate. Player 1 uses all types of passes and makes passes to 4's target hand, which must always be displayed (Figure 11.79).

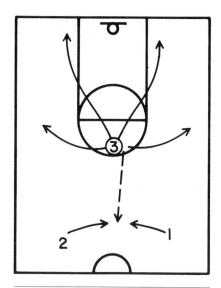

Figure 11.78. One-on-one plus post.

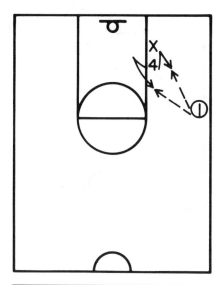

Figure 11.79. Spin and receive the pass at the low post.

Pass to the Posts: *"Jack Pot"*

Half-court three-versus-three is involved in this drill. Figures 11.80, 11.80A, and 11.80B are only examples of passing to the post and splitting the post. In the drills, these procedures may occur at any place on the half court. Three players are on offense for a designated period, and then they change over to defense. Keep score. Which three get the most points on offense? During the course of the play, the offense gets a point every time the ball goes to a post player, followed by a properly-executed split-the-post. Coach yells "jack pot" to the scorekeeper, who records the point. Other scoring rules: made field goal, +2 (ball goes back to the offense); turnover, -1 (ball back to the offense); offensive foul, -1; defensive foul, +1 to the offense (ball back to the offense, no free throws taken, in all cases of foul); and offensive rebound, +1. If the defense rebounds, give ball back to the offense. *Note*: When splitting the post, passer goes first.

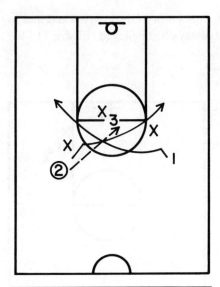

Figure 11.80. Example of jack pot, high post.

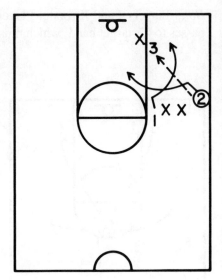

Figure 11.80A. Example of jack pot, low post.

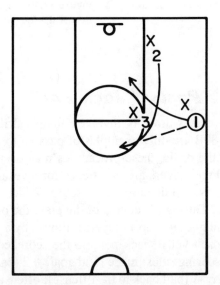

Figure 11.80B. Example of post play, jack pot.

Low Post Reaction to Defensive Positioning

Figures 11.81 through 11.81B are pertinent to the basics of low post play. In Figure 11.81, player 1 slaps the ball to start the drill. With X on his left hip and slightly overplaying, 4 calls out "behind left," projects his *right target hand* (in this case), and receives the pass from 1. After receiving it, he passes the ball back out to 1, for the purposes of the drill. No shot. *Note*: In a game situation 4 is not expected, certainly, to call out "behind left," but this, and the other drills, teach him to be *aware* of the location of his defender, automatically. Player 1's pass to 4 must be properly executed and fundamentally sound (across-the-chest bounce pass, look-away lob, overhead pass, etc., always to the target hand).

The reaction drills continue in Figure 11.81A as 4 calls out "behind right." Player 1 delivers the pass to 4's target hand, and 4 passes back out. In Figure 11.81B, X has taken position directly behind 4, so 4 calls out "behind," receives the direct pass, and then returns the ball to 1 as the drills continue.

Four players participate in the drill for Figure 11.82: players 1, 4, 5, and defensive X. Player 4 is being fronted and is shut off from teammate

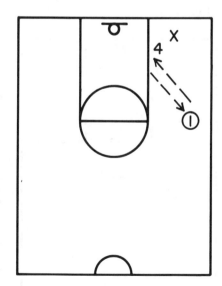

Figure 11.81. "Behind left."

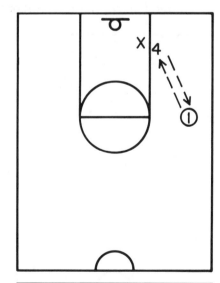

Figure 11.81A. "Behind right."

1's pass. Player 4 calls "front!" (in a *game* situation, he always calls "front!"), and 5 flashes out to the elbow, giving 1 at least two options: a lob to 4 or a high post pass to 5. For drill continuity, the ball is passed back to 1. No shot is taken.

Comment

The following teaching reminders apply to Figures 11.81 through 11.82:

- At the low post, be aware of the defensive player's location.
- When ready to receive the pass, be sure your body is in balance and low, with knees flexed.
- Always give the passer a *target hand*, depending on the location of the defensive player.
- Meet the pass by reaching out, or in some cases by making a *jump step* to meet it.
- Read the floor when you receive the pass. What can you do individually? Is there an open teammate? Did you check the baseline as you received the ball?
- If you are being *fronted*, you must call out "front!".
- The *pump fake* is an important part of a low post player's arsenal, especially when going in for the muscle shot. Sometimes two or three consecutive pump fakes are more effective than one, and the *step-through* move can be incorporated with the pump fake.

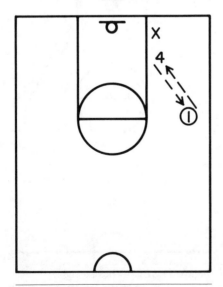

Figure 11.81B. "Behind."

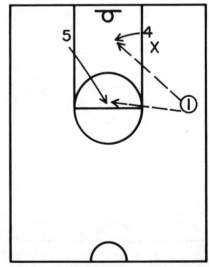

Figure 11.82. "Front."

Hook-Shot Drill

Figures 11.83 and 11.83A depict a rebound-and-hook-shot drill that develops the offensive skills of the low post player, who is the lone participant, with a basketball. Figure 11.83 shows the left-hand hook shot, and Figure 11.83A requires a right-hand shot. The drills are non-stop, left to right, or vice versa. Standing close-in, just outside the foul lane with the ball, and facing the basket, the player tosses the ball across the basket, on the glass, runs across the key, and rebounds it on the opposite side. When he rebounds, facing the basket, he pivots, turns, launches himself with a twisting move in the air, and makes a sweeping hook shot, using the glass if his pivoting position places him at an angle with the basket. In Figure 11.83, he attempts a left-hand shot; in 11.83A, a right-hand shot. After each shot, the player retrieves the ball and goes to the other side, continuing the right-hand, left-hand sequence.

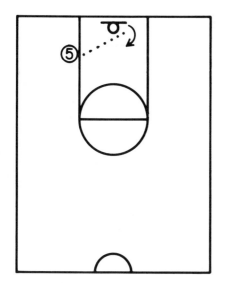 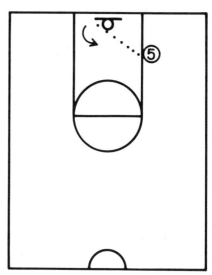

Figure 11.83. Rebound, left-hand hook.   **Figure 11.83A.** Rebound, right-hand hook.

Fundamental Screen Drills:
The Down Screen

Sometimes the *down screen* is called the *jam down*. Participants: coach with ball; players 1, 2, X1, and X2. Coach slaps the ball to signal start.

Player 1 pivots around, facing 2 and X2, and moves to plant a screen-barrier on X2. Player 2 feints for the basket, comes over the screen, emerges to receive the pass from the coach, and takes a jump shot. For purposes of the drill, player 1 rebounds and passes back out as the drill continues. Xs, 1, and 2 rotate. *Note*: The player (2) receiving the screen must remain in place until 1 sets the screen on X2. Jab-feints are important. On defense, communication between Xs is all-important, with the X *behind* the action calling out the action and reaction (Figure 11.84).

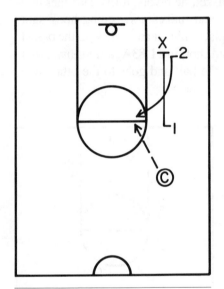

Figure 11.84. Down screen.

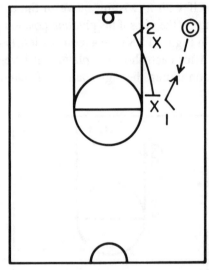

Figure 11.85. Up screen.

The Up Screen

Participants: Two Xs, 1, and 2; coach with the ball. From the corner area, the coach slaps ball to start the drill. Player 2 feints for the basket, then moves to set the screen on X1. Player 1 swings over the screen to receive the pass and takes a jump shot. Player 2 rebounds and passes out to the coach as the drill continues (Figure 11.85). *Note*: Same as those for Figure 11.84.

Lateral Screen at the High Post

Participants: Two Xs, 1, and 2; coach with the ball. From the deep wing area, the coach passes to 2 after the signal for the drill to start. Player

1 had jabbed for the basket, then screened on X2, and 2 moved over the screen for a pass. Player 2 may dribble in for a lay-up or take a close-in jump shot (Figure 11.85). *Note*: Same as for Figure 11.84. On defense, is the coach emphasizing *defensive switching, fighting through screens, or both*?

Lateral Screen, Opposite Side

This is identical to the drill illustrated in Figure 11.86, except that it is conducted on the other side of the floor (Figure 11.87).

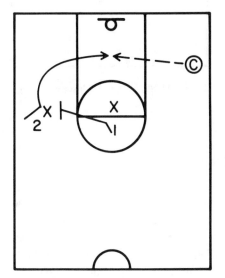

Figure 11.86. Lateral screen at the high post.

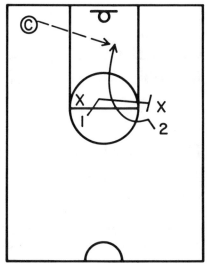

Figure 11.87. Lateral screen other side.

Lateral Screen at the Low Post

Participants: Two Xs, 1, 2, and the coach with the ball. After the signal to start, player 1 crosses the key down low to set a screen on X2. Player 2 jabs for the basket, then crosses over the screen to receive the pass, delivered by the coach from the wing area. *Note*: The moves in this drill are very pertinent to the double-low-post action in the Red and White series Rotary. On defense, Xs are expected to work very hard and aggressively in this drill, with lots of talk and communication. The action is in a very critical area, down low in the key (Figure 11.88).

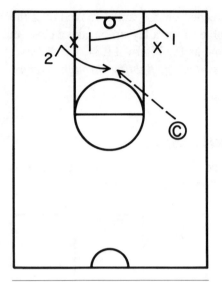

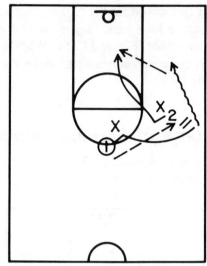

Figure 11.88. Low post lateral screen.   **Figure 11.89.** Hand-back screen-and-go.

Hand-Back, Screen, and Go

Participants: Two Xs, 1, and 2. From the point, player 1 passes to the wing, 2. Player 1 jabs, follows the pass, receives a hand-off pass, and rubs off his defensive opponent, X1, on 2's back. After his hand-back and screen, 2 rolls for the basket as 1 dribbles. Player 1 passes to 2 for a dribble-drive or jump shot (Figure 11.89). *Note*: On defense, coach may have X2 stepping back, X1 sliding through, and both switching to negate the screening effect. On offense, the pick-roll (or an option) will be successful, nonetheless, if executed properly.

Lob-Pass Drill

Participants: 1, 3, 4, 5; two Xs, guarding 4 and 5. After this drill is practiced and perfected, the action can be applied to a defensive fronting situation and added to the list of special plays. A similar example is in chapter 3, Figure 3.22.

Player 1 passes to wing 3. Player X4 fronts 4, shutting off the passing lane; 4 yells "Front!", signaling 5 to flash out toward the elbow. With the underbasket area uncovered, 4 steps under to receive a lob pass from 3. If X5 doesn't come out with 5, the pass goes to 5 for her jump shot or other action. *Note*: Players 4, 5, and Xs rotate duties. Include rebounding, both defensive and offensive, in the drill. This action is effective against both zone and player-player defenses (Figure 11.90).

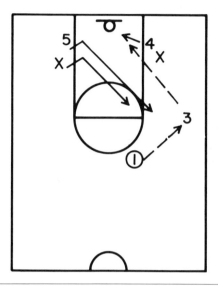

Figure 11.90. Lob-pass drill.

Developing and Maintaining Important Statistics

Developing and keeping pertinent statistics, in both practice sessions and games, is important to successful basketball competition at all levels. Five proven statistical models are presented in this chapter: two for practice sessions (Figures 12.2 and 12.3) and three for games (Figures 12.4, 12.5, 12.6). Figure 12.1 is a model of a Daily Practice Worksheet prepared by the coach in advance of practice sessions.

While different coaches at different levels may have diverse opinions on the relative worth of certain statistics, most do need and want information, in one form or another, about the proficiency of players and team.

The major objectives of the three game-models in this chapter are two-fold. First, in deference to old-fashioned ways, they furnish a format for

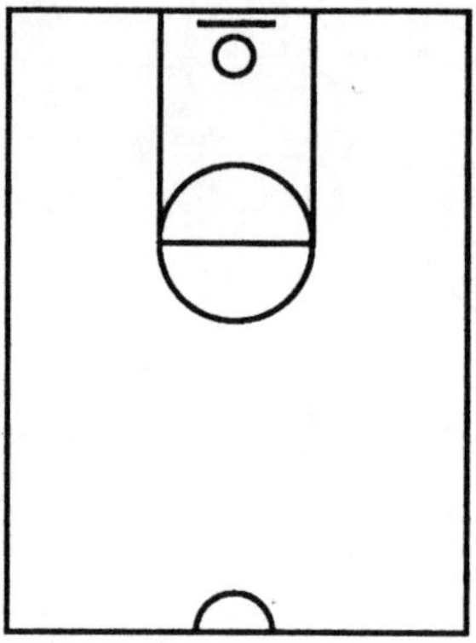

Time:

(In Charge)

Notes:

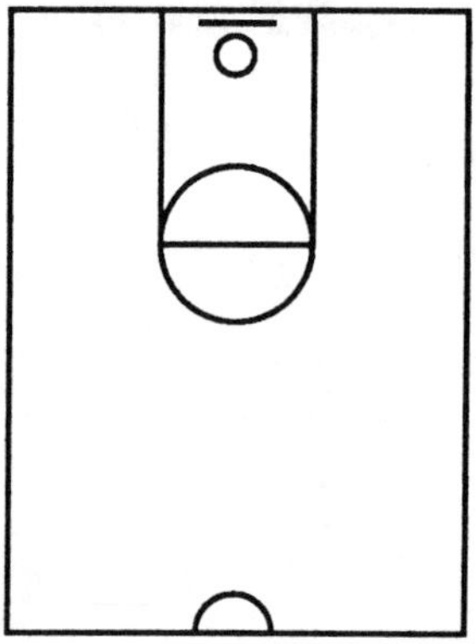

Time:

(In Charge)

Notes:

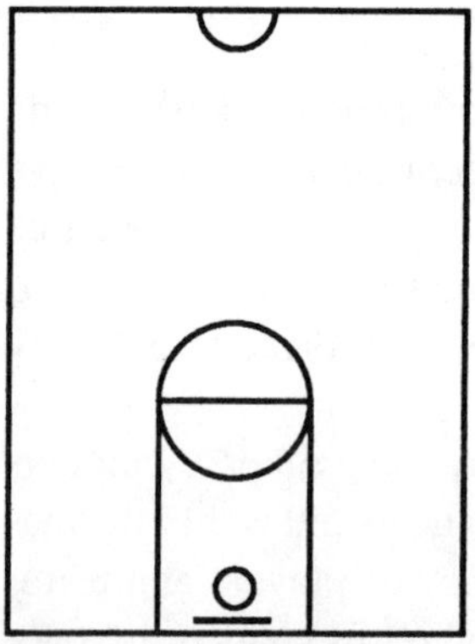

Time:

(In Charge)

Notes:

Figure 12.1. Daily practice worksheet.

recording on-the-spot information that, without further treatment, can be reviewed and then, as desired, transferred to cumulative worksheets for seasonal records. Secondly, the information on the worksheets may be utilized as indirect input for microcomputer or other computational machinery to analyze after a game is over. Of course, if the computer equipment is portable, if an operator is always available, and if it can be operated both at home and away, some of the input may very well be applied directly to the keyboard during a game; in this case, the statistical information contained on Figures 12.4, 12.5, and 12.6 need not be maintained on the worksheet forms.

Managers, assistant managers, assistant coaches, team statisticians, and volunteers are available for the maintenance of the five worksheets. Many schools have either microcomputers or adaptable computer facilities for the more complex aspects of evaluation and analysis. It is probably safe to say that machine computerization, valuable and important as it is, will never completely replace the old-fashioned, human, pencil-and-paper effort. Keeping good statistics requires both.

Daily Practice Worksheet

Practice sessions go more smoothly and efficiently when they are carefully planned in advance. The Daily Practice Worksheet consists of one full-court diagram and two half-court diagrams on one sheet, with space for notes and comments. It is a valuable form for the busy coach. Drills are planned, drawn, and entered on this sheet, which fits a clipboard for easy reference (Figure 12.1).

Since the coach and his or her assistant sometimes conduct drills simultaneously at each end of the court (half of the team at one end, half at the other end), the two half-court diagrams are placed on the worksheet with this aspect in mind.

Practice Free Throw Record

This record assumes that practice time is available for every player to shoot 25 successful free throws, usually at the end of practice. Whether or not the scope ("make 25") is applicable as a daily practice depends on the coach's planning decision. Using six baskets in the gym, the team can finish this exercise in fifteen to twenty minutes. Two players operate at each of the six baskets, rotating as shooter and rebounder-scorekeeper.

Percentages are included at the bottom of the form, for easy reference. Placed on a cumulative graph or fed into a computer for interpretation, percentages are a valuable and interesting reference for players and coaches alike. Individual players are responsible for turning in scores at the end of practice (Figure 12.2).

Name	Made	Attempts	Percent	Date and Notes
	25			
	25			
	25			
	25			
	25			
	25			
	25			
	25			
	25			
	25			
	25			
	25			
	25			

Percentages

25/25	100	31/25	81	37/25	68
26/25	96	32/25	78	38/25	67
27/25	93	33/25	76	39/25	64
28/25	89	34/25	74	40/25	62
29/25	86	35/25	71	41/25	61
30/25	83	36/25	69	42/25	60

Figure 12.2. Practice free throw record.

Graph of
Daily Free Throw Percentages

Players exhibit great interest in this cumulative record, which reflects the daily free throw practices. They compare their efforts with other players' efforts and draw inferences concerning their own progress.

The graphic information derives from Figure 12.2, the Practice Free Throw Record. The percentage column of this form furnishes the information that is transferred to the graph. A series of connected dots, each representing a daily percentage record of between 100 and 49, is drawn across the graph, day-by-day, and the dates involved are shown across the top of the graph. A graph is maintained for each individual player (Figure 12.3).

In the interests of competition and motivation, it is recommended that all graphs be posted on appropriate varsity information boards in the gymnasium. There is a place on the form for brief comments by coaches.

Game Statistics Chart

This Game Statistics Chart, comprised of twelve columns of variables (items), is maintained for both teams, home and visitors. Two statisticians are therefore required, one keeping a worksheet for the home team and the other keeping a sheet for the visitors. This chart is very difficult to maintain during the course of a game, and many times the two statisticians will seek volunteer assistance.

The major purpose of the Game Statistics Chart is to furnish a worksheet for the compilation of the twelve performance items, from which, at the end of the game, the information is quickly transferred to an *official* statistical form. Secondarily, the purpose is to furnish information of interest to all players. The chart can be passed around, while the official form is for the coach's and/or athletic department's files.

The following notes are important: (a) The coach of the visiting team expects to receive, before leaving the gym after the game, a comprehensive, accurate *official* copy, reflecting the information on the worksheets for both teams, (b) the worksheets (visitors' and home team's) can provide the information that is called in to local media after the game, if the completed official forms are not available at the time, (c) in the maintenance of the form, some question always arises about crediting *assists*.

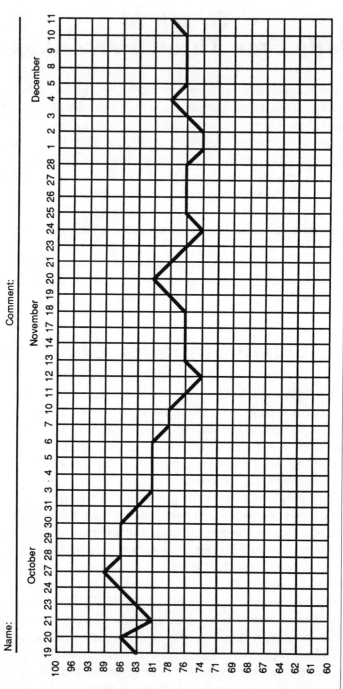

Figure 12.3. Graph of daily free throw percentages.

Some coaches insist that credit is given for an assist only if a pass is delivered to a teammate driving to the basket for a lay-up. A more liberal interpretation gives credit to the passer if he or she delivers the ball to a teammate for *any* resulting successful shot, including jump shots from any location in the half court. At any rate, the statistician must always seek an interpretation of this item before the game starts.

One line has been filled in as an example of how to maintain the Game Statistical Chart (Figure 12.4).

Offensive Efficiency Index (OEI)

A popular rule of thumb for a rough estimate of a team's offensive efficiency is the "one-percent factor." Every possession of the basketball is recorded consecutively, and at the end of the game (and at half-time, if the coach wants the information at that juncture), the total possessions are divided into the total score; the premise is that if the dividend result is 1 percent or better, then the team's offense has operated efficiently, win or lose. The assumption, of course, is that a *possession* should always be worth one point, successful free throws included (Figure 12.5).

A significant number of coaches view this information with great respect and attention. The form included in this chapter as an example is self-explanatory and easily maintained during a game.

Record of Minutes Played

One of the five forms meriting special attention is the Record of Minutes Played. This chart is not too difficult to maintain during a game, away or at home, and the information it records furnishes a means for determining the comparative productivity and proficiency of individuals who play unequal amounts of time in games. The Record of Minutes Played form is used in a very close relationship with another of the three game worksheets, the Game Statistics Chart, which is comprised of twelve columns of variables (Field Goal Attempts, Field Goals Made, Offensive Rebounds, etc.). Using *per minute* averages of these variables instead of *per-game* averages produces fairer and more valid evaluations of performance by all players (Figure 12.6).

Game Statistical Chart

Score: ( ) ( ) Final:

vs.

Name	#	FGA	FGM	FTA	FTM	TP	FF	ORB	DRB	TO	A	ST	BL
Jones, J	10	IIII II /8	III /4	III /3	II /2	10	4	III /5	IIII I /8	II /3	II /4	I /1	I /1
Totals:													

Figure 12.4. Game statistics chart.

Game: _____ vs. _____ (here) (there)   Date: _____

Score: (^{H}) (^{F})   Opponent: (^{H})(^{F})

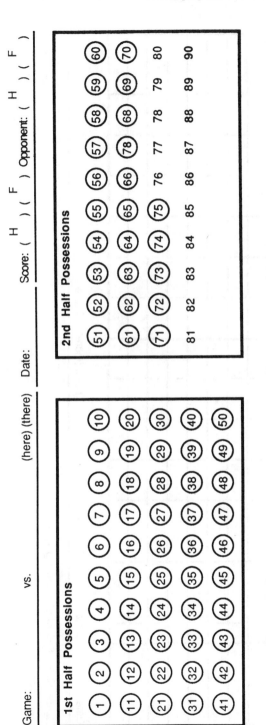

1st Half Possessions

2nd Half Possessions

Circle every possession consecutively.

Recap: Total possessions: _75_   Total points scored: _80_

Offensive efficiency index (OEI): _1.07_ % (total points divided by total possessions)
Example: 80 points + 75 possessions = 1.07 (excellent OEI)

Figure 12.5. Offensive Efficiency Index (OEI).

First Half | **Second Half**

Name	#	Clock Time In	Clock Time Out	In	Out	In	Out	In	Out	In	Out	In	Out	Total Min. Played
Jones J.	10	9:30	6:50			10:00	6:15			2:00	000			8m25s

Date: _____ Game: _____ vs. _____ (here) (there) Score: _____ ( ) ( )

Figure 12.6. Record of minutes played.

Glossary

Basketball coaches do not all speak the same language. The standardization of terms and expressions is far from complete, especially from one section of a country to another, and from one country to another. Perhaps the development of a universal language in basketball is too much to expect. However, coach-player and coach-coach understandings are important, no matter how they are communicated. A coach wants to be sure that everything stated in practices and games is understood without too much time-wasting explanation; by the same token, there must be coach-coach language commonality at clinics, lectures, and discussions, and particularly if a coach is writing a book.

If the New Option Offense, and this book which describes it, has some vocabulary and usage peculiar to itself, then explanations are in order. The purpose of the following material is to meet that expectation.

Assist—A culminating pass that leads directly to a score, for any type of shot. A former interpretation gave credit for an *assist* only if the pass was made to a teammate cutting for the basket and scoring without an ensuing dribble.

Alley-Oop—A passing term, borrowed from football. The passer, with fakery, delivers a soft, high-parabolic pass toward the under-basket area, where a receiver maneuvers and leaps high to receive, control, and lay the ball in the basket.

Banana Route—In the New Option Offense, an unacceptable way of cutting for the basket without the ball. It is a "lazy route," one that circles and veers away from the basket. A defender has little trouble in shutting off a banana route. A proper route includes the initiating V-Cut followed by a direct power-cut.

Basic Structured Motion—A pattern made during the course of planned individual routes in the basic framework of a team's offensive plan.

Blocks—The lower, painted squares on each side of the free throw lane, in the under-basket area.

Body Balance—A physical, major factor in the success of an individual on both offense and defense. Body balance in basketball is controlled by the proper positioning, movement, and use of head, hands, and feet.

Coast to Coast—A term usually associated with a full-court dribble-drive or a fast-break, full-court action of some kind, end-line to end-line.

Continuity—An offensive system that is option-oriented, that keeps pressure on a defense by passing and moving in an attack that does not have to regroup if a field-goal attempt has not presented itself; "if one thing doesn't work, the next one will, in the flow of action."

Cutting Against the Grain—The aggressive movement of a player, without the ball, from the strong side of the half-court to the weak side, usually by slashing across the key area.

Double-Team—A defensive move in which two defenders (sometimes called "trappers") go to the player with the ball, harassing, ganging up, and combining their defensive tactics, hoping to cause a poor pass, a poor shot, or a turnover.

Entry Pass—The pass that initiates a sequence of play, usually but not always delivered by the point (playmaker). In most cases, the pass also serves as a signal, or key.

Exchange—In the New Option Offense, the horizontal, cross-key, coordinated move of the two low post players as they exchange low post places of operation in the under-basket area. Natural screens are created, as the players crisscross in the lane, asking for the ball from outside point and wing players.

Flex—An offensive principle, in a continuity-type offense, that is designed to cause a defense to expand and open up its inside vulnerability.

Floor Balance—The floor is "balanced" during a pattern or sequence when the offensive players are deployed in such a way that, if they lose possession of the ball by turnover or a missed shot, they will not be outnumbered and vulnerable in a fast-moving transition.

Free-Lancing—A development on offense in which an offensive individual takes advantage of a defensive lapse or, reading an opening, improvises a "surefire" scoring option during the course of structured movement and continuity.

Fronting—A defensive act of placing and positioning oneself in front of an offensive opponent, stationary or moving, in such a way as to prevent the reception of a pass, or to discourage the attempt; in effect, being in a position *between* one's offensive opponent and the ball.

Get Down in the Chair!—An exhortation, voiced by the coach in games and practices, to forcefully remind a careless defensive player to simulate sitting in a chair, get in body balance, and assume the aggressive boxer stance.

Get on the Boards!—A coach's vocal expression during a game, warning the team that it must box-out (block-out) properly in rebounding.

Give-Go—An individual offensive move, in which the player, with the ball, passes, makes a deceptive move to gain a step on the defender, and makes a cut for the basket, without the ball, hoping for a quick return pass.

High-Low Action—A feature of John Wooden's UCLA teams in the championship years. The high post player, with the ball, turns, faces the basket, and dumps (passes) the ball down, usually to a low post player who has maneuvered to get open for a close-in shot in the under-basket area.

Jam-Down—Sometimes referred to as "down screen." As the ball is moving outside, one or more players move down (from outside) and set screens for waiting, stationary teammates, who emerge (pop out) from the screening action, hoping for an open-player pass.

Jump Stop—In New Option Offense teaching, the proper way to meet and receive a pass when moving to the *outside*, back to the basket. A very short jump is made when *meeting* the ball, both feet land on the floor at the same time, even across, shoulder-width apart, and *planted* aggressively at time of reception. There is good body balance, and the ball is protected as it is pulled in toward the chest.

Leaning—The tendency of a five-unit zone defense to shade and shift toward the strong side (ball side) of the half-court.

Make Them Play D!—A coach's admonition during the game, reminding the team that there must be continuous ball and player movement against the defense, including movement *without* the ball.

Move Your Feet!—During practices and games, the coach calls out instructions for a player to *slide-step* properly, in the manner of an active boxer or baseball catcher, never crossing the legs and feet while guarding and shutting off an opponent.

Natural Screen—Offensively, when two moving temmates cross paths, a natural, sometimes unplanned, screen results, causing defenders to switch assignments and make mistakes. A natural screen is not to be confused with a moving screen, which is a violation.

Off-Guard—Traditionally, in the back-court two-some, the off-guard is the bigger, stronger of the two; expected to be more of a force on defense than the point-guard partner; expected to be a primary "rifle-man" (jump-shooter), and an assistant to the point guard in advancing the ball toward the front court.

Open Player—A requirement tied to the Option concept, that the offensive player in the most advantageous location on the floor at a given time, receive the ball by way of an "unselfish" pass.

Overloading—An offensive tactic against a zone defense in which the objective is to outnumber the defenders in a given area of the half-court, and in which the ball and players move and rotate strategically until an open shot is possible somewhere in a high-percentage area.

Packing It In—The compression, contraction, and drawing together of a team's defensive formation when, for strategic reasons, the players sag away from opponents *outside*, do not play aggressive defense *outside*, and give primary attention to the restriction of passing and moving actions *inside*.

Passing Game—An offensive term, used sometimes in describing or referring to Motion, Option, Continuity offenses.

Pattern—A set of planned, designated, individual routes, usually rules-oriented, with expectations of scoring options and free-lance opportunities during the development.

Penetration (Penetrator)—A dribbling action, in which the person is able to drive through the defense for a lay-up, a close-in jump shot, or a pass to an open teammate in a favorable position.

Player-Player Defense—A team's defensive system, in which each member is assigned a certain individual opponent and is responsible for preventing that person from scoring.

Principle of Verticality—The principle that a defender in the under-basket area should not be assessed a foul for body-contact with the shooter if he or she, when defending against the shooter, remains "vertical": that is, remains standing in place, in set position, with body and arms extended straight upward to the fullest extent (even if in close contact with the shooter's body).

Reading the Floor—A player's alert evaluation of the significance of the floor locations of teammates and opponents at a given time, and his or her decisions based on that evaluation.

Rub-Off—During *scissors* or *splitting the post*, one or both offensive cutters hope to use the stationary post player as a barrier-screen, which would stop or slow down the defensive opponent or cause the opponent to change direction.

Safety Valve—An offensive player who is located, or set, as an alternate rceiver of a pass, in case the primary receiver is not open. Usually associated with out-of-bounds or situational plays.

Scissors—Sometimes called "splitting the post." The routes of two teammates cutting over the post player (teammate) in a pattern that resembles a pair of open scissors.

Screen and Cut—Sometimes called "flash screen," or "brush screen." The passer, outside, goes opposite the pass he or she made and sets a very quick, temporary screen on a defender on the weak side, then whirls and spins for the basket, hoping to receive a return pass for a lay-up.

Shift—A feature of zone defense action. The totality of the *slides* of the five defending individuals, as the offensive team passes and moves. A zone defensive team *shifts*; its players *slide*.

Skip Pass—A pass, that, for strategic reasons, skips or bypasses a teammate as the ball is moving in the half-court action. A pass from point to corner or deep wing, passing over the head of a teammate; a corner-to-corner pass; a pass from wing to wing, from one side of the court to the other, bypassing the point player. Against a zone defense, a major intent is to skip-pass faster than the zone can shift, and catch the zone leaning.

Soft Defense—The direct opposite of hard-nosed, aggressive, *pressure* defense. The offensive opponent is guarded loosely *outside* (for example, out at about 20 feet). The individual's soft effort is often a part of the team's overall plan to sag away and clutter the critical inside areas.

Square Up—Moving from inside to outside, the player receives a pass with his or her back to the basket, jump-stops in body balance, pivots, turns to face the basket, "squares up" aggressively, protects the ball, and goes into the threatening triple-threat position. This is a major offensive requirement, stressed at all levels of play. "When you receive a pass with your back to the basket, you square up!"

Stack—A part of a team's offensive formation (in an initial set, or during the flow of action) in which at least two players align themselves along one side of the free-throw lane, usually with backs to the basket and facing the action. Planned, assigned offensive actions follow the alignment.

Strong Side—For the offense, the side of the court on which the ball is located.

Sweet Spot—A term borrowed from both golf and baseball, alluding to the spot on the club-head or bat that produces the most powerful drive or hit. In New Option Offense terms, a sweet spot is a specific location on the floor, usually close-in, that is preferred by a given player for a field-goal attempt.

Swing Pass—A part of the New Option Offense in which the ball swings from one side of the court to the other by means of crisp passes from wing to point to wing. Sometimes referred to as a *reverse* or *reversal*.

Target Hand—The arm and hand that an offensive player extends to indicate the location of a pass to be received.

Two-Player Game—Improvised movement of two players and the ball in response to an opening in the pattern. Players concentrate passes to each other to enable one to gain a favorable shot.

V-Cut (V-Jab)—The initial, deceptive move of a cutter that resembles a "∨" a "<," or "∧." Dependent on fundamental footwork skills, the move activates either a drive toward the basket or an effort to gain a step on a defender, anywhere on the floor.

Window—In the jargon of rebounding, the transparent backboard at each end of the court; also called "the glass" and "the boards."

Index

About the Authors

Lee Walker, a native of Indiana and a graduate of the University of Washington, is a believer in the John Wooden philosophy of basketball—organization, fundamental technique, and the concept of team play. He was a teacher and coach in the Tacoma public schools for 19 years, after which he coached highly successful teams at Tacoma's McChord Air Force Base. His teams placed second and first in the Air Force national tournaments for two consecutive years, and his Air Force all-star team placed second in the worldwide championships. Walker is the author of numerous articles for coaching journals and has written one other book, *The Option Offense for Winning Basketball.* Lee and his wife, Lucia, have three grown children and live in Tacoma. In his leisure time he enjoys attending numerous sporting events; he is an avid reader and a collector of traditional jazz and Dixieland music.

Jack Donohue, a native of New York and a graduate of New York University, has coached the Canadian national basketball team since 1972. Prior to that, he taught and coached basketball at the high school and college levels—he was Kareem Abdul Jabbar's mentor at Powell Memorial High School in New York City. Donohue, well known for his motivational skills, is a popular speaker and basketball clinician. He and his wife, Mary Jane, who have six children, reside in Lismer, Ontario.